Pieces of Justice

Pieces of Justice

by
KEN R. ABELL

RESOURCE *Publications* • Eugene, Oregon

PIECES OF JUSTICE

Copyright © 2016 Ken R. Abell. All rights reserved. Except for brief quotations in critical publications or reviews, no part of this book may be reproduced in any manner without prior written permission from the publisher. Write: Permissions, Wipf and Stock Publishers, 199 W. 8th Ave., Suite 3, Eugene, OR 97401.

Resource Publications
An Imprint of Wipf and Stock Publishers
199 W. 8th Ave., Suite 3
Eugene, OR 97401

www.wipfandstock.com

PAPERBACK ISBN: 978-1-4982-3783-3
HARDCOVER ISBN: 978-1-4982-3785-7

Manufactured in the U.S.A.

Scripture taken from the HOLY BIBLE, KING JAMES VERSION, Public Domain.

For my maternal grandfather, Percy Lawrence Major, a strong and persistent man who taught me many important life-lessons—not the least of which were truths having to do with the black and white of right and wrong as seen through the eyes of age and experience.

&

For Anita Irene, a gentlehearted woman who, across the years and miles, has never failed to inspire me. Her steadfast determination in the midst of those rocks and hard places of discouragement often challenges me right down to my socks.

&

For our sons and grandchildren. May each one come to the understanding that doing justice, being merciful and walking in the grace of humility are truly vital to achieving and maintaining genuine contentment.

&

For my friend, Ralph Yoder, whose insightful and thought-provoking exegesis of a particularly complex passage of Scripture instigated a storyline featured on these pages.

Contents

Acknowledgements | ix

chapter one	Passages	1
chapter two	Revelations	56
chapter three	Chases	112
chapter four	Judgments	166

Acknowledgements

ONCE AGAIN I AM extremely grateful for the time and copyediting expertise that Kathi Ellicott freely employs on my behalf. She has done so for coming up on twenty years, which means we have enjoyed a rich and meaningful friendship that is truly valued. It's been too long since we gathered for a summit to solve the world's problems at a hole in the wall joint in Lyndon.

ALSO BY KEN R. ABELL

Nonfiction

An Ordinary Story of Extraordinary Hope

Fiction

Days of Purgatory
Shadows of Revenge
Echoes of Evil
Nightmares of Terror

Websites

www.wantedman.org
www.danceswithcorn.com

chapter one

Passages

"To everything there is a season, and a time to every purpose under the heaven: A time to be born, and a time to die; a time to plant, and a time to pluck up that which is planted; a time to weep, and a time to laugh; a time to mourn, and a time to dance; a time to cast away stones, and a time to gather stones together; a time to embrace, and a time to refrain from embracing..."

~Solomon~

"A rainstorm is coming."

Gilgal stood statuesque, while Deacon Coburn had his head tilted back, eyes squinting at a cluster of thunderheads. He nodded in approval of his assessment, then swiveled in the saddle to survey the lonesome beauty of Mora Valley, which never failed to stir a sense of wonder in his soul. He sought input from his traveling companion by leveling his gaze on him.

"Rain?" Whitey Fitzgerald grunted, waving his hands excitedly. "That's what you said yesterday and the day before that yesterday. And the day before several other yesterdays as I recall." His mount was a sorrel molly mule named Jezebel, often shortened to Jezzy. He pressed up in the stirrups. "A drop ain't fallen since we left Dodge City and I'm done dried out."

"I've been wrong lately, but I'm right today."

"You be wrong again. I betcha."

"You're awful argumentative for a barber."

"Argumentative? What... who... me?"

"Ain't barbers and bartenders supposed to be agreeable?"

"I just be conversating."

"Please. You're more stubborn than your mule."

"Now you done crossed a line," Whitey shot back, eyes twinkling. "My Jezebel ain't got no more stubbornness than a certain scruffy looking preacher-type man I happen to know."

"I ain't so pigheaded that I can't read the sky."

Fitzgerald click-clicked as he craned his neck to have a look-see. From horizon to horizon it was a darkening slate of gray dotted by mountainous embankments of black streaked clouds. "I don't care what the signs say, it ain't going to rain just now. I betcha. If'in it does I'll strip down to my altogether and do a dance whilst I bathe in the showers of heaven."

"I ain't sure that's a sight I want to be seeing."

"Let me ask you something," Whitey countered snappily. "Ain't it springtime? And ain't it supposed to rain in springtime? I've chewed on so much grit that when I be doing my evening necessaries I got sand coming out of me, and I mean to tell you, it ain't pretty."

Coburn bit down on a chuckle. "There's another picture I have no wish to glimpse." He took an easterly gander. A mile or so away, beyond a rolling dip of grassland, he spotted a copse of trees. A smile lifted his bushy moustache. "That's Wolf Creek yonder. It's a mite early, but what say we make camp, then you can splash and get as wet as your heart desires."

"That be a fine idea," Whitey replied, unknotting a dusty neckerchief. He pulled it loose and gave it a good shake, then tucked it away in a pocket. "The best one you've had since you come to me and asked: What say we go for a ride on the trail for the sheer fun of it?"

"Fun? I might've made a mistake."

"The dickens!"

"You ain't having any fun."

"What? I be giddy."

"Your grumbling fooled me."

"Grumbling? You mistake my charm for grumbling."

"Ah-huh." Coburn nudged the silver-dappled buckskin. Gilgal began walking at a lazy pace. "I'm frequently charmed and grateful for your company, so I suppose you're right."

Fitzgerald eased Jezebel alongside the gelding. "Of course I be right," he said, grinning widely as he produced a lighthearted click-click. "In fact, I be as right as rain, which, just in case you be wondering about the matter, I still insist there ain't going to be none today."

"I'd not wager on that forecast."

"You ain't never been one to gamble on nothing."

"And you, Whitey, are an entertaining man."

"I be what folks call a rascal."

"A colorful rascal, I dare say."

"Are you making a remark?"

"Talking honest, is all," Deacon answered slyly. He adjusted his position and arched his back to stretch out a kink. "Black and white, my friend. Black skin and white hair to go along with a black and white outlook on the ways of the world."

"Ain't that the truth?" Whitey guffawed and clapped his hands gleefully. "The Lord Almighty was in topnotch form when he arranged all the jigsaw pieces of me."

"I'll tell you something else," Deacon said, nostrils twitching as he sniffed the air. "The Lord Almighty controls the storehouses of rain, so you best be ready to bare your butt."

"I done already told you, it ain't going to rain."

An instant later, a cloudburst came in a sloshing deluge. The sound of it drubbing the ground was akin to the stampeding hoofbeats of a herd of cattle. Coburn removed his hat and turned his face upward, eyes closed and mouth open. The taste was tingly sweet upon his tongue and he took pleasure in the soaking freshness; so much so that rumbling laughter erupted and it took a second for him to realize he was the source of it.

Then he heard a shriek of a hoot that popped his eyes open. Whitey Fitzgerald had hopped off the mule and was disrobing with all the dignity of a back-alley lady of the evening. Each article of clothing was draped over the saddle until he was swathed in buck-naked glory. He skipped about singing and hollering so far off-key that the tune was unrecognizable.

"I ain't needing the sideshow," Deacon said glibly. He finger-combed the drenched tangle of disheveled curls, then slid his hat on. "I'll be settled in amongst those cottonwoods whenever bath-time is finished." He jostled the reins and the horse broke into a lithe canter. Amusement materialized on his face, crinkling his eyes. His heart was content and at peace.

Late in the afternoon, Lucinda Enochelli arrived in Abilene via the Chicago, Rock Island and Pacific Railroad. She disembarked from the train and had an overly familiar chat with the Negro porter who carried her burnt orange carpetbag and scuffed leather suitcase. She touched his arm and giggled girlishly as he provided instructions to a nearby hotel.

It was apparent that he had much discomfort because of her brash manner, but she was oblivious to it. She swished her skirt and bobbed her head close to his lips in appreciation, then picked up her luggage and strolled off, thick hips swaying in an exaggerated way. She was a voluptuous woman who wore dresses cut to spotlight her top and bottom assets.

The Kansas weather was partly cloudy with a westerly breeze. After being cooped up on the train for the better part of two days she enjoyed being on the move. The air felt invigorating, which caused her to speed up and fill her lungs with a purpose. She increasingly lengthened her stride to loosen muscles and get her blood flowing.

Her cheeks were rosy and she was feeling mischievous when she sashayed into the Austin House on the corner of Third and Buckeye. She paused in the doorway to take it all in. The lobby was empty except for the dandified clerk, but she could see that the dining room off to the side was doing a booming business. She flashed a beguiling smile at the middle-aged man managing the desk, then walked over and dropped her bags.

"Welcome, ma'am. I trust our accommodations will fulfill your expectations," he said affably. He was stylishly attired in a white shirt, paisley vest and bowtie. His eyes dipped to briefly view the casual presentation of cleavage. "How may I be of service, ma'am?"

"That depends," Lucinda replied, moistening her lips. She decided there and then that if she got bored the man might be a pleasurable diversion. She had never been the marrying kind, but when it came to messing around, she was earthy and easy. "What do you have in mind?"

"A room, ma'am," the clerk answered, flustered.

"Would it be a private room with a bed?" she asked, eyebrows rising. She picked up a pen linked to the registry book by a long string braid. Her signature was a sweeping flourish of loops. "Can you imagine how sweaty we could get between those sheets?"

"I'm a married man, ma'am. And the piano player at my church."

"Not to worry," she said straightforwardly. "I'll be gentle. I've had a married man now and again, and at least one piano player, but he didn't tinkle the keys in no church-house."

He shuffled nervously. His complexion had become blood-red.

"Relax, mister. I'm just funning you." She reached down the front of her dress, and took note that he immediately averted his eyes. She jiggled a bit and retrieved a billfold from the cup of the undergarment. "Here's two nights payment in advance. I expect to complete my business in that interval. If it turns into a longer stay I will take care of the charges when I depart."

"Thank you, ma'am. That'll be fine." He pushed a key on a large wooden ring across the desk. "Room 4 at the top of the stairs and down the hallway. Shall I deliver your baggage?"

"Do tell, aren't you the devious one? You flummox me, sir," she teased coyly. She locked her eyes on his as she shoved the wallet back to its fleshy hidey-hole. "Claim respectability, but wanting to take a lady to her bedroom." She lifted the luggage and started for the staircase, then stopped and inquired, "By the way, you wouldn't happen to know Deacon Coburn?"

"I'm not acquainted with that name."

"Are you sure? Think again. Deacon Coburn."

"Never heard of the man."

"You're not at all helpful, are you?" she retorted, dismissive and contemptuous. Then, true to her straight-shooter temperament, she gave him a mean-eyed sneer before ascending to the second floor. She hurried along the corridor and was more than happy to get to the room. A weary sigh accompanied the closing of the door. She placed the carpetbag and suitcase at the foot of the bed, and swiftly went and threw the window open.

Her sunhat came off and was unceremoniously tossed aside. It took her less than a minute to be free of her outer garments. She hung the dress, camisole and striped stockings on one of the pillars of the four-poster bed, then got an ivory-handled hairbrush from the burnt orange satchel and, in her corset and bloomers, went to the mirror above a chest of drawers.

She gave her shoulder-length raven hair a thoroughgoing brushing, delighted by the fact that despite approaching too terribly close to sixty, there wasn't a single strand of gray showing anywhere. Her eyes, as black and shiny as polished onyx, sparkled as she admired the fullness of her figure. She spun around and released the top several hooks of the binding underwear.

"I could plainly pass for forty," she said in an enthusiastic murmur. "I still have it where it matters most. That foppish desk-jockey has no idea that he missed out on the most satisfying relations of his life." She flipped the hairbrush onto the dresser. She fluffed the pillows and sprawled onto the bed. After bouncing around some she found a measure of comfort.

She laced her fingers behind her head, crossed her ankles together and stared at the ceiling, vaguely worrying that she had embarked on a fool's errand. There were doubts in her mind, but those were trumped by daring and a mysterious darkness in her heart. Tomorrow, Lucinda Enochelli would follow the lead that had brought her this far.

Avis Lahay was crying. The tears were flowing freely, but she kept her voice soft and muted. She sat alone in the darkness at the window in her room above the Suncurl Café. Her thoughts were being consumed by the travails of a friend, and the forthcoming ripple-effect consequences of those tribulations, which could not be avoided or forsaken.

She looked up as if in supplication. The moon was in the first quarter phase; above Santa Fe it cast a dull yellowish-red tint. A sigh slipped off her tongue. She was twenty-four years old and could feel the weight of an enormous responsibility coming down upon her that would forever change her life. She flexed her legs to make the bentwood rocker do its job.

The chair was a solid piece of craftsmanship. Back and forth she went without a squeak of complaint from the joints. She sniffled and wiped her eyes. Her gaze drifted downward. She saw nothing out of the ordinary to draw her attention. This segment of San Francisco Street, a bustling thoroughfare during daytime hours, became park-like quiet shortly after sundown.

She stood abruptly and crossed the room to a roll-top desk. After firing up a pair of oil lamps, she took a seat in a large wooden swivel chair. She removed a maroon notebook from an almost hidden pigeonhole compartment. Her thinker riffled over various topics as she slowly thumbed through the pages until she came to the first blank one.

The soft leather journal, its edges engraved in a pattern of interlinked circles, was the twelfth edition of her daybook. The daily discipline of self-examination and meditation had been integrated into her life for a decade and she couldn't imagine ending the practice because of the deeply spiritual aspects involved in her chronicling feelings and happenings. She twirled a gray metallic fountain pen like a miniature baton, then began writing.

April 19, 1888

Dear Diary: Enough already. These days when I'm alone all I do is cry. I can't seem to stop. Even now my vision is blurry because of tears. I stay strong and keep up a brave front for others, but as soon as I close my bedroom door the waterworks start. I suppose it's only a natural release of tension and sadness, but just the same, I'm fed up with it.

I have tried to submerge my emotions in books, which have always been a refuge for me. There's nothing like being carted away on the currents of a well told story. Last week, for the first time, I read The House of the Seven Gables by Nathaniel Hawthorne. It features the precariously poor Hepzibah Pyncheon and is dark, which certainly matches my mood of late, but the hint of witchcraft and the supernatural were disconcerting to me.

I had no problem identifying the themes the author explored. Guilt and retribution and atonement are realities that everyone has to sort through over the course of life. I think I have a positive and forward looking perspective on those universal concepts, but the notion that the sins of past generations are handed down across the years to become uncontrollable motivations that compel present actions troubles me and will require much contemplation.

Yesterday and today, in between nursing and chores, or popping in to see a young gentleman, I revisited an incomparable Shakespearean favorite, which gave me lots of smiles and a few laughs. Twelfth Night has comedic overtones that never fail to lighten my heart. The twins, Viola and Sebastian, separated by a shipwreck, are thrust into a sometimes convoluted romantic plot where confusion and mistaken identity are essential elements.

I have likely read Twelfth Night a dozen times. It never fails to amuse my imagination, but this time through, I had an enlightened insight that'd previously escaped me. It occurred to me that a subject in the storyline that resonates with me is the portrait of women seeking to survive and triumph in a world dominated by men. I can definitely relate.

There have been and are exceptions of course, but I've had many encounters with boorish men who think females are fragile and inferior creatures. In the realm of horses and cowboys where by choice I am regularly occupied, I hear the snide whispers and derision directed at me. If the mouthy malcontents had any sense at all they would realize those attitudes are a reflection of their own insecurity, though don't ask me to feel sorry for them anytime soon.

I don't know. Perhaps I think too much, but the dynamics of the troubling situation has me out of sorts. The fact that life has many unfair undercurrents is not new information to me. I am well aware of how easily troubles can come out of nowhere, but none of my experiences with hardships and difficulties changes the current stresses and heartaches.

Mom is a rock. By all outward appearances nothing rattles her. It matters not that the doctor's inability to do much is an ongoing dilemma, or that his depressing prognosis offers no hope. She plugs along meeting the needs of others as best she can. I lean on her for all I'm worth. She inspires me. I'm sure she has her private moments of grief, but no one would ever know. She serves and smiles while never once having a discouraging word to say.

The sickness happened so fast. I am having problems accepting the arbitrariness of it. I pray that Deacon and Whitey will arrive soon, though to the best of my knowledge, neither of them have any idea of the goings-on here. According to the telegram Whitey sent me near the end of March, they're simply on the trail to make memories.

> *The plan is for them to have a stopover here, which is exciting news. How long they stay is yet to be determined, but it was made clear that their expectation is for me to tag along with them whenever they leave here. When I first saw the wired invitation I was one hundred percent agreeable, but now, I'm not sure it will be possible for me to saddle up with them. Things are fluid and changing so quickly that I may be forced to bow out.*
>
> *After all, being dependable and conscientious are hallmarks that I desire to continue cultivating so as to be an honorable woman of character. Deacon and Whitey will understand, though perhaps, as I take all the variables into consideration, there could be an option that might be extremely beneficial, contingent on timing and emotional upheaval.*
>
> *As I wrote that last sentence I cringed at the grimness of it. Reality is such a soulless taskmaster. The circumstances are utterly gothic and outrageous. A person's life has been reduced to a shivering waiting game—a person who I love courageously awaits death and there's nothing anyone can do to halt the inevitable process. As this virus or whatever it is has progressed I've decided that the medical profession is groping around in the dark.*
>
> *I am so anxious to talk things through with Deacon and Whitey. It will be wonderful to be around them. I can almost see the glint of wisdom in Deacon's eyes and hear Whitey's habitual click-click. We've not all been together in a number of years. They better be a wellspring of information because I've not had a letter from Abbey in far too long.*
>
> *That's enough unloading for now, though there is such disarray in me that I could mark up another page or so without even trying hard, but will not indulge in that rather unbecoming exercise of selfishness. My goal is to be third, not first or second. It's still early enough in the evening for me to do some visiting and Bible reading before bedtime, so I need to scoot.*

Avis Lahay sat back and read the entire entry, lips tightening and hands fidgeting. She closed the notebook and slipped it into its secret slot in the roll-top desk. Standing, she snuffed out one of the oil lamps and turned the other's flame low. She rubbed her eyes and pinched her cheeks, then fastening a bright smile in place, she sallied forth to be a conduit of mercy.

Darkness was in full command when Charley Jondreau finished bedding the stock down. He gave his dapple gray's mane an affectionate stroke, then stepped away from the San Juan River and climbed the slight incline to the campsite. The sky was a star-speckled mural that spoke of the exquisite wonder of creation. He paid heed to its language as he soundlessly crept past scrub cedars as though he was an extension of the night.

He went to the spot where he had stowed his gear. It was a cleared niche amongst sagebrush. He spread the groundsheet, then got into a cross-legged squat so his back was against the saddle. He looked into the deep shadows on the far side of the campfire and said, "A grassy flattop of bottomland at the water's edge, eh. Fifty yards of excellent grazing."

A chuckle came back to him. Max Dawson cleared her throat. "Ten years."

"A riddle?"

"Not at all."

"Enlighten me, eh."

"No inklings, Charley?"

"Ten years? Tell me true."

"We've ridden together for a decade." She was munching on beef jerky as she sat on her heels in her own nest betwixt and between clusters of sagebrush. Her bedroll was ready and she had a poncho bundled over her shoulders. "In all that time, have I not learned that you are a most trustworthy man? You always take care to find the perfect place to picket our animals."

"Many years, many miles."

"We ought to do something."

"Meaning?"

"We should mark the anniversary, Charley."

"Are you getting girly on me?"

Dawson laughed effortlessly. "And I thought we were friends."

"More than friends, Max. We're blood, eh."

"Thicker than blood, Charley."

"What's your idea?"

"Shoot a mule deer and feast on roasted venison," she replied cheerily. "After we've had our fill of fresh meat we can gather a bushel of berries and put your grandmother's pemmican recipe to use. It's been a fair piece of time since we enjoyed that fine cuisine."

"We can do that," he said, removing his floppy-brimmed hat. He turned and hung it on the saddle horn. "Pick the berries now and get them dried. Kill the deer closer to autumn."

"Unless we get haunted by Mr. Crowe."

"Making him buzzard bait is what unites us, eh."

"Not quite, Charley." Finishing her dried beef, she relaxed onto her backside and fluttered the clumpy wrinkles out of the poncho. Beneath the heavy cloak, as she often covertly did, she slipped a hand into an inside pocket of her waist length jacket and removed a leather billfold to hold it over her heart as though it possessed unusual and extraordinary powers.

"What is your meaning, Max?"

She expectantly pressed the secreted wallet against her chest for it contained a venerated personal belonging. "You threw in with me because of an inflated sense of duty. Hunting Crowe down motivated us in the beginning, but if we kill him tomorrow our partnership is not going to be dissolved. We may be together to the bitter end and if so, no regrets on my part."

"Me, neither."

"We've done hard riding."

"Some, but mostly it's been first-rate."

"Will we succeed, Charley?"

"Success is being loyal and steady."

"Do you ever have doubts?"

"Doubts? About what, eh?"

"Bringing Crowe to justice," she said, hissing a low sigh. "I mean, come on, Charley. The stuff we've seen; the violence and bloodletting? We get him dead to rights and he disappears into thin air at will. How many times have we cornered him? His magic may be too formidable."

"His medicine is evil, not all-powerful."

"He bests us again and again."

"Smoky Crowe will not do so forever, eh. His reign will end." A knot of wood flamed blue and popped. Jondreau stood and went to the campfire, and after stirring the coals, banked it for the night with a couple logs. "The sweat of truth must persevere. Good cannot take a holiday or put up a white flag because it has a setback now and then. We press on against all odds."

"There's no quit in me. You know that, Charley."

"I hear frustration. Discouragement, even."

"Ten years."

"Honor is not measured in time."

"I don't have your deep calling to deep sensibilities," she said, somewhat prickly. She carefully returned the billfold with its valued remembrance to its reliable home. "All I want is to finish what we started, but I have uncertainties troubling me down to my socks."

"What is the question that bothers you?"

"Will we ever see Crowe dead?"

"He will die. I have *seen* it."

"I have great respect for your gift, but could it be a bit more specific?" she asked, getting to her feet and inching to the fire. "A when and where Crowe will fall would be nice to know."

"The Great Spirit doesn't operate according to our itinerary."

Dawson laughed thinly. "Perhaps he should."

"We know so little of what goes on in the heavenlies."

"My concerns are earthbound. I want Crowe executed."

"Good will triumph over evil, eh."

"How are you so sure, Charley?"

"I have faith."

"Your faith is strong, mine not so much."

"No one asks for hard tasks, Max," he said flatly. He sat on his haunches across the campfire from her, studying her face in the pale firelight. "The path we're on is the one set out for us by the Great Spirit. We are on the side of good; foot-soldiers pitted against evil."

"Too lofty for me to grasp."

"No harm or foul, eh," he replied, casually twiddling his thumbs. "In the context of my understandings of the Great Spirit and his ways there are complexities about good and evil that no one can possibly fathom. You and I are mere pawns on a grandiose chessboard."

"Explain that to me, Charley."

"I cannot, eh. It simply *is* because the Great Spirit is the master of history." He traced a palm over his scalp, which had a two-day crop of stubble. "In this earthly realm, whether we like it or not, we struggle and do battle in age-old trenches dug by the forces of good and evil."

"I get foggy when the discussion turns to good and evil," she said, poking a stick at one of the burning logs. "All I know is that wrongdoers need to be judged and punished."

"Good and evil exist as living powers, Max," he assured her in a stern tone. "From eternity to eternity evil is at war with good. Evil viciously engages any and all means necessary to annihilate good, eh." He rocked on the balls of his feet. "Bible words refer to the mystifying time before time when Jesus saw Satan hurled as lighting from the paradise kingdom."

"Color me a skeptic, Charley." She backed up. "I'm hitting the sack."

"See you at dawn, eh." He double-checked the fire, then wandered off in the direction of the river. He stood at the top of the bank and tilted his head skyward. The reflection of infinity in the stars beckoned him. Arms outstretched, he murmured prayers in awe of his smallness. It was an hour before he ceased his reverent meditations and retired to get some shuteye.

At *WT Ranch* near Wagon Wheel Gap, Caleb Weitzel stirred awake. He scrunched around to reach for his wife, but even before his eyes adjusted to the darkness he realized her side of the bed was empty. Not only was she gone, but the heat of her body had dispersed from the sheets. His ears pricked and a shiver touched him. He turned onto his back and listened to the notes of a wooden flute. He sat up and tossed off the covers, blinking rapidly as he got up.

The floorboards chilled the soles of his feet. He padded to the other room and paused in the doorway. The Navajo woman sat on a woven woolen rug encompassed in a jittery glow from the fireplace. Her hair, twined in a thick braid, hung down her spine to the small of her back. Her body swayed ever so subtly as she played a sad-sounding song. A smile crested on his lips and he tiptoed to the tall-backed oak rocker, which creaked as he sat in it.

Sally Twosongs abruptly stopped. "I hope I didn't wake you."

"I had to get up in a couple hours, *lucero*."

"I thought I was being soft and quiet."

"I missed your warmth before I heard your prayers," he said, giving a nonchalant shrug. "Apparently when it's the middle of the night my little bright star shines the brightest."

"You are such a sly one, Caleb."

"Do you ever sleep anymore?"

The flickers crackled like popcorn. Hank got up from beside her, stretched and yawned as though bored. The tricolor collie whined and gently nuzzled her cheek with its damp nose before wandering off to curl up at the front door. She exhaled a breathy sigh and put her flute on the hearthstone, then shifted around to face him. "My heart is heavy, my spirit restless."

"I hadn't noticed, Sally Twosongs."

"And I hadn't noticed that you work too much."

"That sounds like a diversion."

She aimed a teasing grin at him. "Maybe so, maybe not."

"That's not helpful, Sally Twosongs," he said directly. "It's been over a week since you slept the night through. I'm getting more than a bit concerned, especially since whatever it is that has gotten under your skin is out of bounds limits for you to share with me."

"That's not been intentional," she replied, furrowing her brow. "My thinker is messed up and I'm searching for discernment. Sorry if I've not been open with you about all this."

"All what, Sally Twosongs?"

"A dream. That's what's been disturbing my sleep."

"Dreams are not unusual for you."

"I realize that, Caleb."

"So what's the problem?"

"I can't see enough of this one, which is vexing."

"Unloading on me could be a constructive way to go."

She scooted closer to him and lifted his feet onto her lap. She began massaging them with a spontaneous tenderness. "I see tiny fragments and even those are distorted, as if through a glass darkly. The sound of tribal drums are thunderous and compelling. There are branches of leaves and a sea of humanity dancing, but I cannot recognize any of the people except one."

"Who?"

"Charley Jondreau."

He gulped audibly and stiffened. "Are you sure it's Charley?"

"Yes," she answered, eyeing him curiously. "What's wrong, Caleb?"

"I'm not sure. Tell me more if you can."

"Charley is in extreme danger."

"How can you know, Sally Twosongs?" he asked edgily. "If all you can see are bits and pieces, and those imprecise and unclear, how can you be so sure Charley is at risk?"

Her hands were still busy rubbing his feet. She looked him full in the face. "I sense an overpowering evil surrounding him. His life is in jeopardy. Before or after what's taking place in the dream I cannot say, but denial of my perceptions would be foolishness. He needs me."

"Needs you? We haven't seen Charley Jondreau in ten years."

"*You* haven't seen him."

Tension was rising in him. "What are you suggesting?"

"He is ofttimes in my dreams, Caleb."

"That's unfair. I can't argue against a dream."

"I need to go on a vision quest."

He flinched. "What?"

"A pilgrimage to lobby the Creator on behalf of Charley," she replied, fixing her gaze on him. "I will walk into the wilderness and be alone to pray and fast and be put to the test. This shall be done, Caleb. I will take a flute, a walking stick and water, but that is all."

He was puzzled; shocked, even. Alarm stained his expression. Sudden-like he swung his feet off her lap and stood. He went to the fireplace, grabbed the iron poker and pulled aside the chainmail to jab at the logs. Sparks and cinders flew up the chimney. He added a blocky chunk of fuel, then closed the guard and huffed a grunt. He returned to the rocker. "When?"

"The Creator will speak. I will know."

"This is bizarre."

"Bizarre? No, you are being unkind."

"Our daughter," he said, dry and cottony. "I'm getting it."

"Getting what, Caleb?"

He scratched at his jawline, which was taut and twitchy. "Yesterday some strange things came out of Bethsuelo's mouth that were confusing, to say the least." His facial muscles had a case of the jumps. "She was giggling happily and sitting on a pony as I groomed it. Then her eyes went blank and she said: *Don't worry, Daddy. Jesse will be with Mommy.*"

"What? That makes no sense."

Hank leapt to its feet and yapped once. He raised a finger and gave it a command to behave and stay-put. The dog displayed reluctance, but obeyed and dropped onto its buttocks. Weitzel folded his arms over his chest. "When I asked her what she meant, she crunched her nose in that funny way she does and informed me that she was hungry."

"*Jesse will be with Mommy?*"

"Wait, it gets weirder." He cocked an eyebrow. "Later she was watching Jesse muck out stalls and I overheard her tell him: *Mommy is going away, but you will find her, Jesse.*" His head was wagging in bewilderment. "The kicker came when I was tucking her in last evening. I kissed her cheek and she hugged me like always. She settled on the pillow, and her eyes widened and got as glassy as marbles. She spoke in a squeaky voice: *Mommy must help Charley.*"

"Were you planning on telling me all this?"

"I just did, Sally Twosongs."

"Aren't you the slippery one?"

"In my defense, I was wholly distracted," he said, hastily holding a hand up. "I intended to talk it over with you when I came to bed, but you had candles lit and sweet promises hiding behind the prettiest of smiles. I was straightaway lost and for that, I don't apologize."

Her dark eyes twinkled delightfully. "You were obliging and pleasured me well, so I suppose I must let you off the hook." She gave his forearm a squeeze as she hobbled closer. "I will have a chat with Bethsuelo and try to determine what's going on."

"Don't make a big deal of it. She just a little girl." He cupped her chin for a moment, then slipped his hand around her neck to start toying with the braid. "I simply chalk it up as to her being her mother's daughter. I'm just not sure if I can handle two mystics in my life."

"What choice do you have?"

"None. Love compels me to acceptance."

"And what of Charley Jondreau?"

"I'm buffaloed, Sally Twosongs."

"As am I, but is it an option for me to refuse the call?"

"In all likelihood, no," he answered grimly. She rested her head against his thigh. He kept fiddling with the braid while staring at the fire. He tried to comprehend the undertaking because he wanted to be supportive, but the developments had him anxious. Fear crept into his mind, but Caleb Weitzel dispatched it to the nether regions of nothingness. He took his bride back to bed, where they cocooned beneath the blankets, entwined in the silence of abiding affection.

When the first blades of sunlight sliced over the mountaintop, Hans Weitzel and Jesse Axler already had *WT Ranch* a half-hour behind them. The twelve-year-old held the reins loose as he guided the two-mule team toward the settlement of South Fork. The roadway was roughly parallel to the Rio Grande, which was flowing high and fast with winter run-off.

Hans Weitzel, who had immigrated to America from the state of Hessia in Germany in 1850, was in his sixty-fourth year. He remained strong and vital, thick-chested and solid, full of an innate kindheartedness that could be obscured by a straight from the shoulder rejection of superficial social niceties. His patience for stupidity was always a drop shy of bone dry.

He took off his tweed cap, flipped it from hand to hand and surveyed the rutted trail ahead. The air was brisk and bracing, scented by the budding freshness of wildflowers. He returned the hat to his squarish head, then gave the driver a clap on the back. "You're doing a fine job, young man. No doubt you'll be making this trip by yourself come autumn."

"You think so, Mr. Weitzel?"

"If not then, next spring for sure."

"I hope, but it's not likely."

"What makes you think that, Jesse?"

"Mom and me are having a go-around."

"About responsibility?"

"Yep, that covers it. She thinks I'm still a child."

"It's just a stage, Jesse. Cut her some slack."

"I try, I really do."

"My mother treated me the same way when I was your age. It's all part of growing up." Weitzel moved his Henry rifle from at his feet to balance it on his thighs. "You just keep your head down, do for her all you can, be courteous, and stay on the track you're on. I've known you for eight years and my two cents worth is that you're already the kind of man I trust."

"Thank you, Mr. Weitzel. That means a lot."

"Take it to heart, Jesse. I don't dabble in falsehoods."

"I know that, sir."

"This morning I stood back while you hitched up the mules and readied the wagon," Hans said, eyes narrowed. "You did everything by the book, then when all was done, you took a walk-around to check every detail. That, young man, is the way to approach every task. It's an attitude and perspective that eliminates or corrects the silly mistakes common to us all."

Jesse nodded as his lips contracted into the slenderest of grins. "My Dad always says that it's better to give a job an extra once-over and not need to, than to skip it and get stuck in a tight spot between a rock and a hard place that could've and should've been avoided."

"Wisdom to apply."

"Yep." Jesse inclined sideward and a frown creased his brow. He had his father's lean build and laidback disposition, but carried his mother's coloring—dark brown hair, and skin the tawny shade of a summertime tan. "That back left wheel needs greased and some attention."

Weitzel listened deliberately. "Yeah, it does."

"I'll see to it."

"I'd expect nothing less."

"No big whoop, Mr. Weitzel. A cinch chore."

"Your father surely doesn't think you're a pipsqueak."

"Nope," Jesse replied, jiggling the reins a tad. "If anything he supposes me to be doing more man's work. I ain't sure what my mother's problem is, but it wears me out."

"Mothers can be difficult in such matters."

"Why? I don't get it."

"You don't need to *get it*, young man," Hans said sternly. "There's a unique bond between a mother and son that resides in a secret chamber in her heart. Call it nature's way of civilizing men. You can't fight it and ought not to even try to because the end result of that is nothing but heartbreak and bitter tears. You have to always respect your mother."

"Even when she's wrong?"

"Even when she's wrong," Hans answered, laughing heartily. "More importantly, even when you *think* she's wrong because she has intuitions you'll never know. And I'll tell you this; if you want to live a long life don't ever tell your mother you figure she's wrong."

"Makes sense."

Weitzel tapped his knee. "Don't sweat it too much. Time is your partner, and quicker than later, all these complications get smoothed out, Jesse. As far as I'm concerned you're already one of the men of *WT Ranch*. We stand together to provide and protect."

"I get that easy enough."

"Don't be so sure," Hans said, terse and determined. "There's nothing easy about it. You must have a special care for the womenfolk and not just the youngsters. Amanda and Bethsuelo are your prime priority now and that's just the way it is, but there's much more."

Jesse squinted a confused scowl. "How so?"

Weitzel regarded him closely. "Eliza, Naomi, and Sally Twosongs each have strength, independence and sturdy backbones, but if anything ever happens to me, your father or Caleb, then you'll have to step up and fill the gap. It's a lifelong calling that can never be shirked."

"Being responsible has no end?"

"An applicable inference, young man." He glanced over a shoulder to observe their back trail for several moments. He turned frontward in time to see a herd of elk lope up from the river a hundred yards ahead. The animals crossed their pathway and rapidly disappeared into the timberland. Hans Weitzel, satisfied that all was well, sat back and relaxed to enjoy the ride.

Brenda Hawkins gloried in the sunshine. The warmth of it soaked down to her bones. She was hatless, with her face turned upward and eyes closed. There were no interruptions on any horizon that could steal her happiness or intrude on the sheer beauty of the day, which was perfect and extraordinarily wondrous; she relished everything about it.

The picnic had awaited such a day. She wore a daffodil yellow dress with a ruffled collar at the neckline. Its pleated skirt billowed around her like the petals of a bouquet as she sat on a thick blanket spread on a gentle slope of grassy pastureland near a slow-moving river. Gigantic weeping willows lined the riverbank on both sides.

She periodically searched for a glimpse of her nine-year-old who was exploring or fishing, but mostly she just enjoyed the intensity of the sun. She had never seen so much splendor in the sky; it was a crystalline blue that had no end and roused oodles of hope in her heart. The feelings accentuated the sunbeams to heat her from the inside out.

"Ma!" Stace called excitedly. She looked and saw him running up the hill toward her. His face was beaming. She cherished him and was so proud—he was serious-minded and possessed a sensitive conscience. Every once in awhile she would catch a peek at the man inside the boy and on those occasions, her heart swelled and expanded her ribcage.

"What do you have there?" she asked, shading her eyes.

He skidded to his knees and almost crashed into her. "Look!" He opened his right hand to show her a roughhewn stone. He held it in his palm as though it was a glittering diamond. "Can you see it? I found it over there and had to dig it out of the dirt. It's petrified wood."

"It's lovely, Stace."

"Can you see it?" he queried again, eyes lively.

"Yes, of course. It's right in front of me."

"No! Look," he said, a pout darkening his forehead. He urgently placed a fingertip at the center of his prize. "Can you see the heart? It's right there! Can you see it, Ma?"

She bent low to examine it. Her face became an awe-filled smile. There, where she had simply seen ridges, was a perfectly formed heart shape. "Wow, Stace. It's a treasure."

"I'm going to keep it forever," he promised, putting his arms around her neck to squeeze with all his might. "It will be a reminder that no matter what, you are always in my heart."

It was then that Brenda Hawkins woke up, quivering helplessly. There was no picnic, no grass, no river, no willow trees, and a complete absence of sunlight. Her lips and mouth were parched and cracked. She was aching and crying, and oh, so cold; the arctic cold relentlessly stabbed at her like sharpened icicles—she couldn't resist or escape the frozen daggers.

The curtains were drawn shut. She was sick and dying in her room above the Suncurl Café. Quilts were piled on to offset the frigidness in her bloodstream. Her muscles were stiff and weakened, so her ability to move beneath the burdensome covers was curtailed. Her health was drastically deteriorating. She had to exert much effort to swallow and to even breathe.

"Brenda?"

Her eyelids flickered open. "I was warm, Avis."

Avis Lahay dabbed a damp sponge on her patient's fevered brow. "That's good."

"Stace is my hero."

"He loves you so much, Brenda."

"Isn't it strange how God works?"

"He is indeed mysterious."

"Not so much when death is camped on your doorstep," Brenda replied, her voice a whispery rasp. "I see the past so clearly now. My mistakes are washed away. I have peace, and am glad about the decision to put my life in Las Vegas behind me and start fresh because one friendship led to another. Do you remember the train trip from Dodge City?"

"Autumn of '82," Avis answered amiably. "My right arm in a sling and Stace treating me like I was delicate china that'd break." She took a seat beside the bed. "You and I chattering like schoolgirls. Mom scolding us to go to sleep. Yes, I remember it all very well."

"Meeting Delores was Providential."

"I agree wholeheartedly."

"I don't know how or why I got this illness," Brenda said, gasping for air in a strained and painful sounding spasm that seemed to constrict her throat in a choke-hold. She fought for control and when it came, her breathing improved. "I am grateful that Stace has a support system. He's not going to be cut loose to fend for himself as I was for my upbringing."

"I will do all I can to guide and raise him."

"Please live your own life, too."

"Don't worry about such matters, Brenda."

"Whatever happened to Bob Cooney?"

"I squashed that big talker like a bug."

"He was a nice enough fellow, wasn't he?"

"To others perhaps, but as far as I'm concerned he was seriously lacking in the chivalry department," Avis said, severe and disparaging. "He had big plans, but mostly those had to do with getting me in bed. He became extremely insistent one evening last week which resulted in a slap he'll not soon forget. I gave him the heave-ho and have no sorrow about doing so."

"Maybe Cupid's arrow will find you."

"Maybe, but if not, so what?" Avis asked rhetorically. "I'm truly not all that interested in romance. Perchance I'm wrong, but for the foreseeable future, Stace is the only young gentleman I have any desire to keep company with because he's polite and fun to be around."

"I'm pleased that he has his Aunt Avis."

"He's a blessing to me."

Brenda groaned and faltered as fatigue took over. "I pray that Stace has good memories of me." She sagged into the pillow. "When my time here ends, I don't want any fuss or fanfare. Make my funeral short and simple. Get me boxed and buried as promptly as you can."

"I will see to it that your wishes are respected."

Brenda nodded, biting her bottom lip. Her eyes shuttered shut. Tears dribbled down her cheeks. She puffed and panted. The lines of her face tied into knots as she laboriously wheezed air into her failing lungs. She struggled and stiffened. The grating noise of her agony filled the room. A convulsion gripped her, then Brenda Hawkins collapsed into a fitful sleep.

Avis Lahay wept quietly as she waited for the inevitable.

At the Austin House in Abilene, Lucinda Enochelli was having breakfast. She ate only one meal a day, but at whatever hour she chose to do so, she indulged a voracious appetite. She demonstrated thoroughness while demolishing her third serving of bacon and eggs. She didn't quite lick the platter clean, but used a slice of crusty bread to swab every drop of yolk.

A rail-thin, roundish-faced waitress offered cheery banter as she removed the dishes and topped off her cup with hot coffee. Lucinda dismissed her with a brusque backhanded gesture, then picked up the latest edition of the *Abilene Reflector*, compliments of the hotel. A bold headline immediately intrigued her. She sipped her steaming drink and perused the article.

OPERATION CROWE

The Ute renegade Smoky Crowe, whose reputation for cunning and cruelty has never been surpassed, remains the scourge of the frontier. For decades his brutal butchery has terrorized the southwest, leaving an unprecedented trail of destruction and bloodshed. The shadowy and ghostlike outlaw has repeatedly eluded all efforts to capture or kill him.

Though there has not been savagery attributed to Smoky Crowe since last summer's slaughter of innocents in borderline backcountry, the despicable marauder is still on the loose. A grassroots movement of citizenry from the territories of Arizona and New Mexico has petitioned for action to be taken sooner rather than later. The expectation of further violence has government authorities preparing for a massive preemptive strike.

A spokesman for the War Department in Washington announced plans for Operation Crowe, a full-scale campaign to rid the country of the vile pillager. Detachments of Calvary units will be launched in a coordinated search and destroy mission in early June. When pressed to respond to the widespread speculation that Smoky Crowe has supernatural abilities, a high-ranking official rejected the idea as "fanciful hooey and poppycock".

Lucinda scrutinized the article a second time, smiling shrewdly as she swallowed the last mouthful of coffee. She had an interest in Smoky Crowe, which increasingly fascinated her since she'd first read about him in eastern newspapers during a lengthy incarceration. Over the years, her curiosity was satiated because of sensationalist scandal sheet coverage.

She folded the tabloid and tossed it on the table as she stood. In her travels westward, she had formulated a strategy that she intended to implement this morning. Armed with the only clue she had, she would visit the *Abilene Reflector* office to scrounge for information. To that end, Lucinda Enochelli grabbed her purplish handbag and embarked on her grand enterprise.

Deacon Coburn and Whitey Fitzgerald were lollygagging. The sun was at ten o'clock in a sky populated by tumbles of fluffy clouds, but the companions were not even close to getting on the trail and had no urgency to do so any time soon. Both were bare-chested, wearing only boots and one-piece thermals with the arms of the underwear tied at the waist.

The campsite in a grove of cottonwoods on Wolf Creek had the adornments of a tenement neighborhood on laundry day. Their gear and supplies were scattered, and most of their clothes were draped over low hanging branches of a tree. The garments were long-dry and freshened by the airflow of a warm zephyr, but packing up was not yet on their agenda.

Coburn, suffering the aftereffects of a headache, sat on the edge of his saddle which straddled a deadfall stump. His knees were pulled up, elbows propped on them as he read his Bible. The page corners were dog-eared and yellowy, and in several places throughout the book there were splotches of coffee or sweat marking spills and drips, but the black leather cover remained shiny because he still routinely gave it a fussy oil rubdown.

"I soon be prepared to make the bacon sizzle," Whitey said, putting a pot of Arbuckle's on a flat stone at the edge of the campfire. "Whatcha be reading this morning?"

"Just got to the nineteenth chapter of Revelation," Deacon replied, glancing up from his studying. His eyes flinched against a splash of sunshine. "Want to hear the first few verses?"

"I be all ears if you be ready to explain what I don't get."

"It's Revelation, Whitey. I ain't persuaded anybody *gets* all of it."

"It be a certainty that you gets it better than me."

"I ain't as smart as you think, my friend," Deacon said, chuckling. He straightened his posture and read aloud. "*And after these things I heard a great voice of much people in heaven, saying, Alleluia; Salvation, and glory, and honor, and power, unto the Lord our God: For true and righteous are his judgments: for he hath judged the great whore, which did corrupt the earth with her fornication, and hath avenged the blood of his servants at her hand.*

"*And again they said, Alleluia. And her smoke rose up for ever and ever. And the four and twenty elders and the four beasts fell down and worshipped God that sat on the throne, saying, Amen; Alleluia. And a voice came out of the throne, saying, Praise our God, all ye his servants, and ye that fear him, both small and great.*"

Fitzgerald click-clicked. "*Both small and great.* I gets that just fine."

"That's worthy of shouting far and wide."

"To be sure it be," Whitey agreed as he put slices of bacon in the frying pan.

"The Almighty is no respecter of persons," Deacon said matter-of-factly. "His desire is for all to know and receive the unmerited favor of grace. Rich and poor, princes and paupers, kings and peasants, generals and privates. *Both small and great.* There are no exceptions and no one is excluded, however, there is a caveat. The bottomless well of grace is for all to partake of, but we must each come to God on his terms, and that's where *fear* becomes a requirement."

"It ain't about being scared, is it?"

"A failing of language, Whitey. The commonplace definition of fear doesn't fit its usage in Biblical references to *fearing* God," Deacon replied, hunching forward. "Solomon proclaimed that *the fear of the Lord is the beginning of knowledge: but fools despise wisdom and instruction.* His father had no qualms or misunderstandings. He wrote that *the fear of the Lord is clean, enduring forever: the judgments of the Lord are true and righteous altogether.*"

"He be God and I be Whitey is what I knows."

"And that's it exactly," Deacon stated emphatically. "King David put a fine point on it in the thirty-third Psalm. *Let all the earth fear the Lord: let all the inhabitants of the world stand in awe of him.* To *fear* God is to bow in humility before the One who spoke creation into existence. God opposes the proud, but pours out the tender mercies of grace on the humble."

"I tries to keep my heart low and meek before the Lord."

Coburn puckered his lips. The horseshoe of his dense moustache wiggled. "It's where we live day-in and day-out, isn't it? When our heart stays knelt before God we grow in grace under his mighty hand and when needed he lifts us up from the mud and mire. And in the process of growth we come to comprehend that he is God and he can do whatsoever pleases him."

"And all we have to do is trust him."

"I reckon that's it in a nutshell."

"We went down a gopher hole," Whitey said, flipping the bacon in the cast-iron skillet. "What I wants to know about that Revelation passage is whether it be the past or the future?"

"Maybe not either or, but both and," Deacon answered, shrugging.

"Past and future? How can that be?"

Coburn's shrug became an eyebrows tented expression of ambivalence. "God's Word is a living document. Prophecy is layered and multidimensional. There is much wisdom in embracing the riddles and ambiguity of Scripture." He raised a finger in emphasis. "If the infinite One who put the foundations together while the morning stars sang a chorus can be explained by the finite minds of men, then we are no longer discussing the God revealed in the Bible."

"Well, God be God, and there ain't no other."

"That's absolute truth," Deacon said earnestly. "Here's conjecture to make your brain work overtime: What if those visionary scenes in Revelation are past, present and future?"

"Too much," Whitey replied, click-clicking rapidly. "I knows enough to know that I ain't got the faculties to swim in those murky currents. Besides the grub is ready." He forked half the bacon onto a tin plate and delivered it, then took the remainder for himself and sat on a short makeshift stool he had cobbled together. "We be quite a pair, ain't we?"

"Because we talk theology?"

"No. Have we been in a cat-fight?" Whitey speculated, jerking a thumb at him. "We got scars like a couple old dogs. You look like you been whipped front and back."

Coburn laughed, head bobbing. His eyes bent downward and he drew a finger over the lumps of tissue that crisscrossed his chest. "Nope. Just carved by Smoky Crowe. Now that you broached the subject, it looks to me like that crazy-eyed pariah took a knife to your back."

"No, sir," Whitey said, munching on an oversized bite. He jabbed his fork at him in an exaggerated gesture. "Master Fitzgerald thought he had to teach me some lessons, but I outfoxed the miserable coot. Took the whuppings and faked him out just fine, thank you very much."

"More than conquerors. That's what we are, Whitey."

"We done triumphed over adversity."

"By God's grace," Deacon added, smiling broadly. He winced, eyes slamming shut for a perceptible instant. He massaged his forehead. "I got a nasty ache lingering upstairs."

"Sorry, but there be no powders in my kit," Whitey said sincerely. "I'll keep my eyes peeled for proper species of willow trees so as to make you some bark tea. When we be in Santa Fe I'll get a supply of medicine. For now, the coffee is robust and tasty. Drink your fill."

"Will do." Deacon got up and went to the fire. "Then we best sort out this mess, bundle our belongings and get moving. We'll be lucky to get five miles put behind us today." He poured a cup of caffeine and drank it down in four gulps. He had a refill, then rolled his head in a circle to release a crick. After polishing off the entire pot, he got busy and took care of business.

An hour later, the cohorts were on horseback riding southward.

∽ ∽ ∽

At a farmstead north of Abilene, Anna Mueller had been working since sunup. Six loaves of bread were baked, and in a rite of springtime the house, a two-story frame structure, was in the midst of a thorough top to bottom cleaning. The windows were all open and the stuffiness of an enclosed winter was departing on the wings of a gentle breeze.

Anna was sad. Her exuberant labors chased dust bunnies away and made the woodwork shine, but all the scrubbing and mopping could do nothing to displace the cobwebs of sorrow creeping through her soul. She had prayed endlessly; she had even been encircled by the elders of the community and anointed with oil, but all the heartfelt efforts were to no avail.

The deeply entrenched sadness preyed upon her sensibilities. Not yet twenty-five, she was the mother of twin boys whose ninth birthday was less than a week away, and she yearned to be set free of the darkness within, but the view that she was reaping judgment plagued her. All she knew from her nurture and rearing was to bear down harder, so she put on a brave face and pretended all was well as she kept her apron sashes tied tight and served her family.

She was in the large kitchen and readying to take a break. The water was on the boil for sassafras tea. She prepared it, placed a cozy over the pot and set it, along with a cup and saucer, on the table. As it steeped, she sat and tore open an envelope that her husband had brought from town yesterday afternoon. The letter was from her aunt and she read it anxiously.

> *March 16, 1888*
> *WT Ranch, Colorado*
>
> *Dear Anna: I received your late-January letter yesterday. I was dismayed by your news. There is heaviness in my heart. I am so sorry for your loss. Words pale and are a poor excuse for conveying my compassionate sympathy. I cannot imagine the utter agony of your grief. To suffer a fourth miscarriage is a tribulation that must test and try your faith. You are in my prayers.*
>
> *Shed tears, ask questions, and holler at the Lord if necessary. Write out your grievances to him in no uncertain verbiage to vent all the doubts and turmoil, then burn the pages as a prayerful offering. There are no easy answers to this woeful misery, but be assured and encouraged that the gloom will not prevail for God is in the midst of it with you.*
>
> *I know that what I am about to suggest is not conventional thinking and may cause much opposition, but it's in my mind and I must share it or else I will be guilty of not being honest and forthright. I am not meddling, but rather, expressing concerns for*

your overall health and wellbeing, which has been weakened by the trauma of losing four children.

Perhaps it's time for you and Abraham to take precautions. The marital bed ought not to be a place that causes distress, or worse, results in permanent harm to you. I doubt that your body is strengthened by these spontaneous abortions. Who knows if another pregnancy might not result in disastrous hemorrhaging? I urge you to vigorously consider my counsel. Be thankful that you have Eli and Seth. Pour your love and energy into their hearts.

Life here continues with its rhythms and patterns. The ranch is doing well, which is gratifying because of the long hours and hard work. There never seems to be completion to the tasks that need to be done. The division of labor between the men and women is fair and equitable, which is conducive to solidifying good relationships.

Jesse and Amanda are hale and hearty. They have their moments of competition and scraps, as brothers and sisters do, but mostly they get along and look out for each other. Amanda has yet to have her hair cut, which is problematic because of the care it requires. Fixing her up in pigtails can be an exercise in frustration that annoys both of us.

Amanda is a character. Whenever I mention a haircut she resists the idea and pushes her bottom lip out in a pout that is hilarious. Our son thinks the braiding is high entertainment. He'll sit and make witty comments that goad her into giggling, which of course makes the job more difficult. I often have to shoo him or else the chore would never be finished.

Jesse is chomping on the bit to be a man, which is a source of tension between us. He's strong and reliable, but I think he has too much responsibility for a twelve-year-old. Pete is not at all helpful in alleviating the conflict between mother and son—if anything, he exacerbates it. Mr. Axler tells me that I am too protective. I'm sure we'll work through it all, but just now, the friction is tetchy. You will likely soon be dealing with the same disquiets with your boys.

I must end this so as to get it posted in a timely fashion. Please be comforted in the knowledge that I hold you before the throne of grace. Heaven is assaulted with prayers on your behalf. Stand strong on the promises of God. He is faithful. Take care, dear Anna.

Blessings,

Aunt Naomi

Anna exhaled a huge sigh. There was moisture glistening in her bluish eyes. She returned the letter to the envelope and slipped it into the pouch pocket of her apron. She poured a cup of tea and held it under her nose to enjoy its sweet fragrance. After sniffing it for more than a minute, she took a sip and a feeble smile made its presence known.

She heard footsteps on the backdoor stoop. She turned to see her husband come in with a stony expression darkening his countenance. She stood to greet him. Before she sat, she ruffled folds out of her gray dress. She wore the plain garb prescribed by the brethren. Her tresses were secured in a bun beneath a white brimmed covering. "Will you join me for a cup of tea?"

Abraham Mueller was gangly and as skinny as a sapling. He had a ruddy complexion and deepset eyes which were currently churlish. "I do not desire tea. I have a matter to discuss."

"What are the boys doing?"

"They are busy. I instructed them to hoe the garden," he replied, sitting stiffly across from her. "Seth is a hard-worker, Eli's a dreamer stopping to watch clouds time to time."

"Different personalities, is all."

Mueller scowled, head shaking in disgust. "That is not the topic of our discourse. I was distraught by your actions last night," he said rudely. "Your behavior was intolerable."

"If anyone should be *distraught*, it is I by your behavior," she answered, steadily holding his gaze over the rim of the cup at her lips. "I am not yet in the mood for such doings."

"It has now been months since you lost the baby," he told her, harshness slinking into his tone. "You've had your menses. You are healed. I expect you to fulfill your wifely duties."

"Are you prepared to give me your word?"

"I care not to converse on such matters."

She felt a hot rush of anger flush her cheeks. This was not new territory for them; circles had already been talked around the issue. She put the cup onto the saucer and realized that her hand was trembling. "I'll honor that, if you'll reciprocate and respect my wishes."

"I have marital rights, Anna. Attend to the admonitions of Brother Raffens."

"I have emotions, Abraham," she said, voice stressed and eyes full of resentment. "My heart cannot endure the piercing desolation of losing another child. Until you give me your word that you will not spill your seed inside me I shall not receive your physical attentions."

"You shalt make yourself available to me, or else."

"Or else what, Abraham?"

"Not a query to make, Anna."

"I do not take kindly to being bullied, nor do I cower at threats."

"I have marital rights, Anna," he repeated, steely-eyed.

"I have emotions, Abraham," she responded, mouth clenching. Her face was blotchy tints of crimson. In a startling display of defiant independence, she haltingly unknotted the strings of her covering and removed it from her head. "If you force yourself upon me as you attempted to do last night, I will pack a bag and go on a long vacation to visit Aunt Naomi."

Mueller balked, eyebrows crooking low to hood his eyes. "You dare not!" He shoved the chair back and it almost tipped over as he stormed to his feet. He glared at her. The silence that germinated in the room became a vine sprouting barbed thorns for all the unspoken sentiments suspended in the air. He started to speak, but clamped it off and hurriedly departed.

Anna Mueller, born and raised in a prominent River Brethren family in Pennsylvania, went to the window and watched the man she loved scuttle to the barn. She remembered their affection and how enjoyable their bedroom carrying-on used to be. Her heart ached because of the ugliness between them. Melancholy engulfed her and hot tears blurred her vision.

In New Mexico, Charley Jondreau had ridden ahead of his partner to scout the outskirts of the northern edge of the Angel Peak badlands. The sun was high, occasionally playing hide and seek with cotton-ball clouds that were slow-movers. He rode in confidence, particularly because a red-tailed hawk was soaring in a slothful pattern low in the sky ahead of him.

The dapple gray, stalwart and trail-wise, had developed a feistiness in recent days that Jondreau found amusing. He spoke to the stallion and its ears twitched. The animal snorted and pranced playfully. He started to lean forward, then a bolt of surging energy cramped through him and his backbone stiffened into an upright posture. His mouth wrenched open and his head jerked backwards with such force that his floppy-brimmed hat fell to the ground.

An enormous groan tore from his throat, followed by a gasp that took his breath away. His nostrils flared; the acidy smell of the skunk was heavy on him. His eyeballs rolled back and disappeared as his hands clenched on the reins. The horse whinnied, stood stockstill and waited to be released, but Jondreau was occupied elsewhere, mesmerized and caught up in the pageantry of otherworldly proceedings. What he clearly saw and heard riveted his attention.

The rolling thunder of drums had his feet moving in an animated two-step amongst a multitude of dancers, none of whom he was acquainted with, yet an overwhelming sense of kinship burned in his veins. Thousands and thousands were undulating in unison and waving large leaves whilst singing a wondrous rhapsody of celebration.

Transfixed by an outpouring of awe, he was clothed in ceremonial Iroquois regalia; a formal feathered skullcap, wampum jewelry around his neck, a ribbon shirt, breechcloth and leggings. His face was decorated with charcoal and streaks of radiant paint. His feet, shuffling continuously, were encased in intricately beaded doeskin moccasins.

The grandeur of the powwow thrilled him. His mind and senses were on overload attempting to process the scene. He held a hawk-feather fan over his heart, head bowed and free hand raised in supplication. He crouched low and spun around in a whirl that began slow and measured, but progressively quickened as his upper body bobbed side to side.

Round and round he went, lifting his knees high and planting each footstep with authoritative double-taps. The drumbeat rose and fell, increasing and decreasing in speed and loudness as the gyrating throng of humanity bounded and skipped in individual displays of ancestral folklore that somehow melded together as a perfect mosaic of movement. He became more and more buoyant, then abruptly halted when he spotted a personal heroine.

All the saliva on his tongue dried up. His pulse throbbed against his temples. He blinked and his mouth gaped open. His grandmother was there watching him with pride and joy shining forth from some inner fountainhead. Her fiercely brave eyes were enthusiastically focused on him. She sat on a blazing red blanket, her snow-white hair long and loose on her shoulders.

Charley Jondreau beheld her in reverence. Tears of gladness gathered in his widened eyes and fervent rivulets streamed down his cheeks. His heartbeat was synchronized with the cadenced drumming. He touched the tip of the hawk-feather fan to his forehead and respectfully genuflected to her, then in a swirling burst he launched into a foot-stomping honor dance. His shoulders dipped and weaved, and jubilant hoots pulsed from his voice box.

The pounding drumsticks on stretched animal hides mutated into galloping hoofbeats. He twitched free of the clairvoyant foreknowledge, hands shaking and head swiveling from pillar to post as his faculties came into alignment to see his strawberry-blonde pard's high-spirited arrival. She leapt off her red dun before it even came to a full stop.

"What was it, Charley?"

Jondreau, distant and detached, gawked at her, speechless and hollow-eyed.

"Charley? Are you alright?"

"Beautiful, eh," he murmured wistfully. He pinched the bridge of his nose and violently exhaled to expel the pungent aroma of the phenomenon. "More beautiful than starlight."

Dawson knelt to pick up his hat. She dusted it off and handed it to him. "Starlight?"

"A beacon on a murky night."

"An odd metaphor, don't you think?"

"Guidance from the great beyond, Max."

"What was it that you saw?"

"A congregating of tribes."

"A parley? Explain more fully, Charley."

"The constant was the drums, eh."

"And the meaning?"

"I know not. In age I was as I am now," he replied, flipping his hat on. He filled his lungs and patted the dapple gray's mane. "The insight will come again, eh. I'll understand." It was a reasonable expectation, however, Charley Jondreau was wrong—he would never again see *that* vision inside his head; it was a onetime gift from the Great Spirit. He gave her a deadpan shrug accompanied by a prodding smile, then chuckling, goosed his mount and rode onward.

"Why'd this happen, Grandmom?"

Delores Solrizo stared at the lad sitting on the steps. Her eyes, which at fifty-two could still be mischievous and teasing, were now laden with empathy and apprehension. She was in a bentwood rocker on the boardwalk veranda of the Suncurl Café—inside was a beehive of activity as volunteers sorted and boxed donations of foodstuffs to be delivered to the poor and needy.

"Ain't no answer, is there, Grandmom?"

"None that make much sense here and now," she replied sadly. She collected her thoughts and shifted forward. "Life comes with no guarantees. Sickness strikes whosoever it will."

Stace Hawkins, sandy-haired with a splash of freckles across his nose, had a handful of agates that he was counting into a drawstring bag. He popped the last few glossy balls in, then glanced up, shaking his head slowly. "It ain't fair. And it ain't right, either."

"You're correct, Stace. It's extremely unfair."

"There's nothing can be done about it."

"We can and are praying, Stace."

"I think God is making a terrible mistake."

"An honest conclusion," she said, careful to keep her feelings in check and her voice on an even keel. It was noontime. Horse and wagon traffic on San Francisco Street was sporadic, but there were an assortment of pedestrians going to and fro in enjoyment of the warm sunshine. She moistened her lips and asked, "Have you talked to your mother about all this?"

"Nope."

"Why not?"

He turned to her, eyes squinting and brow wrinkling into a corkscrew scowl of total puzzlement. "She's dying. She's got enough to worry over without me being a burden."

"Are you afraid for her, or for you?"

He pondered that for a long while, staring down at his hands and jiggling the cloth bag so the alleys clattered together. "I ain't sure I like what I'm thinking, Grandmom."

"Why is that?"

"Because I'm more afraid for me."

"Why does that bother you?"

"It's selfish, isn't it?"

"Not really, Stace. It's quite normal, I would suppose."

"I just don't know," he said, sounding old and weary. "Mom is going to heaven to be with Jesus, so I shouldn't be afraid for her, but she's hurting so much it makes me angry and afraid and lots of other junk." He pressed his knees against his chest. "How come God's so mean?"

"He's not, but it certainly seems that way sometimes, doesn't it?"

"He's making me mad." He got up and plopped into the bentwood rocker beside her; the Suncurl Café had a dozen of the chairs in strategic places throughout the building. "If God is so strong and all-powerful why does he allow Mom to suffer? That's being outright mean."

"There is much about God that we can never grasp, Stace."

"Why is God so hard to understand, Grandmom?"

"He is, that's all there is to it," she answered softly. "I have a rather basic belief system that helps me through the pains and troubles that come to test us time and again." She made sure she engaged his eyes. "Faith. We must come to God in faith, which doesn't do much to solve the problem of human suffering, but gives us a proper place to stand for a starting point."

"Faith is trusting?"

"Yes, trusting God to be God."

"Who else would God be, Grandmom?"

Her eyes brightened. "There's a profound verse in Romans that is foundational to my faith: *And we know that all things work together for good to them that love God, to them who are the called according to his purpose.*" She began rocking gently. "It may be challenging to comprehend when we're in the middle of dilemmas or misfortune, but I have had enough heartaches redeemed to be fully persuaded that God faithfully keeps his promises."

"Are you sure?"

"Indeed, I am."

"Well, I got a problem," he said, frowning cheerlessly as he nibbled on his bottom lip. "I've never had a father and now I'm going to be motherless. What will happen to me?"

"I beg your pardon?"

"What will happen to me, Grandmom?"

"Where'd that foolishness come from?"

"That's what Aunt Avis asked me."

"What's that tell you, mister?"

He tilted his head, perplexed. "I don't know."

"Grandmom and Aunt Avis are your family."

He nodded, clipped and somewhat cautious. His eyes veered to the street. "Yeah, but that doesn't stop me from being scared or wondering about what I will do without Mom."

She reached over and took hold of his hand. "We are going to be crying together. Aunt Avis, too. And praying. And sharing stories to encourage each other. We will hold on tight, and be strong and tender as we say goodbye and take your mother to her final resting place."

"I'm afraid, Grandmom," he said, lips quivering.

She pulled him out of the chair. He didn't resist, but instead, sagged against her like a ragdoll. She hugged him close as he forced his face against her neck to stifle the choked sobs that broke free and gushed out. Her heart-rate sped up. She locked onto him, then Delores Solrizo, full of faith forged in distress, called upon God to bathe the nine-year-old in merciful grace.

Whitey Fitzgerald removed his black coachman hat, scratched his head and joggled his back to loosen a twinge. He moved around in the saddle. The molly mule never varied its pace so as to stay walking alongside the gelding. He returned the headgear to a low angle on his forehead and glanced at his colleague. "Do you remember when we were at Fort Union?"

"I'm aging, but my mind ain't turned to mush yet, Whitey," Deacon replied, shooting him a scoffing sideward smirk. "We were just there two days ago, so yeah, I remember."

"You being a cheeky saucebox ain't flattering."

"I just spelled out the facts."

Fitzgerald grinned smugly. "I be rubbing off on you."

"I reckon."

"Can we get to what's on my mind?"

"Only if you speak your piece."

Fitzgerald spat a short chuckle. "You be in rare form, my friend. One snappy comeback after another." He inclined his head upward and took a long gander at the compelling blueness of the sky, then gave him an inquisitive look. "We was getting ready to put on the feedbag in the mess hall when that loudmouth refused to serve me and called me a *jungle bunny nigger*."

"I amended his attitude quick enough, didn't I?"

"Any quicker and he might've crapped his pants."

"Which would've been entirely appropriate since the man was so full of it that it was slopping out his big bazoo," Deacon said, shoulders hunching dispassionately.

"I be a nigger man, I ain't at all arguing against that," Whitey remarked, rolling his eyes and click-clicking. "I be proud of who I be, but is people ever going to stop being ignorant?"

"No chance, Whitey."

"No chance? You ain't a-gonna explain?"

"What's to explain? Human nature ain't ever going to change."

"Ain't you a fountain of pessimism?"

"Not at all pessimistic," Deacon volleyed back, lips puckering. "Realism birthed in a lifetime of observations. I've been young and now I'm older and supposedly wiser. I ain't seen any indication that humanity's motivations will ever change this side of eternity."

"All the Good Book in your head and that be your outlook?"

"On a grand scale, yeah it is," Deacon replied pointblank. "Individually we make efforts, and there are small pockets and fleeting moments when we succeed, but the consensus of history is that humans are boiling caldrons of bigotry rooted in the sinfulness of the heart."

"I ain't cheered by your assessment."

"It ain't an original view, Whitey," Deacon said, eyes crinkling. "King Solomon covered this territory in Ecclesiastes: *The thing that hath been, it is that which shall be; and that which is done is that which shall be done: and there is no new thing under the sun.*"

"That relates to pithy heart issues?"

"I've weighed it out and that's where my understanding takes me," the man from Conoy Creek answered succinctly. "Since the fall in the garden, our primal instinct is for me and mine. We are tribal. Self gets elevated and is disgracefully deceptive. Until Jesus returns, or we die and are glorified, self-centeredness will wage war against humankind's noble intentions."

"And self-centeredness and self-preservation wins most battles?"

"Self, unfortunately, is the dominant beast within."

"What hope is there then?"

"Hope comes when believers boldly walk in the light we've been given," Deacon opined, thumbing his hat up his forehead. "What snags us again and again is that it's too easy to not be willing to pay the price. We get comfortable and complacent, and let stuff slide and get too accepting of ignorance. Or become too involved in the tiny circle of our lives."

"I be guilty of that very thing."

"We're all guilty of that more often than we'd like to admit," Deacon said, making a backhanded gesture off to his right. A sizable herd of pronghorn sheep were feeding on a grassy hillside. He watched them for a spell, then cleared his throat and spoke hesitantly. "Or, we can have the best aims and objectives, and be deceived by the sin nature within."

Fitzgerald eyed him closely. "You be sounding sorrowful."

"I'm a prime example of how deception leads to destruction."

"You need to be explaining yourself."

Coburn puckered his mouth, eyes flinty and narrowed. He rode a hundred yards or so before he started to be transparent in a voice so thick that his usual rasp had a tremble in it. "I left home when I was eighteen. I intended to do justice and make a difference by rectifying an ugly wrong. I wanted to be a vessel that would mete out righteous judgment on slavers."

Fitzgerald jerked in the saddle, as though it had pinched him. "What?"

"My father tried to warn me, but his ways and mine clashed," Deacon replied, gazing straight ahead. "My conscience was tender. I read *Narrative of the Life of Frederick Douglass, an American Slave* and Harriet Beecher Stowe's novel *Uncle Tom's Cabin*. In my outrage over the sin of slavery I deceived myself into believing that *I* had to dismantle it.

"I became involved with well-meaning abolitionists who had a bend toward the radical. I raised funds, learned the ropes, took risks, and though conflicted, justified my choices in Bible language. Soon I was an active conductor on the Underground Railroad. I made numerous safe passages and helped dozens to reach freedom, but one particular failure marked me."

Fitzgerald was shock-eyed. "I canst believe my ears."

"Saul and Maggie," Deacon said, paying no consideration to him. His eyes were moist, his tone deadened. "Maggie was pregnant and they arrived at a clandestine way-station a half-step ahead of a posse of slave-catchers. I was taken out with a bullet, then a rifle butt to the back of the head. When I came to and saw the bloodthirsty debauchery done to those poor people, something inside me snapped and solidified into hunger for vengeance.

"I buried Saul and Maggie, their baby too. In April '61 when Fort Sumter was fired upon and President Lincoln put out a call for ninety-day volunteers, I went straight to Washington City to enlist. I was attached to the Army of the Potomac as a sniper. In the ghastly bloodletting, I almost lost my soul. I definitely lost whoever I was before deception triumphed in me."

"I canst believe my ears," Whitey said once more, click-clicking and shaking his head in rabid incredulity. "After nearly twenty years of me making you pretty and you just be telling me all about this now? I swear, Deacon, you be tighter than a donkey's arse in a sandstorm."

"I ain't sure what you want me to say, Whitey."

"There be times when you still be a walking riddle to me."

Coburn gave a half-hearted shrug. "I ain't a gabby chatterbox."

"You was an abolitionist! Whew doggies," Whitey exclaimed, slapping a knee. "I be like a hog in a mucky pigsty I be so pleased to be riding at your side." A grin encompassed his face and his shallow chest swelled in pride as his shoulders stiffened. His head bobbed in affirmation. The gratified expression and body language remained entrenched for five miles or more.

Meanwhile, in the northwestern quadrant of New Mexico, Max Dawson and Charley Jondreau were traversing the rugged terrain of a steep-walled canyon. The midday sun was high and hot, creating multihued bands in the variegated gullies and rock formations. There wasn't a cloud or concern on any horizon; peacefulness permeated the stillness.

Their mounts were compatible, taking cues from the partners. On occasion, his dapple gray could flex a domineering streak, though not so much as to be a hindrance. Her red dun, with a distinctive triangular splash of white on its chest, held its own just fine. Both stallions carried the *WT* brand. She had traded in her soot-gray mare two winters ago.

Dawson coughed lightly. "Have you ever had a woman, Charley?"

"Out of nowhere you ask such a thing?"

"My brain's on a wander."

He grinned curtly. "An odd place for it to roost."

"Not so odd, methinks. A fair question."

"I've sown some seeds, eh."

"No, I mean, have you ever been married?"

Jondreau, leading the pack mule, tossed her a slanted smile. His lips and jaw tightened so as to take on the bearing of a bulldog—an outward manifestation of his inner workings. "Are you bored with the scenery?" His dark and brooding eyes glinted a subtle taunt. He kept the look fixed on her for several moments. "Ain't you got more important stuff to think on?"

"I was wondering, is all."

"Strange wonderings."

"It's quiet and calm, Charley. I figured yakking was in order."

He gave a half-shrug. "Long ago and far from here, I had a Mohawk woman, eh. In English, the meaning of her name was Snow Maiden. Her voice was beautiful, her body warm and vibrant, her soul old and wise. We had a longhouse near a village situated where Chippawa Creek flows into the great waters of the Niagara River. One spring, she gave me a fine son."

"You have a son? Where?"

"Had, eh. Had a wife and a son," Charley replied tonelessly. "Six months after the boy wailed his first cry, a plague of influenza swept across the countryside. Many died. Snow Maiden and Jean Pierre now keep the fires burning and await me at the altars of tomorrow."

"I feel like I should say I'm sorry, but that's so trite."

"No reason for such words."

"Your sorrow is unseen."

"Its reflection is strong inside."

"I empathize, Charley."

"Life does what it does, eh," he said, glancing back at the mule. "We put loss behind us, but forgetting is an impossibility. Our hearts carry the scars of mourning as is proper. Snow Maiden and Jean Pierre are close to me. One day we will celebrate being together again, eh."

"Does it ever get easier?"

"Easy is for fools," he replied bluntly. "You know that, Max. Nothing worthwhile is ever easy. The grievous wounds on our hearts are to be reminders, eh. Death stalks us all. We, the living, do well to carefully number our days for the sunrise holds no promise of breath."

"Sometimes the brevity of life is heavy on me, Charley."

"As it should be."

"I try imagining the future, but can't envision anything beyond putting an end to Smoky Crowe's reign," she said, eyes pulling tight. She took her Stetson off and flipped her hair. "The Ute witch is ever before me, but on the other side there is nothing except blackness."

He nodded. "Whatever tomorrows we each have will come in layers of newness; whether troubles or delights, we'll not experience the offering until the Great Spirit awakens us."

"I'm not in disagreement."

"Days pile on top of each other to become months and years, eh."

"And the years are our lives."

"As are the moments of every day."

She laughed loudly. "I get the message, Charley."

"Concentrate on the now and suck the marrow out of it, eh." He rested his hands on the saddle horn and chuckled softly as slyness crept into his eyes. "What about you, Max?"

"Shine more light on it, Charley."

"Have you ever had a man?"

Dawson toyed with the snakeskin hatband and flashed a smarmy smile. "We've ridden side by side for many years and miles, Charley. Has there ever been a man in the picture?"

"Remember the Bluetick Tavern in Little Black Water, Max?" he asked, amusement in his voice. "I guessed maybe Bronco Bob had a chance with you, but you hustled him, eh."

"Aren't you the wise-apple?" she replied, scoffing. "Truthfully, before we partnered up there were a few ne'er do well suitors, but none ever got past the pawing me stage. I've not yet come across a man who stirred me in that way, so my ripeness has never been picked."

His head tilted as his eyelids fluttered. His shoulders hunched in a shiver, then he gave her an intense stare. "Somewhere on the trail ahead you will meet an unbedded rusty-haired man. You will make each other very happy. He is the one the Great Spirit has for you." He pointed at her. "For you, on the other side of Smoky Crowe, there are years of domestic bliss."

She swallowed hard, startled and wary. Her brow creased in doubt. A small tightness formed in her craw and she felt dryness in her mouth. She fidgeted with the snakeskin hatband again, then tucked her hair under the hat and eyeballed him. "That's crazy, Charley."

"No. Your future, Max. I have *seen* it, eh."

Eliza Weitzel had her granddaughter snuggled on her lap, occasionally jostling her from one knee to the other, so as far as she was concerned, the importance of the day was settled. She was in a roughhewn chair that had been cut from a tree stump. It had cushions on the back and seat, and was one of four such examples of unique workmanship on the veranda.

It was midafternoon, and a considerable amount of anticipatory excitement had taken hold at the main house of *WT Ranc*h. The women were gathered and waiting for the buckboard to return from South Fork loaded with supplies. When it arrived, there would be a flurry of activity parceling out dry goods and sundries, followed by a communal meal.

"Grandpa and Jesse are coming," Bethsuelo said, serious and firm.

Eliza smiled gently. "Not quite yet, muffin. Another hour or so."

"No, Grandma. They're just over there a ways. Not far at all," Bethsuelo insisted, waving toward the direction from which they would come. "Can't you hear the squeaky wheel?"

Sally Twosongs slipped off the rocker swing and went to the top step, head inclined and tensed to listen. Lines knitted across her brow. "I don't hear any such squeaking."

Naomi Axler stood. "Neither do I."

"There ain't no squeak," her daughter said glumly. The eagerness for the wagonload of store-bought provisions didn't extend to Amanda Axler. The ten-year-old was in a pouty funk because she had wanted to tagalong on the trip, but those plans were summarily nixed by her mother. "Bethsuelo is making it up to tell a story. There ain't no squeak and she knows it."

"Mind your manners, young lady," Naomi ordered, eyes tightening on her. "You should know that my patience for your tiff has worn paper thin, so be wise and heed the warning."

Amanda's mouth puckered sourly. "Yes, ma'am."

Naomi gave her a nudge. "You owe someone an apology."

"I'm sorry, Bethsuelo," Amanda said meekly. "I didn't mean nothing."

Sally Twosongs bent low to make eye contact with the girl. "I could use some help in the kitchen, Amanda. Will you please join me to mix the dumpling dough for the stew?"

"Yes, Sally Twosongs," Amanda answered, jumping to her feet. They scampered inside, and when the door closed behind them, Naomi slumped onto the rocker swing, sighing.

Eliza was sympathetic. "Is motherhood putting you through the mill?"

"I'm often at my wit's end," Naomi answered wearily. "Jesse is growing up far too fast and demanding man-sized responsibility. Amanda is at a stage where she gets moody and lets her feelings stick out like she was a porcupine. If it isn't one squabble it's another. There are days when it seems I'm constantly at loggerheads with my children."

"Relax some, Naomi," Eliza said, hugging Bethsuelo close to her bosom. "You are doing a wonderful job. Jesse is a fine young man. Very reminiscent of Caleb at the same age. Yes, Amanda is a spunky firecracker, but she's mostly respectful and always tenderhearted."

"I probably worry too much. A mother's tension I suppose. My mind has been much distracted of late." Naomi shifted her backside and smoothed folds from her skirt. "Whenever they get here there better be mail. It would be good to have some news from Abbey."

Bethsuelo sat up straight. "LC is safe, Aunt Naomi."

Naomi frowned. "Pardon, honey?"

"LC is safe. He has a new friend."

"LC?"

"She means Langton," Eliza explained, raising her eyebrows expressively. She gave the little one's nose a playful tweak. "Bethsuelo is convinced LC is his *real* name."

The women exchanged an inquisitive look. Just then, three rifle shots rang out, which was the signal that the buckboard was close to its destination. Two hundred yards away, it emerged from the cover of aspens as the echo of gunfire dispersed. Eliza Weitzel and Naomi Axler stared peculiarly at each other—the incessant squeak of a wagon wheel could be clearly heard.

In the wide open spaces north of Abilene, Lucinda Enochelli guided the rental buggy off the dusty road onto the ruts of a laneway that led to a farmstead. The house, a two-story building with an overhang roof, sat atop a smallish hillock. A barn was a fair distance behind it, along with another outbuilding, and off to the side, what appeared to be a two-seater privy.

She took it all in, steering over bumps on the way to the residence. Her mouth was parched, and there was a cramp crawling around between her shoulder blades. She tugged on the reins and the horse dutifully slowed to a stop. She disembarked and shaded her eyes against the sun, then bopped up and down on the balls of her feet to get circulation flowing.

The front door opened. A woman clad in a drab outfit stepped onto the porch. Her face was pinched and her demeanor standoffish. "May I be of some service to thee, ma'am?"

"A glass of lemonade or something sweet and wet before I die would be nice," Lucinda replied, dour and brazen. She strolled determinedly toward her. "Is this the Mueller place?"

"Yes. I am Anna. I shall return shortly."

Lucinda nodded brusquely. She waited for her to be inside, then climbed the stairs and surveyed the broad veranda. Positioned across from each other were two straight-backed benches of the kind found in a chapel. She took a seat and began fanning her face. The afternoon was warm, and the ride from town had her sweaty and disagreeable.

A lanky man in a straw hat rounded the corner of the house and stuttered to a stop when he saw her. He eyed her cautiously as he came onto the porch. "I am Abraham."

"Is Anna your wife?"

"Yes."

"Sit down then. She's getting me a drink."

"And you are?"

"A woman dying of thirst," Lucinda answered sharply. "Do you have any other hairball questions to ask?" Her hand was still acting as a fan. "Lucinda Enochelli, if you must know."

Mueller remained standing. "Are you in need of assistance?"

"No," Lucinda snapped, shaking her head. "I woke up this morning and decided I wanted to tour some godforsaken backcountry, so here I am. If I had to live here in nowhere land I'd take a gun out and shoot . . ." She cut off the remainder of the sentence because she caught the thirtyish man in the homespun clothes secretively snatching peeks at her bustline. He made every effort to be furtive, but she had much experience in identifying his sneaky tactics.

Since puberty, when her upper deck became prominent, she always enjoyed the effect her bubbies had on men of all ages and stations. She became coquettish in putting her assets to good use. She presently rolled her shoulders forward, which caused the square-cut neckline to dip even lower. His discomfort was obvious. She licked her lips and said, "Why, Mr. Mueller. I was under the impression that River Brethren men were delivered from seamy lusts of the flesh."

Mueller, red-faced and shifty, turned away. "Your enticement is sinful."

"Sinful is where the fun is, Mr. Mueller," she quipped, laughing throatily.

The door opened and Anna came out carrying two glasses of lemonade. "Abraham, I did not realize you had arrived from the barn. Would you like me to get you a drink, too?"

"Thank you, no."

Anna gave him a second-look, showing surprise at the aggression in his tone. She handed their visitor a glass and sat across from her. "It's sweet and wet as per your request, ma'am."

"Anna," Abraham said somberly. "Your hospitality is commendable, but not necessary or warranted. This woman has come here for an intent that may not be at all on the up-and-up."

"Apologies for your delusion, sir," Lucinda retorted, eyes glaring hotly. "I assure you that my motivations are honorable. The clerk at the newspaper office bade me to come here."

Suspicion shadowed his face. "To gain what advantage?"

"First off, the whippersnapper gave me decent directions," Lucinda answered wittily. "He inferred that you folks would have information as to the whereabouts of Deacon Coburn."

"What business does a woman like you have with Deacon Coburn?"

Anna cringed. "Abraham!"

"A woman like me?" Lucinda enquired, feigning wide-eyed offense. She caused fingers to tremble over her cleavage. "And what kind of woman do you suppose I am, sir?"

"Thou art loose and immoral."

"Mayhap so, as far as it goes, but it's a small man who condemns with such exceptional ease," Lucinda said snidely. "What goes around comes around so be careful, Mr. Mueller."

"You dare to lecture me?"

Lucinda sipped her lemonade, pursed her lips and spoke over the rim of the glass. "Your verdict puts me in good company, sir. Mary Magdalene was a loose and immoral woman, and if I remember my Sunday learning accurately, she hung around with Jesus." Her eyes never strayed from his face. "Your caustic judgment may come back and bite your ass, Mr. Mueller."

Anger was visible in him—his complexion darkened and his hands were flexing. He took a glowering step closer to his wife. "Anna." His voice buzzed indignantly. "I will have no further contact with vulgarity. Ours boys are working in the barn. I will join them and expect you to do the same when this woman departs." He turned on his heels and scurried off in a huff.

Lucinda dismissed his temper with a devil-may-care chuckle. She finished off the tasty beverage and smacked her lips. "I haven't got all day, Anna. Do you have pertinent information as regards Deacon Coburn? Perhaps knowledge as to where I could locate him?"

"Deacon is my uncle, but I never really knew him," Anna replied, anxiety evident in her posture and the set of her face. "He was gone from the community in Pennsylvania before I was born. He stopped in to visit with us a couple years ago, but we haven't seen him since '86."

"Where does he call home nowadays?"

"Nowhere I would guess," Anna said tersely. "He has moved from one town to another so much I doubt he calls anyplace home. He may still reside in Dodge City, at least when he settles down for a spell, but I cannot say so having any assurance as to being correct."

"Dodge City will be my next stop."

"If you don't mind, how do you know Uncle Deacon?"

"That's neither here nor there, is it, Anna?"

"It would be polite of you to provide a reply."

"Politeness has never been an affectation of mine."

"As you have demonstrated quite well."

Lucinda put the glass on the floor, then got to her feet. "You best toddle off to the barn to be scolded." She whipped past her and hurried to the buggy. Afternoon sunshine highlighted her bouncy black hair. Seated in the carriage, she handled the reins as if she was a seasoned teamster, and in short order, Lucinda Enochelli had the horse trotting toward Abilene at a rollicking gait.

That evening, at Delmonico's Restaurant in Dodge City, block-bodied Willy Phips was all sixes and sevens, and in no mood to be disturbed. He had a Panama hat low on his forehead and his skillful hands were busy shuffling the tools of his vocation. Nostalgia was in him and he pined for the good old times because try as he had, there was no action to scare up.

The gambler and gadabout, who for over half of his fifty-eight years, had plied his trade on the swankiest riverboats and in the wildest gaming houses from coast to coast, now sat at a table against the back wall, minding his own business playing solitaire. He flipped each card over and studied it as if the proceeds of a jackpot depended on where he put it.

He felt alone and out of place. The ticking clock had no scruples or mercy; time kept altering or revolutionizing all it pertained to, and his sense was that the world was turning too fast and the changes were not at all an improvement. He came to town two days ago in hopes of looking up a plump and sassy whore he had cohabited with in '83 and '84, and to see for himself if the newspaper reports and grapevine gossip jelled with reality.

Upon alighting from the train—to his enduring disappointment—he soon determined that Dodge City was duller than a multitude of teetotaler Quakers vigilantly resolved to keep the Sabbath Day holy; the news of the downfall of a hotbed of excitement was too true to be real. The onetime *wickedest city in America* had become a sleepy agricultural community.

He made every effort to revisit all the untamed hang-outs, but wandered aimlessly because the rowdy saloons and dance halls were no more, which curtailed the merchandising of sin that had made the cowtown infamous. The proprietors of barrooms and brothels had become legitimate or simply took their money and entrepreneurial skills westward.

It was as though the hand of God had aligned the universal forces of morality and judgment against Dodge City in 1885. An inferno on Front Street gutted establishments on the main thoroughfare about the same time as an epidemic of splenic fever among the longhorns resulted in a quarantine that shutdown the Great Western Cattle Trail.

The fiery destruction of Front Street and the halt in trafficking of Texas cattle were twin cataclysmic happenings that coincided with the cresting wave of a do-gooder movement that was swelling across the country. In 1885, while burnt out buildings were being demolished and cattle were dying, public officials enforced the 1880 Kansas Prohibition Law in Dodge City.

Now, to an oldtime highroller cardsharp, everything was wrong. Willy Phips was in the grips of a dose of the doldrums. He'd searched for the bubbly soiled dove his loins so thoroughly desired, but gave up, concluding that she had either died or moved on. The only familiar face he had seen was the Western Union operator, but Phips had no intention of reaching out to him because he recalled Butch Mackenzie's reputation for being surly and irascible.

The eatery was sparsely populated. In days of yore when Dodge City was the reckless and undisputed *Queen of the Cowtowns*, Delmonico's was known as The Lone Star, a joint where prostitutes circulated freely amid the poker and faro games. All that thrilling atmosphere and ambiance was gone; replaced by routine dreariness that was boredom personified.

There was a cup and saucer near his right hand; the contents of which had begun as black as midnight, but at present, despite the citywide ban on liquor, had golden hues and was more alcohol than coffee. He had been surreptitiously boosting the Arbuckle's from a silver flask kept in an inside breast pocket of his frock coat—never to be bereft of rye whiskey he carried four such containers secreted in slots of his loose fitting clothes.

Willy Phips, a hard-eyed and cynical man, put the cards down and emptied the cup. He tapped the table to get a waitress's attention and motioned for service. He intended to salivate over a juicy beefsteak smothered in onions and afterwards, unless a better offer arose, he would return to his accommodations at the Central Hotel and sip whiskey until sleep overtook him.

At the Axler household in Colorado, Pete sat on the top step of the front porch whittling, with Jesse beside him cleaning a Spencer rifle. The moon had yet to make an appearance above the wall of mountains. Father and son labored effortlessly, encased in a flickering bubble of pale light from kerosene lanterns hooked on brackets mounted on the pillars of the veranda.

"Did Mr. Weitzel say anything about the bobcat we saw?"

"Not a word. Where?"

"We were on our way home," Jesse answered, ramming the rod down the barrel. He did so in a precise and methodical stroke. "It couldn't have been more than a mile from here."

"Too close for my liking. A bobcat's a nuisance."

"Mr. Weitzel wasn't pleased."

"I'd guess not."

"The cat was bold," Jesse said earnestly. "It stood in the middle of the roadway staring and snarling at us. When Mr. Weitzel lifted his Henry rifle, it scooted and disappeared."

"Our chickens will be an invitation to it."

"I could camp out in the coop."

The former lawman jiggled his blade across the chunk of oak. A sliver peeled off and dropped onto the heap of shavings between his feet. His seemingly permanent frown deepened as he mulled over the proposition. He had a glance at the bluish-black sky, where dots of stars were beginning to shine as unsteadily as momentary winks. "That's top of the line thinking, son."

"Mom ain't gonna like it."

"I'll square it with your mother."

"Are you sure, Dad?"

"Yep."

"I'll get a bedroll when I'm done here."

"And keep that Spencer close," Pete advised calmly. "The wildcat will smell you, which ought to keep it away. You likely won't get a chance at a shot, but if you do, kill it."

"If all's quiet tonight," Jesse said, "I could do some riding and wandering tomorrow, and be on the lookout for it. Get on the hunt before sunup and stick to it until noontime or so."

"More top-drawer thinking."

"Best opportunity to spook it will be early morning."

"That's a fair reckoning," Pete declared, hands staying busy. "Bobcats are solitary and generally nocturnal hunters, but like to do some peak prowling at dusk and dawn."

"You'll square me being gone with Mom?"

"Yep." Pete nodded, eyes tapering into slits. He straightened his back, stopped sculpting the wood and gave his son a consequential look. "Is there something you need to be telling me?"

"Whatcha mean?"

"You're overly concerned about your mother."

"Ain't you noticed the tension between us?"

"Am I blind?" Pete asked, grinning. "It ain't nothing out of the ordinary. Just the way it is with mothers and sons, Jesse. If I was you I'd keep plugging away and it'll work itself out."

"Mr. Weitzel told me much the same."

"I suppose he would."

"We got to talking about responsibility, Dad."

"An interesting topic. Any surprises?"

"That it has no end."

"You already knew that, Jesse."

"Did I?"

"Yep," Pete replied, chuckling cheerfully. He had the knife working at a moderate clip that kept chips flying. "Your nature has always been serious and levelheaded. You were born to it and there's no earthly reason to kick against it. In all your growing up learning, I can count on one hand the number of times I had to tell you something more than once."

"That's good, no?"

"That's good, yes," Pete corrected, accompanied by another chuckle. "You see a job that needs doing and promptly get to it. Take that wheel for example. Many others would've let greasing the axle wait, but you had it done twenty minutes after the wagon was unloaded."

"I told Mr. Weitzel I'd see to it."

"And so you did. That makes you a man of character, son."

Jesse wiped a rag over the barrel and stock of the carbine. He finished buffing and rested the rifle in the crook of his arm. "Mr. Weitzel referred to me as one of the men of *WT Ranch*. I ain't ever thought of myself in that way, but he hit it hard and kind of convinced me."

"Why would you need convincing?"

"I ain't sure I could put a finger on it."

"He's right, Jesse."

"You agree?"

"It ain't something I ever thought needed saying aloud."

"That *is* a big whoop. The womenfolk?"

"Nothing you can't shoulder, son," Pete said candidly. "You keep an eye out and stay the course. Be ready to jump in and help. There ain't a manual on the subject that I know of, which means you have to trust your instincts. Whenever trouble shows up you'll know what's required for you to stand strong for others. You ain't no greenhorn when it comes to responsibility."

"You ever worry about failing?"

"Worry ain't got no point."

"It nags at me on occasion."

"Give it a swift kick, son." Pete shifted around until he was facing him directly. "I may not have the right words in me or get them out so as you can take hold and make sense of it, but you're made of stuff that's solid under pressure and I am proud to be your father."

Jesse gave a tight-lipped nod. "I best get to the chicken coop."

"Sit awhile longer," Pete said, voice thick and eyes glistening. "You got time. We'll patrol the perimeter together in a bit, then get you settled in." He returned to his prior position and his hands automatically got to whittling. In their understated style, the conversation picked up and took a turn toward ranch business that rapidly became a to-do list of tasks.

While her husband and son were occupied by man-talk, Naomi Axler was at the kitchen table with oil lamps burning. Amanda sat across from her using knitting needles with the same disciplined exactness that her father put into action carving wood. Naomi beamed a smile that had no end as pride swelled in her bosom and put a lump in her throat.

Moisture filled her soulful brown eyes. Lately her emotions seemed to be a swirl within that often got away from her. There was no rhyme or reason for the moodiness that overcame her to make her edgy and frustrated. She blinked the dampness away. She had a bulging envelope in hand that had arrived with the supplies from South Fork. Excitement thrilled through her as she tore it open and bent back the creases in the letter from her vagabond gypsy niece.

January 12, 1888
Dakota Territory

Dear Aunt Naomi: Hello from the land of frozen tundra. We have been in a deep freeze for the past three weeks. The skies are continually heavy and leaden-gray, but there is just a thin blanket of snow that the wind manages to whip into a frenzy on a daily basis. It has now been nineteen days since the sun made an appearance from behind the bulwark of clouds, which I suppose, accounts for the general malaise affecting many of us.

Despite the dreary weather and sometimes harsh conditions, Langton and I are well. We remain sojourners with a band of Lakota Sioux who have accepted us as their own. At first, due to so many wrongs done to them by people who look like us, our relationships were tenuous and awkward, and we were treated as outsiders, but over time that has changed. This spring will mark our second year as white-skinned members of the nomadic clan.

An elderly man named Standing Wolf has adopted us as his kinfolk. From what I have ascertained he is a medicine man of some repute and used to be active in the councils of his people, but of his own accord, chose to withdraw from tribal politics and decision making to concentrate on spiritual needs and caring for those requiring extra attention. It is good for Langton and I to know him for his heart is inflamed with compassion and mercy.

We are camped on a bend of Wounded Knee Creek—in Lakota it's called Chankwe Opi Wakpala. It is an offshoot of the White River, which itself is a tributary of the Missouri River, so if the aspiration so struck, I could put a canoe in the water here and paddle all the way to St. Louis on the mighty Mississippi River. Now that would be an adventure to enjoy!

In these dismal winter days we spend many hours burrowed in our tepee, but boredom is not an issue, though Langton may disagree and tell you different because he always wants to be out running with his friends. He has made a special connection with a daring and likeminded youngster named Yaz, who is somehow related to Standing Wolf, but I am unsure of the exact familial lines. The boys are the same age and it is a joy to see them together.

Langton is thriving in this environment. He is treated as an equal amongst his peers, which he naturally reciprocates. I am so proud of his innocence and relational tenderness. I suspect if cut deep enough there is bigotry in our midst, but to my knowledge, my son has not been subjected to it or even seen it displayed, which encourages and blesses me.

His education is a one of a kind affair, not confined to a classroom or contained only within books. It is wonderful to teach him life-lessons in the context of our day by day scratching to provide for basic necessities. He knows the value of teamwork and communal sharing. The perspective that the village must function together is being ingrained in him.

I marvel at how quickly he picks up new ideas and insights. His mind is sharp and curious. He has a grasp for the language that eludes me. He easily communicates in English and Lakota, or a blended mix of the two that is somehow eloquent. To see him interact with his chums is to be amazed for he demonstrates a take-charge leadership role.

There is a protocol for the men to pass knowledge on to the next generation, and Langton is included in this upbringing ritual. Through fathers and uncles of his friends, he is developing all kinds of hunting and fishing skills along with tracking and trailing and wrestling. It is great fun watching him tousle about learning the ins and outs of takedowns and such.

Be assured that his formal education isn't being neglected. I tend to those requirements of his schooling. He is being immersed in reading, writing and arithmetic, which he seldom handles as a chore. He cherishes books and stories. On a regular basis Yaz joins us for a daily tradition of me reading a chapter or two with a dramatic flair. We are currently working our way through Treasure Island by Robert Louis Stevenson. Both boys are enthralled by it.

I do as much writing as possible—not as often as I would like, but enough for Standing Wolf to have taken it upon himself to arrange for a lap-desk to be built for me. Its top is covered in tanned buffalo hide. I also acquired a Sioux name that humbles me; Speaks With A Quill, which in Lakota, as near as I can get it is, WóglakA Kičhí Waŋ WíyakA. Don't ask me to pronounce it because I cannot wrap my tongue around the tonal syllables.

My latest article should be in an upcoming edition of Harper's Magazine. It is the first installment of what I hope will become a novel featuring a dog's escapades keeping a frontier woman safe, which is obviously fictionalized from my journey with Old Blue. I posted the manuscript at Fort Robinson when we were there in early November. Your August letter awaited me. I so enjoyed the news from WT Ranch and pray that everyone remains in fine fettle.

I keep the following to myself, and thank you ahead of time for having an understanding ear. I hope me venting my feelings is not too burdensome for you. I miss our face to face talks, when we were alone and cried without regard to decorum. After my husband was murdered you allowed me to honestly release all the raging pain without judgment or platitudes, which was a precious treasure. You helped me through a terrible darkness in '83 and '84.

Unfortunately, I am discovering that the miles and years make no difference to my sorrow. The empty spaces in my heart are valid. I miss Sam so much that it hurts. I wake up in the night reaching for him. A thorny snag arises and I think that'll be no drawback because Sam will figure it out lickety-split. I'll see something wondrous like a sunset or a particularly beautiful landscape, and my first inclination is to point it out to make sure he sees it too.

Sam is always close to my heart, both figuratively and literally. On the day he asked me to marry him we were on a picnic at a place we dubbed Willows Rest. It was a grove of coyote willows beside a small trickle of a creek. I was a mere child of eighteen, with no experience at all with boys or men, other than what I'd read about in romantic tales. It didn't matter because I was proverbially head over heels in love and he was similarly smitten.

> When I think about the whirlwind nature of our courtship, comprehension sinks in about the connection Sam and I shared; it was remarkably special and far beyond what customarily transpires between prospective sweethearts. God created us for each other. We had ten great years living a dream that others never have the courage or opportunity to pursue.
>
> I am grateful for all we had together, however, my thankfulness does nothing to still the undercurrent of sadness from having a tidal pull on my sentiments. I can still see the burning intensity of his eyes when he popped the question after putting a spindly chain and gold locket around my neck. I now wear that cherished jewelry beneath my clothes so it rests against my skin close to the pitter-patter of my heartbeat. A picture of Sam is framed inside the pendant.
>
> A day doesn't go by that I don't press a palm over it and think of him. Is that normal or morbid? My guess is that bereavement has many expressions and is so personal that all who suffer through the traumatic loss of a loved one has to determine how to navigate through the choppy waters in ways that comfort or make sense to them.
>
> This has been beneficial, Aunt Naomi. I hope it's not a discouragement to you. Thanks for being supportive. I do think of and pray for you often, as I know you do the same for me. I cannot say when we'll return to WT Ranch, but it grants me much freedom to know that we are always welcome. Give my best to all and take care. Write as soon as you possibly can.
>
> Much love,
>
> *Abbey*

Naomi was nibbling on her bottom lip and tears were on her cheeks. She held the correspondence tight. She would read it again—quite possibly several more times. After she drafted a response and got it in the mail, she would file her niece's letter away in a box of esteemed memories to be retrieved whenever she had an urge for another visit.

"Are you alright, Mom? Did Abbey have bad news?"

Naomi jerked in surprise. "Why do ask?"

"You're crying."

"Am I, Amanda?"

"What's wrong, Mom?"

"Abbey is Abbey," Naomi replied, wiping away the wetness. "She has toughness and tenderness, which is fine combination for us to emulate." She slipped the letter into the envelope as her lips strained into an uncertain smile. "As for your mother, I've decided that I don't know what's wrong with me, Amanda. I'm weepy and grumpy, then grumpy and weepy."

"Don't worry, you're tough and tender too, Mom."

"Hope so. I haven't felt tender latterly."

"Everyone has bad days, Mom. You'll be fine," Amanda said thoughtfully. She bounced to her feet and gathered her knitting into a checkerboard patterned handbag. "Goodnight."

Naomi was momentarily rendered speechless by the seriousness of her tone. By the time she was ready to voice a lyrical catchphrase the ten-year-old was gone from the kitchen. "Sleep tight, wake up bright," she purred under her breath. She tinkered with the wick of an oil lamp, somewhat flustered and ill at ease. Her legs were jittery and she felt feverish. It was then that Naomi Axler thought it wise to bundle up in bed and seek a fresh start on the morrow.

When Jack Whistler strolled into Delmonico's Restaurant in Dodge City, his belly was growling. All he wanted to do was silence it, but the joint was nearly deserted because it was almost closing time. He surveyed the room and took in all the details. He placed an order for a meal, applying charm and forceful persuasion that pushed the waitress to compliance.

Jack Whistler could develop situational deafness when he didn't receive the answer he wanted. He received negative replies as an affront, which depending on circumstance and locale, required cajolery or intimidation. He routinely projected a combination of oily smoothness and an audacious confidence that belied his eighteen years.

Stocky and fearless as a child, he had grown into a tall and sinewy man who collected information the way a naturalist gathered specimens to be studied and shelved in the devoted pursuit for knowledge. He strolled to a table against the back wall. He swung a chair out and sat across from a florid-faced man swabbing a plate with a biscuit. "How goes it, Slick Willy?"

"Who the hell are you?"

"An old friend."

"I don't know you, punk. Take a walk."

"We've met, Mr. Phips."

"Where and when?"

"The Wyanhell Roadhouse," Jack replied, eyes piercing and intent on him. "You were in a poker game when Kid Greer disrupted it to scatter Ben Slaton's brains across the floor."

Phips thumbed the Panama hat up and gave him a cock-eyed grin. His shoulders slanted forward as his chest expanded proudly. "I saw it all, but I don't recollect you being there."

"I arrived in Las Vegas a couple days later, Slick Willy."

"I must've been drunk."

"You were tipsy when we met."

"Couldn't be helped," Willy said humorously. His grin got wide and wrinkly. "I was a celebrity and all-comers wanted to buy me a drink so I could regale them with my eyewitness account." He spoke in a girlish sing-song voice that seemed odd given his bulky girth. "The whiskey flowed like water. I even got cash from a newspaperman for an exclusive telling."

"I know. I listened to every word of that interview."

Phips stared studiously at him. He shoved his eating irons aside and gruffly planted his elbows on the table. A flare flashed in his eyes and he wagged a finger at him. "You're that acrobat kid who followed me around for weeks doing handsprings at the drop of a hat."

"That'd be me. Jack Whistler, at your service."

Phips laughed uproariously. "You have any idea how much money in side bets I made off the dares and double-dares you took? A cartwheel here, a triple somersault there. I was flush and feisty. The best was the twisting backward dismount off a galloping horse. Made me a fortune."

"I don't recall ever getting my cut of the winnings."

"We were never in partnership, Jack."

"Live and learn."

"What you doing here?"

"Been around the world and back again," Jack answered, adjusting on the chair as the waitress delivered a plateful of beef and beans. He nodded thanks, then dug in and spoke as he chewed. "Seen the pyramids in Egypt, lived with Tibetan monks and French mercenaries. I've dined on delicacies that looked god-awful, but were mouth-watering tasty."

"Ain't you a frigging fancy pants?"

"And you, Slick Willy? What are you up to?"

"Looking for the past and not finding it," Willy said, picking up the deck of cards. He began to lazily shuffle them top to bottom. "You should've been here when this outfit was The Lone Star. Standing room only and poker or faro around the clock. And painted ladies so sweet and juicy you'd gladly hand over greenbacks just to get them to hang around your chair."

"Change is the way of the world."

Phips sneered. "To hell with change."

"One needs to stay a step ahead of change."

"What do you know, Jack?" Willy asked impishly. His eyebrows wiggled. "You're still a snot-nosed schoolboy with a streak of scalawag in you." In a graceful motion he reached inside his frock coat and came out with a flask, which with the sleight of hand of an opportunist gamester topped off the cup in front of him. "Dodge City never used to be depressing."

"I passed through here in November of '82."

"We missed each other. I came in late October. It had everything," Willy said, forlorn and pensive. He took a long drink of rye and swallowed in a gulp. "My God, in '84 there was a bullfighter ring not far from where we're sitting. Mexican vaqueros put on shows using specially chosen longhorns. I was diddling a buxom gal and at the tables nightly, raking in plentiful dollars." He scoffed in disgust. "Now all the fun and games are gone to blazes."

Whistler finished his meal, and with a twinkle in his inquiring gray eyes, extended a hand to grasp the cup of liquor. "Here's to the optimistic hopes for all the tomorrows to come." He tossed it off and winced as it went down his pipes. "That burns like the bite of a rattler."

"You're just a child, Jack. Whatcha know about smoothness?" A chuckle wove its way through his voice. "I got a suite at the Central Hotel. Let's move this party over there. I'll tutor you in whiskey and tell you some whoppers from yesteryear that'll curl your hair."

"An offer not to be bypassed," Jack said merrily. He possessed the traits of a sponge and regularly sought chances to soak in chapter and verse. From their previous encounter, he knew that the gambler was an effortless raconteur who conveyed data without realizing its import.

Phips rummaged in a pocket and came out with a wad of bills in an ornamental money clip. He slid payment and gratuity for both meals under his plate, then stood and was heading to the door at a rumbling pace. On the boardwalk, the men hurried along side by side, bantering and cracking wise. The camaraderie, folksy and free-spirited, blossomed long into the night.

The kitchen was cheery. Light invaded the darkness and permeated it—nightfall had been reduced to murky shadows straining against a barrier of brightness. Three oil lamps were situated on the table and a row of candles were lined up on the counter, appearing to be sentinel soldiers standing at attention. Eliza Weitzel sat beside her husband with a newly opened letter from Max Dawson in hand. She read it in a poignant voice that was once used to fill a classroom.

February 3, 1888
Taos, New Mexico

Dear Hans and Eliza: Long overdue greetings, my friends. Life is good. Charley and I are both enjoying respite from the trail. We're wintering with Daniel Twosongs at his place on the outskirts of Taos. He is a generous host and well versed in many topics. Daniel and Charley keep me enlightened and challenged with their inexhaustible discussions.

We arrived in late November. Had intended to be here earlier, but got bogged down by a blast of bad weather in the Cimarron Range. We hunkered in a crevice of a cave on the edge of Baldy Mountain for more than a week—first waiting out a snowstorm, then having to deal with the drifts that required much digging. We slugged our guts out, but are no worse for the effort.

It occurred to me when I sat down to write this that I hadn't done so since a year ago January. I apologize for not being a more regular correspondent. Much has happened; some new and some just same old same old. I would like to tell you that Smoky Crowe has met his Maker because of our due diligence, but unfortunately I cannot.

The quest to kill the Ute butcher continues. We've done some rough riding and have gotten close, but his magic is powerful, so Smoky Crowe is still on the loose. A troop of U.S. Cavalry, with orders to hunt the renegade down and arrest him, forcefully recruited us last spring. Neither Charley nor I had much regard for the expedition.

Following our lead in tracking Crowe, the soldiers were mostly saddle worthy, but trotted out a naiveté that dumbfounded us. To a man, the squad expected to have the assignment accomplished inside of a few weeks. We had good clues and sign on Crowe, and were making plodding progress, but then what has become all too predictable occurred.

By mid-summer we had ranged over into the flatland of eastern Colorado and came into contact with our adversary. While the ridiculously flamboyant Sergeant had Crowe sighted in his binoculars and men were hooting and acting like idiots in celebration, there was a puffy cloud of smoke and when it diffused, the rampaging outlaw was nowhere to be seen.

Shortly thereafter, Charley and I extricated ourselves from under the thumb of the military. We made a middle of the night getaway and were long gone by sunup. For all we know we've been branded as deserters, and there could be paper out on us, which doesn't hassle or slow us in our pursuit. We go where the trail leads, though doubts are assailing me.

I am seriously beginning to wonder if we will ever achieve success. I hate myself for saying so, but perhaps Smoky Crowe is so blessed by evil that he is untouchable to us. He has a supernatural knack for making fools of us. He appears, then disappears. He resurfaces and we respond with vigor and persistence, then when we approach, he vanishes again.

I cannot tell you the number of times Smoky Crowe has looped around or past us while we were on full alert. It frustrates me to my core. Charley not so much. He views each incident with a calmness that defies understanding. He is clever and steadfast. And he is convinced beyond ever having reservations that we will end Crowe's life. I sincerely hope he's correct.

My mother and father have been on my mind. My motivation for doggedly chasing Crowe is rooted in what he did to my parents. He took vengeance on my mother and slaughtered her in a furious blood-sport in which no mercy or quarter was given. Daddy, enraged and obsessed, went after him and got pierced by a fatally poison arrow for his troubles.

I don't know. On down times like this, when I have time to reflect and evaluate the dimensions of my life, I worry about the future. What does it hold? More of the same? Is my destiny locked on an unchangeable course? Are there any other options for me? Even as these questions beset me, I know that as difficult as the mission is, I must suck up any misgivings and press onward. To quit or even delay the duty is a genetic impossibility.

In October we were closeby, so we made a quick venture to the old Weitzel homestead. It brought back a ton of memories. I am pleased to report to you that the Freiheit archway remains intact. The charred black cross is also still standing as a landmark of sorts. I visited my father's grave, which brought forth a flood of detestable tears.

He only ever wrote me one letter and I carry it with me always. Three sentences burned into my psyche. This sounds nutty, but as I knelt at his burial place, with a hand resting on one of the rocks piled on the site, I swear, I heard his voice say the words. I was alone, but I heard what I heard. It was so real that I actually looked over my shoulder and expected to see him.

The puritanical couple who now owns the property were friendly enough, though there was judgment in the looks given to us. Charley sloughed it off, as he does all such small-minded things, but their attitude got under my skin. I bit my lip, and to *my credit, kept my mouth shut as best I could. We departed on reasonably good terms, I think.*

At the first warm spell in March we'll be back at it. Taking all our experiences and knowledge of Crowe into consideration, we have talked through many possibilities, and settled on a plan. We intend to spend the spring crisscrossing the Angel Peak badlands. We expect to have an element of surprise that'll arouse him out of his winter slumber.

That's all I got. Will see you when we see you.

Sincerely,

Max

"That girl writes an excellent letter."

Eliza nodded agreeably. "She's not much of a girl anymore, Hans. She must be pushing thirty, or even a bit more. I worry on her and pray for a breakthrough that'll set her free."

"Lightning could strike Smoky Crowe and burn him to a crisp right in front of her, but I'd not count on that," he said, chaffing his hands together. "It seems to me that the Almighty holds back direct intervention because he requires good to willingly pay the price to defeat evil."

"It's bedtime. I'll not be drawn into a theological debate," she replied tartly. "I will, however, ask that you bow your head and be in accord with me as I implore the Lord."

Hans Weitzel smiled gently and gave her hand a firm squeeze. Eliza closed her eyes and waited until the silence became the fragile stillness of meditation, then she dauntlessly entered it with phrases of praise lifted from Scripture, followed by devoutly claiming the promises of God on behalf of Max Dawson. When she said amen, both husband and wife were teary-eyed.

Avis Lahay was on her knees at the bedside of the dying woman. A single candle sliced into the darkness as she silently begged God to set her dear friend free. The urgency gripped her with such force that it set off waves of dizziness. An emotional tug of war had her mind churning between chaotic eruptions of anger and devastating lamentations.

Her sorrowful pleading could no longer be contained. The tumult of words escaped from behind clenched teeth as a desperate whisper. "Why, God? Why are you putting her through this agony? Why? What purpose does it serve? In the name of Jesus, please show yourself benevolent and merciful, and take her to heaven. Please, please release her from the wretched pain."

Brenda Hawkins gasped. The burbling clamor of it filled the room. She fought for air, which was a laborious battle that increasingly became unwinnable, but with whatever reserves of strength that remained, she instinctively clung to life. Her bodily functions were actively shutting down, yet she demonstrated a fierceness that contradicted the ravaging weakness.

Avis pushed to her feet. She leaned close to brush aside stringy strands of hair matted on her sweated brow. "Don't fight anymore," she murmured solemnly. "There's nothing more to be gained, Brenda. Take that short step through the door and see the place prepared for you."

Brenda convulsed and shook. A strenuous breath got trapped in her gullet and gurgled stridently. Her eyes were glazed and unfocused when the swollen lids creaked open. "Tell Stace to be a good boy." Her voice, awash in fluid, was scarcely audible. "Take care of him."

"I promise I will."

"Tell him I'm proud of him."

"I'll do so often, Brenda. I promise."

"Keep him on the straight and narrow."

"I will raise him as my own, but will never let him forget you."

Brenda nodded feebly. She stiffened and struggled, lungs rattling torturous rasps. She unexpectedly sat up, eyes bulging. "I see Jesus. I see Jesus. He's *so* beautiful." Then, Brenda Hawkins sank, exhaled a blood-misted wheeze and was no more—her imprisoned soul shattered the chains of mortality and embraced immortality in the presence of her Lord and Savior.

Avis bent over and kissed her cheek, keeping her lips pressed tight for the longest time. She spoke affectionate words in shaky hitches. Helplessness, of the kind laced together by knots of fragmentary questions, clutched at her. She knelt and prayed insistently. Her hands trembled, as now, the weight of shouldering the role of motherhood overwhelmed her. Discernment and courage fortified her, then Avis Lahay went to say and do what needed said and done.

chapter two

Revelations

"But he, being full of compassion, forgave their iniquity, and destroyed them not: yea, many a time turned he his anger away, and did not stir up all his wrath. For he remembered that they were but flesh; a wind that passeth away, and cometh not again."

~Asaph~

In the dream, Deacon Coburn was seventeen. The surroundings, a favorite hideaway on a forested hilltop, were serene and familiar. He sought out and was drawn to lonely places for he relished solitude and a sense of oneness with nature. It was summertime. In the distance he could view shimmers of sunlight frolicking on the Susquehanna River.

A backpack, loaded with abolitionist doctrinal material that was shaping perceptions and providing insights, was at his side. As was a groundsheet and bedroll, for he had been camping for several days. He had his back propped against a mushroom shaped maple tree and when not being distracted by sunbeams on the choppy water, was reading a provocative tract.

There was much turmoil in him, which sparked a moral superiority that goaded him. He heard a rustle of leaves, closed the pamphlet and searched the dense woods. It took a moment for him to spot one of his younger brothers coming up the sloping incline from about a hundred yards away. Josiah was closest in age to him, separated by a mere eleven months.

"I am here," Deacon called, waving.

"I knew you would be," Josiah said as he came close, smiling easily. "I've tracked you to this spot more than once." He squatted on his heels and clasped his hands together. "Father expects you back today. Most of tomorrow will have us busy butchering hogs."

"I intend to be there," Deacon replied, pulling his knees up and altering his position. He scratched at the bristles of beard stubble. "I told Father I would return for those chores."

"He expressed a desire for me to find you."

"And you have."

"We can walk home together, Deacon."

"Does he not trust me, Josiah?"

"He's Father. He insisted I come."

"His grind pushes me in the wrong direction."

"Not knowingly, I don't think, Deacon. It's just his way."

"He refuses to listen to me, or even see my way."

"Should he?" Josiah asked cheekily. "The commandment has no ambiguity: *Honor thy father and thy mother: that thy days may be long upon the land which the Lord thy God giveth thee.*" He did a tiny hop, shifted his feet and took a knee. "Paul had no vagueness in his letter to the church at Ephesus: *Children, obey your parents in the Lord: for this is right.*"

Deacon smiled wryly. "Are we to have a Scriptural duel? If so, note that two verses later Paul penned a counterbalance that also has no ambiguity or vagueness: *And, ye fathers, provoke not your children to wrath: but bring them up in the nurture and admonition of the Lord.*"

"I'm seeking to be a peacemaker."

"I am appreciative," Deacon said, staring downward. "I will not disregard the rupture in my relationship with Father, but for a difference to be made, he must amend his stance."

"He's Father. Do you expect him to soften?"

"I don't know," Deacon answered gloomily. "I want no dissension between us, but Father and I are at odds. We have contrasting viewpoints and opinions. I expect it'll get worse."

"Why?"

"I cannot abide slavery, Josiah."

"What do you propose doing about it?"

Deacon fiddled with the brochure he had been reading. "I am in constant prayer to hear and understand what steps I should take to participate in justice. What comes to mind again and again is to leave the farm, move to Philadelphia and labor for the abolition of slavery."

"Leave the farm?"

"A plausible presumption."

"Father has twenty-five acres set aside for you."

"I don't want it, Josiah."

"Are you daft?"

"Not to my way of thinking."

"What will become of the land?"

"It's yours, as far as it is possible for me to give it, Josiah."

"You'd leave the farm? The community?"

"Yes."

"What about Lucy Elburt?"

"What are you suggesting, Josiah?"

"Everyone knows she's sweet on you."

"She's too loud and brassy for my liking."

"Maybe so," Josiah allowed, shrugging slightly. "According to the rumors chattering around the agreed gossip is that you're the man her mother has chosen for her to marry."

Deacon squinted. "She can choose someone else. I have some say in the decision. I know nothing about nothing, but I can tell you in certainty that I ain't the one for Lucy Elburt."

Josiah chuckled. He leaned in closer. "What of Mother?"

"A man has to do what's in his heart to do."

"Mother will be discouraged and distressed," Josiah said frankly. A dim fog of sadness sifted across his face. "You are to be a River Brethren preacher. That's her dream."

"*Her* dream, Josiah."

"Perhaps a call for you to respect?"

"My sensibilities direct me elsewhere," Deacon replied, low and indomitable. "Mother is the one who taught me to follow the light shining within. I am prompted to be honest and true to the voices of our Negro brothers and sisters crying out from the bitterness of hard bondage."

"When will you leave?"

"It's still if, not when, Josiah."

"Do I hear hesitation and doubt?"

"No," Deacon said distinctly. "I'm wrestling with the issues and expect to be patient in perseverance to gain assurance of praying through to victory on the decision. Your support in prayer is coveted, but I request that this discussion remain confidential and sealed."

"You have my word, brother to brother."

It was then that Deacon Coburn woke up and returned from the recreated past in stages. He lay perfectly still and listened to the night as he fondly remembered Josiah and wondered what had become of him. His lips pursed because there'd been no contact between the brothers since before the war—almost three decades. That recollection dismayed him.

He sat up and leaned forward to grab his boots. He tipped each one upside down and gave it a shake to be rid of any creepy crawlers that might've taken up residence whilst he slept. When he was satisfied that no snakes or lizards were present he pulled the footgear on, stood and stretched. A massive yawn consumed his face as he energetically waggled his arms.

The brisk air was revitalizing. He did a couple deep knee-bends, then stretched again in a deliberate manner. His partner was snoring softly, wrapped up in a tangle of blankets close to the smoldering ashes of the campfire. Coburn stepped lightly past him. He took long strides and went fifty-plus yards before he unbuckled for the purpose of relieving his bladder.

After completing the deed of watering a patch of brush, he wandered until he came to a boulder suitable to be used as a bench. He roosted on it and got comfy. He waited and watched, angled eastward to behold the pinkish-orange line peeking over the edge of the horizon. Alone with his thoughts and memories, he prayed under the inspiration of the sunrise.

Sally Twosongs looked and saw a throng of tribes celebrating a circle dance. She was high and lifted up, as though her spirit had risen to an unearthly realm where the chanting song of the multitude was the rushing roar of a colossal waterfall. Her heart was awestruck, and her body tingled from the top of her head to the soles of her feet.

The panoramic spectacle stole her breath away. Her senses were overloaded and she couldn't process the wide-ranging pageantry. She strained to partake of it all. Her dark eyes were aglow with a passionate concentration, and her ears were pricked and sensitive. The voices of the myriad choir were a melodious harmony woven in unison with the drumbeats.

Nations were gathered in ceremonial garments—thousands upon thousands; of a number no one could count. The teeming swarm of humanity moved in perfect rhythm to the music of drums, horns, flutes, bagpipes, harps and lyres. Her legs began to lift and fall as the pounding cacophony of notes got inside her. Though she was not in the midst of the dancers, it was as though the cadence gripped her; she mirrored their movements and became one with them.

Excitement surged through her when Charley Jondreau came into view. She immediately called his name, but it stuck in her throat and remained unheard. He emerged from a cluster of high-steppers to take a turn leading. He twirled in a flourish as his upper body bobbed and weaved, his face encircled in beams of light. She felt a wave of heated emotions and tried to shout louder and louder, but not a peep came forth.

She awakened to the bleep of gleeful laughter, which caused her to cover her mouth so as to stifle it. Her eyes widened in awe and wonder. She remained still and flat on her back staring at the ceiling as she pondered the significance of the scene. She rolled over to the realization that her husband was already up and at it, then remembered that the *WT Ranch* spring roundup began today, so the men would be gone and busy from dark to dark.

The blankets got tossed aside and her feet hit the floor. She hurried to her shelf of flutes and selected a favorite, then went to the living room and sat in the grayish light in front of the fireplace. A log crackled a greeting. She bowed her head and listened to the interior music. After a moment of contemplation, she duplicated the melody from the dream.

Her imagination soared to heights unknown. Each note took her higher and higher. She had no hesitation and put up zero resistance. She was floating in a beauteous place of peace and seamless symmetry. The tune increased in volume and she was lost within it. Her eyes were closed, her body swaying in sync with the tempo.

She heard humming that matched the canticle of the flute, then padding footsteps eased up behind her. There was pressure against her side that got stronger as the sweet crooning intensified. She kept playing, while enjoying the warmth and voice of her daughter. The two purposefully pressed and seesawed together until the song faded into silence.

"Mommy."

"Yes, Bethsuelo."

"I heard you in my sleep."

"The song came to me in *my* sleep."

"It was pretty."

"Yes, very." She put the flute on the floor and pulled the child close. Hank tried to squeeze between them, but Sally Twosongs gave the collie a dissuading shove. The dog huffed and slobbered sloppily, then plopped down in a sad-eyed sulk. "I often have dreams where I see or hear things in my sleep. Does anything like that ever happen to you?"

Bethsuelo nestled in tighter. "I don't know, I guess."

"That's not really an answer."

"Yes, it is, Mommy."

The fire snapped and popped. A streamer of blue flames sputtered upwards, then became a reddish ridge on a chunk of wood. Sally Twosongs hugged her even closer. "Bethsuelo, this is important, honey. I want you to think real hard. Do you see or hear things while you sleep?"

"I have funnies in my head."

"Funnies?"

"I smile and laugh."

"That must be nice, Bethsuelo."

"I don't know, I guess."

"There you go again, honey," Sally Twosongs said, chuckling softly. "Can you tell me what you meant when you said: *Don't worry, Daddy. Jesse will be with Mommy.*"

"I told Daddy that?"

"Yes, Bethsuelo."

"I forgot, I guess, Mommy." She crinkled her nose. "I'm hungry."

The tricolor collie stood and barked once. Sally Twosongs nudged her daughter and made a gesture toward the door. "You let grumpy old Hank out, then meet me in the kitchen and we'll fix pancakes for breakfast." She rose to her feet and took dawdling steps. Her heart was full of questions for the Creator, but readily let them go, and a smile creased her lips. She possessed a single-minded faith that steeled her against the problematic vagaries of the world.

When the train chugged away from the Chicago, Rock Island and Pacific Railroad Depot in Abilene, Lucinda Enochelli settled in for the ride to Dodge City. The passenger car she sat at the back of had only three other occupants, which pleased her just fine. A newspaper was in hand, but she wasn't reading it yet. Her luggage was on the seat across from her.

She had rolled a cigarette while waiting to board, and now, lit it and inhaled the first drag so deeply that it tickled the bottom of her lungs. She tossed the match on the floor and exhaled short spurts of smoke. Her westward trek put her in a reflective mood that had her mind drifting backwards in time as she poked through a closet of memory.

It was in the boisterous early days of the War Between the States when social upheaval offered opportunities for action to exert change. She was sated and sweaty from a noontime tryst with an aggressive lover. She stood at the window of a loft apartment overlooking a street in Philadelphia. A crumpled sheet was clutched to her bosom to cover her nakedness.

"Coco."

She turned to face Logan Treglor, her latest paramour—he had tagged her with the affectionate nickname based on her dusky complexion. She liked it so much that it had become interchangeable with her first name. He was dashing and thick-chested; her hard as nails partner in all things that skirted lawful behavior. She flipped her raven locks. "Are you spent?"

"For now," he replied, lacing up his boots. "We go get the job done and be back here shortly after sunset, and I'll be ready to ride the bucking pony again." He pulled a shirt on and tucked it into his trousers. "Are you wearing that bed-linen or are you going to get dressed?"

"It's simple and elegant, is it not?"

"We're on a clock, Coco."

"There truly is no rest for the wicked, is there, Logan?"

"The timetable is set and we can't miss any marks."

She dropped the white wrapper and did a wiggly promenade toward him. She folded an arm across her boobs and flashed a taunting smile. "Maybe I'll just go in my birthday suit."

"It'd be a helluva diversion."

"You'd be the one getting distracted, which cannot be since you're the one responsible for the fuse and gunpowder," she said, stepping into her bloomers. She gathered her clothes and sat on the edge of the bed, then began rolling on her stockings. "You do realize that if this goes wrong my father will find you and skin you alive or put you through a cider press."

"If this goes wrong, your father will be the least of our worries."

"I suppose."

"The police will come crashing down, so our retreat has to be flawless."

"We have time for one more run-through of the details." She had her undergarments on and got to her feet to finish dressing. "There's too much at stake for slipups or mistakes."

"Yes," he said, taking a seat at a small table. He picked up a notepad and studied the step by step plan. "It's a good strategy, Coco. We hit it, in and out real quick. No muss, no fuss."

"No muss, no fuss? What the hell, Logan?" She was giving her wavy tresses a slam-bang brushing. "There better be plenty of muss and fuss. We're at war, for crying out loud. Southern sympathizers cannot be allowed to operate in our midst without consequences. This foray is our first shot and it best be rip-roaring. If there's no commotion or shakeup, what's the point?"

"Easy, Coco. You're preaching to the choir."

"Am I?" she queried, hot-eyed.

"You're brackish and full of brine."

"Tell me something I don't know."

"I'm the one who initiated this scheme, Coco."

"I am aware of that fact, buster," she said, giving him a smarmy glare. "You seem a mite lackadaisical, is all I'm saying. This isn't a lark or a Sunday afternoon stroll in the park."

"Is that headline news?" he asked sarcastically. "I'm the one whose ass will be on the firing line. I, more than anyone else, understand the risks, yet you don't see me having the wet willies." He fisted a hand and bumped knuckles on the tabletop. "We hit Southern sympathizer businessmen in their pocketbooks, destroying property and capital. No caving in, no surrender. We strike hard and they'll get the message. The cash flow to the south will be choked off."

"Disruption is what we must be all about."

He slid off the chair and came up behind her. His arms went around her, hands clamping on her breasts. "We're in for a penny, in for a pound, after today. No turning back. If it goes off the rails and our names get published in the newspapers, we'll be black sheep."

She laughed snidely and pressed forward at the waist. She playfully jiggled her backside against him. "I'm already the black sheep in my family, Logan. As you are in yours." She gave him a hefty elbow and spun free. "If this goes haywire there's no going home for either of us."

Lucinda Enochelli jerked free from the past and exclaimed a profanity. The quirley had smoldered down to the nub and singed her fingers. She dropped it and crushed the butt under the heel of her shoe. The train trundled along at a jaunty clip. She muttered the Lord's name in vain and stared out the window, but the emptiness of the plains had no comfort for her. Moisture glistened in her eyes. Everything that could possibly go wrong had done so in spades.

She remembered the aftermath of the firestorm. The target for the arson, a printing company that specialized in pro-slavery propaganda, was demolished. Logan Treglor got trapped inside and became a human torch, screaming bloodcurdling shrieks until the flames mercifully put him out of his misery. His blackened bones and crispy dregs of flesh were discovered beneath charcoal timbers—his identity remained unknown for she refused to rat him out.

Sitting behind bars, on the edge of a steel-framed rope bed, she hardened her heart and refused to cooperate with authorities. "Lock me up and throw away the key, copper. You'll not get a solitary tidbit out of me. Not today, not ever, you scum-sucking maggot."

The jailer, a flat-nosed screw with a pudgy torso and stubby arms, gave her no relief; he bored harder and harder. "You claim no knowledge as to the body in the ruins."

"I claim nothing," she said, and spat a slimy gob of spittle that splattered at his feet. "You can go away and come back in an hour or tomorrow and you'll get the same answer."

"And your name is Coco?"

"Pound salt, copper."

"Surname?"

"Piss off."

"Our investigation will turn up facts, lady," he replied calmly. He smiled, jowls lifting high enough to convert his eyes into slits. "Whoever you are, whatever you want to call yourself, get used to accommodations such as these because you're likely going to a Federal hoosegow."

"Pound salt up your arse, copper."

The engineer hooted the whistle; its shrillness jarred her back to the present. She leaned against the window—the countryside was unchanged. Her mind was still in that stonewalled cell, which actually, hadn't been her first time behind county bars, but became the longest stretch because after many legal maneuvers, it got restructured into a drawn-out prison sentence.

Her eyes were wet; her mouth withered into a taut line. She pulled the pouch that contained her fixings out of a side pocket of her skirt and set to the task of building a cigarette. Her hands made adjustments to be steady against the rocking of the train. After putting a match to the rollup, Lucinda Enochelli sat back and smoked obsessively as she tried to forget.

When Charley Jondreau was twelve years he had one of the best summers of his life. He was with his maternal grandmother Nekoma, camped on a grassy notch alongside of Chippawa Creek. He had built a large and elaborate lean-to hut to her specifications, and though their site was a mere day's walk from the village, it seemed faraway and remote.

He was in charge of the food supply—an assignment he plunged into with extraordinary thoroughness. He snared rabbits and weasels, collected roots, berries and wild onions, as well as picking apples and pears. The bulk of his energy, however, was invested in fishing, which was peaceful and rewarding; they often feasted on catfish.

A routine developed that he treasured. Each morning after breakfast they would sit together, and Nekoma would tell him stories or provide instruction regarding proper respect. On this sunshiny day, she sat on her thick red blanket listening to an explanation of his education. Her legs were crossed and her hands were on her lap, thumbs idly twiddling.

"Reverend Winger is a strict schoolmaster, eh."

"You are learning much?"

"Oui, Grandmere."

"The white man's words can be strange and his ideas different, but you must put them inside you," she said, dark eyes fixed on him. "Weigh them against our words and our ways. I will always be here to help you find the balance between the two worlds you must live in."

"The Bible has many hard sayings."

"I have read much of it," she told him, sternness in her tone. "The white man's sacred book comes from a long ago place when the Great Spirit chose to set apart the Hebrew people. He called out a man named Abram, and from his loins sprang forth twelve Israelite tribes."

"I studied the dreamer Joseph and his brothers," he said, nodding. "The Great Spirit entrusted him with a gift of seeing what could not be seen or understood by others."

Nekoma smiled knowingly. "You, Charley Jondreau, would be wise to take lessons from Joseph. Examine him to know his faults and failings. Search him and make not his mistakes of youthful pride." She raised a hand, palm held upward. "An eagle screamed on the day you were born. A powerful omen of the Great Spirit's blessing on you, never to be forgotten."

"I *see* happenings, then what I saw becomes real."

"The visions in your head, follow them. Always."

"Follow them, Grandmere?"

"Be true to them," she replied, almost reverently. "The Great Spirit has put a finger on you for reasons that have not been revealed to me. His purposes no one can fathom."

"What am I to do?"

She bowed her head and her hair, as pure white as freshly fallen snow, fell off her shoulders. She swiftly pushed it back. "I only know what I know, Charley Jondreau. You are the oldest son of an oldest son. Your mother, my daughter, was the oldest daughter of an oldest daughter. This land will not be your land. Your destiny will take you far from here."

"I am curious about other places, Grandmere."

"It is in your blood, like the ancient ones."

"Why, eh?"

"Why?" She cackled mirthful laughter. "You can ask the Great Spirit silliness, but do not expect he will draw aside the curtains of the unknowable. He alone is faithful. Wisdom trusts him. You must choose his guidance and walk in the footsteps he has established for you."

"I will try to do my best."

"*Do* your best, Charley Jondreau."

"Oui, Grandmere."

"The God of Abraham, Isaac and Jacob is the Great Spirit. There is no other. False idols come and go as freely as the four winds blow, but pretend gods of rocks or woods are weak. Be not deceived," she counseled adamantly. "The Great Spirit inhabits creation. Keep your eyes clear on that or else when sorrow comes there will be no comfort or hope for you."

"What are we to learn from the Israelite tribes?"

"Everything," Nekoma answered, folding her arms together. "The Israelite tribes were warriors and princes who fought valiantly, and the Great Spirit was heavy on them. There was an understanding in them about the mystery of the Great Spirit's ways that the white man lost and cannot find because they search inside buildings made by human hands. It is pitiful."

"I ponder such things, Grandmere."

"It is good for you to do so," she said, gentle and serious. "We, the Haudenosaunee, the tribes of Iroquois people, have not forsaken the knowledge of the Great Spirit divulged to the tribes of Israel. We have stayed strong by keeping the embers close to our hearts."

"I want those embers to burn in me, eh."

"Jehovah. Creator. Great Spirit. Yeshu'a. Gitche Manitou. One God, many names. Many tribes, one God," she said, picking up a gourd bowl of raspberries leftover from breakfast. She sucked on them one at a time, savoring each berry as she continued presenting wisdom. "We worship the One who is everywhere present; the One who shows his secrets in the shadows of the moon and the brightness of the sun; the One who speaks messages in the heavenlies, and through the birds of the air and all the magnificent creatures roaming the earth."

"How did my white ancestors become blind?"

"Arrogance is the downfall of humans. Always," she replied, nibbling on the fruit. "That is the pattern we see in the tribes of Israel. Over and over the Great Spirit provided miraculous deliverance for them from the hands of enemies, but nothing was enough to satisfy them."

"Grumblers, eh."

Nekoma's eyes got thinner as her head bobbed. "Ungrateful, like we all can become when our heads swell with pride. We forget we are reliant on the Great Spirt for life and breath."

"I give thanks in my prayers. Always, Grandmere."

"As I have taught you." She shifted sideward on the blanket and set the bowl down. "A rebellious streak brought the sword of the Great Spirit's judgment upon the Israelites. Babylon conquered them and the peoples were cast into exile amongst the nations. They were adrift and nomadic, and who shall say that the tribes of Iroquois are not descendants of tribal Israelites?"

"An idea to keep my brain busy, eh."

"Get your feet busy, too, Charley Jondreau," she said, chuckling flippantly. "The sun is getting high and this old woman is going to be hungry for fresh rabbit before too long."

He leapt to his feet and ran to the lean-to, his longish hair flowing behind him. He grabbed his bow and arrows, tipped a grinning nod to her, then raced off to hunt and check the series of traplines. His mind was speeding faster than his legs. As he sprinted toward a dense woodlot, Charley Jondreau secured his grandmother's utterances in the vault of his heart.

When Jesse Axler reined the mare to a stop, Hank came off the porch barking happily. Its whole body wiggled as its tail wagged as though it was going to shake loose. Jesse dismounted and took a knee to receive the collie's sloppy greeting. He hugged its neck, but then, a slamming door and squealing laughter gave him enough warning to stand and get braced for a tangle.

"Jesse!" Bethsuelo yelled as she launched herself off the top step. She collided against his chest and he caught her, but the force of her jump knocked him off balance and he thumped onto his backside, clutching her protectively. The horse did a nifty sidestep to avoid them rolling on the ground, while the dog yapped and pawed at them.

Sally Twosongs came outside, laughing at the sight. "Mr. Jesse Axler, would you mind telling me what your intentions are with my daughter?" she asked, a musical lilt in her voice.

"Ma'am?" he blurted, red-faced. The pigtailed girl was plunked on his chest pinning him down. He propped himself up on his elbows. "I just came for a visit, Sally Twosongs."

Her laughter became exaggerated, hands planted on her hips. "Bethsuelo, will you please let that poor man up before his stuffing comes spouting out? He's not one of your dolls." She sat on the top step. "Shouldn't you be doing chores or in the high pasture with the men?"

"Chores are all done," Jesse replied, on his knees. He gained his feet and dusted the seat of his pants. "I'm kind of slacking on the roundup because another duty had my attention."

"Something important, no doubt."

"I've been out hunting a bobcat."

Her brow darkened in concern. "Really?"

"Yes, ma'am," he answered, tucking his hands in his back pockets. "Mr. Weitzel and I spotted it yesterday. I saw signs this morning, but couldn't scare it from cover to get a shot."

"Thanks for tracking it," Sally Twosongs said, pensive and no-nonsense. "Respect it and give it plenty of elbowroom, Jesse. There is much that can be learned by studying its behavior, but perhaps, you gave it a good enough scare that it skedaddled to find different territory."

"Maybe, but I'd not bank on it." Jesse hunched his shoulders. "It's still hanging around. Our chickens are a temptation, to be sure. I'll make it my business to be on alert for it."

"Stay on top of that cat, Jesse."

"I will, ma'am."

Bethsuelo had been squatting between them listening. She stood and her eyes darted hither and thither. Her mouth puckered doubtfully. "Jesse isn't on top of a cat."

He started chuckling, but it rapidly passed. "That's a good joke, Bethsuelo."

"Joke?"

"You made a funny, Bethsuelo," her mother told her, suppressing a grin. "If you see a big cat anywhere around here, you stay far away from it. Do you hear me?"

"Yes, Mommy."

"Hank, you guard my girl."

The tricolor collie produced a drawn out whine and cocked its head.

"I best go." Jesse sidled to his horse. "Get some food, then join the roundup."

Sally Twosongs glanced at the sun—it was nearing midday. "Did you have breakfast?"

"No, ma'am."

"Get into my kitchen, mister," she said, standing. She backed up across the porch and held the door open. "Miss Bethsuelo and I will put together a stick to your ribs meal."

"That's not necessary, Sally Twosongs."

"I'll not take no for an answer, Jesse."

"Yes, ma'am." He went up the stairs, and the girl skipped along behind him. Inside, he dillydallied to the table. As he watched mother and daughter work on his behalf, he felt like he was indulging in laziness. He squirmed and his hands went from his lap to the tabletop and back again; repeatedly. A half-hour later, he was relaxed in the saddle, riding to high country.

The sun was up and shining like a jewel when the woman once known as Coco walked out of prison in October 1868. Unbowed and unbroken, her backbone was ramrod stiff and her head held high, even though she was entirely alone. Her family, if any relatives remained alive, were scattered and estranged. Her father had passed during her confinement; the news of his death was delivered by a stone-faced official reading a telegram from a lawyer.

Her eyes and body language had remained impassive, but her heart was crushed. She listened and realized that she was familiar with the Philadelphia law firm. She filed that knowledge away for future reference because she had no inclination to make an investigation into estate matters a priority. She had life to live. Her rigid resolve was to go forward.

She had survived imprisonment relatively unscathed, mostly due to the vinegary makeup of her disposition, and her willingness to exchange sexual favors with officers in positions of influence. Those numerous liaisons resulted in her having to partake in doses of pennyroyal on three occasions—each time bleeding out the baby put her in the infirmary.

The institutional clothes on her back were ill-fitting and the drab color of mud. She expected to burn them as soon as she was able to acquire other garments, and when she did so, it would be symbolic of the new beginning she intended to put into action. Flames of intentionality snapped and crackled hot in her, which given her grit, could not be extinguished.

Her plan, mulled over for endless hours while incarcerated, was simple; she would put her former life behind her and reinvent herself. The only limits or boundaries to her designs were those that weakness allowed to chisel away at her daring, which as far as she was concerned, meant that there were no restraints because timidity was unacceptable.

After much daydreaming and scribbling out ideas on scraps of paper, she had settled on an exotic background story to match a flashy new name; she would become Lucinda Enochelli. The instant the letters took shape off the tip of the pencil, a thrill went through her. Far removed from any rural sleepiness, the inspirational appellation had a big city old world ring.

Even though she had yet to speak it aloud, swells of pride surged in her veins at the very thought of it. The moniker, culled off branches of her family tree, put a constant smile on her face because it retained a powerful significance that would ever be motivation to keep her pressing onward no matter what circumstances the fates heaved at her.

The penal system had provided her with a one-way ticket to Philadelphia. Two hours after strolling into the sunshine of freedom, she disembarked at the railroad station and made her way to a women's wear retailer. She shopped in a rush, and the goal of new garments from the inside out was accomplished, though it depleted her meager funds.

The dress, low-cut in the front and a bustle on the rump, was sunflower yellow and ruffled, and made her feel flirtatious. She detoured to a back alley where the prison rags were converted into a small bonfire that gave off billows of greasy smoke. Fulfilled by the ritual, she sauntered to a high-traffic intersection in the business district and exercised her wiles by pacing and prowling like a predator. She started crying and *accidentally* jouncing selected men.

Her distress was palpable. If there was any hint of politeness or compassion from her mark, she proceeded to tell a tale of woe about a tragedy that had befallen her family. She had an urgent need to raise funds to travel to California to see her dear sainted mother before an illness killed her. She was convincing, and soon accumulated a stash of greenbacks.

All was unfolding exactly how she had concocted it. She went to a swank hotel, trolled in the lobby for prospective prey, and then entered the restaurant and ordered steak and eggs. While munching slowly, she probed and analyzed any man who arrived alone. By the time her plate was empty and her belly full, she had chosen a distinguished looking elder statesman.

As she departed the eatery in a sashaying swagger, she opted for a route that took her past his table; she contrived a stumble, and was pleased when he leapt to her assistance. "Oh, my! I am so embarrassed," she exclaimed, wide-eyed and distraught. She clung to his offered forearm and squeezed, blushing on cue. "These shoes are new and pinching my toes."

"Don't be embarrassed, my dear," he replied, exhibiting a thick accent. He helped her get steady, a hand cupped at the small of her back as though he was preparing to dance. "New shoes? A sad dilemma. Always unpleasant until the leather gets broken in." He released his gentle hold, took a decisive backward step and slid a chair out at his table. "Please sit a moment."

"No, I don't want to be a bother."

"I insist."

She batted her eyes. "How can I resist such an offer from a kind-hearted, and may I add, handsome gentleman?" She did a wee-curtsy, making sure to lean forward in such a way as to give him a picturesque view. She immediately saw the symptoms—she had him hooked. All else that occurred in the next twenty minutes would be nothing less than teasing foreplay. She sat and introduced herself; the name felt warm and inviting as it slipped off her tongue.

"Sven Klasson," he said, taking his seat across from her. He fingered a neatly trimmed moustache that had a hint of gray. "Happy to make your acquaintance, Miss Enochelli."

"I am indeed a miss, but please, Sven, call me Lucinda." She smiled and moistened her lips in a slow and deliberate manner. "After all, you are rescuing a damsel in distress."

Klasson had a highball of whiskey in front of him. He took a large swallow. "Helping a lady is always my pleasure." He then ordered a sarsaparilla for his newfound admirer.

She nodded thanks. They conversed about this and that, laughing comfortably. She learned that he had emigrated from Sweden as a teenager, and was now a Chicago banker in town for a convention. Every few minutes she would make the necessary shift in posture to give him a private show, and was joyed by the fact that he didn't disappoint—Sven Klasson seized each opportunity, which was the telltale progression she so desired to illicit in him.

They sipped their drinks and when he came close to the bottom of his glass, she looked into his eyes. "I need to get these shoes off," she said, "but I have miles to go before I can do so." She stood and shuffled to his side. "This has been delightful. I'm sorry I must be going." She bent over and gave him a lingering kiss on the cheek. "Thank you for your kindness."

Sven Klasson was done in. One thing led to another, and Lucinda Enochelli spent her first night outside of stonewalls and iron bars in his third-floor suite. She drove him wild. He tried to keep up with her insatiable carnal cravings, and she convinced him that he was taking her to great heights, though truth was, when he finished and collapsed atop her, she was unsatisfied.

For her, the good news was that Sven Klasson was drained dry and completely exhausted. His lights had been knocked out. As he loudly snored in the feather bed, she disengaged from his arms, got dressed and liberated five hundred dollars from his billfold. Before leaving, she blew him an impish kiss, then successfully made a middle of the night departure. It was a pattern of establishing a useable bankroll that would serve her well across the years and miles.

A mere twenty-four hours after being released, she was on a train to New York City, reading a newspaper and minding her own business. Her objective was to become an actress and get involved in the theater. She did so, and for most of two decades, she traveled the eastern seaboard circuit with one troupe or another. Whenever she required an extra influx of cash, she would seduce vulnerable men and relieve them of the heaviness of their wallets.

Then, in early 1886, when age set-off a longing to reconnect to her past, she searched through legal records in the basement of a courthouse in Philadelphia. The dusty boxes were plentiful, requiring patience and perseverance. One day her efforts were rewarded; she came across paperwork in her father's name on letterhead of the attorney who handled his affairs.

She descended on the law firm in a hubbub of untethered emotions. After explanations, much drama and an extensive use of bantering coquetry that beguiled the senior partner, she was able to produce enough information to persuade them as to her true identity as his long-lost daughter. She was escorted to a cubicle of a room and told to wait. Shortly, a safe-deposit box and key was delivered, and she was granted privacy to explore its contents.

Her heart fluttered. She unlocked it and carefully popped the top. Her eyes squished shut. She had no idea what to expect, though there were hopes doing cartwheels inside—hopes that would be realized beyond all her imagining. Her hands were clammy; her breathing became quicker than hummingbird wings as her eyelids lifted in wary anticipation.

Her hands flitted through stacks of ragged leaflets, brochures and old letters. Buried beneath those items was a substantial amount of cash and treasury bonds. The sound of her gasp filled the tiny chamber. It only took a handful of moments for her to calculate that the sum total translated into enough capital that if frugal and wise would last her for many blue moons.

The train clattered over a rough patch of rails, which caused the passenger car to pitch and creak. She returned from bygone days, but truly couldn't get them out of her mind. She recalled sorting through the steel strongbox and being shocked by a peculiar discovery. At the bottom of it was the document that now had her on the quest to find Deacon Coburn.

Lucinda Enochelli got busy and rolled another cigarette.

A pair of rabbits were roasting over the campfire, and twelve year old Charley Jondreau sat on his haunches enthralled by his grandmother. His eyes, humble and attentive, responded to her stories in glints of merriment or awe depending on the theme. Whenever she paused or grew silent for an extended spell, he prompted her with a query or request to hear more.

Nekoma, entrenched in the traditions of oral history, was a remarkable chronicler of earlier times. She released her vivid remembrances in an animated voice that conjured emotion and kept him on the edge of expectancy. She was in the midst of a tale laced by copious amounts of sorrow, which cut him. "I was a mother of two when the Redcoats and Yankees warred over this ground. I knew then that the time of the Iroquois was passing before my eyes."

"How so, Grandmere?"

"The Redcoats and Yankees were dishonorable men."

"Dishonorable?"

Nekoma nodded bluntly. "Lies were told to our people and there were divisions amongst the tribes. Some allied with the Yankees, others with the Redcoats. The white captains and kings made treaties and promises that were written in sand and washed away by the rain. Do not trust those who speak lofty oaths for they are manipulators seeking power and their own fates."

"Oui, Grandmere. Why were the Yankees and Redcoats fighting?"

"For the soil we sit upon, the air we breathe," she answered, cutting and dismissive. She leaned over and used her fingers to dig out a clump of dirt and grass, then held it up and stared wonderingly at it. She shook it at him. "Who can own creation?"

"The Great Spirit, eh."

"*Only* the Great Spirit, the Creator," she said, crumbling it in disgust. She wiped her palm against her thigh. "White men and their territorial kingdoms across the seas, think that muskets and bloodshed purchases land that belongs to them to be parceled out to whoever has the most gold. It is the sickness of greed that breeds jealousy and contempt and warfare."

"Did you ever see the Yankees and Redcoats clash?"

"No, I had babies to care for and other important duties."

"I should've known, eh."

"I wasn't interested in slaughter," she said abruptly. "There were many skirmishes nearby, and our village moved more than once while troops of Yankees and Redcoats scurried all around us like ants. A Redcoat hero was slain on a battlefield beside the thundering waters. We were all supposed to be sad. I was not. Sadness did drape itself over me much later."

"Why, Grandmere?"

Nekoma had a faraway gleam in her eyes. "Our Shawnee brothers under the leadership of Tecumseh aligned with the Redcoats. Tecumseh was wise. His words had power and glory. The Great Spirit gave him a vision to bring unity to all our peoples. The Shawnee warriors fought bravely, but were betrayed by the Redcoat masters at a battle near the Thames River.

"When news of Chief Tecumseh's death came to our community, I wept silent and bitter tears," she told him, shoulders slouching in defeat. "In my lament I saw that the sun was forever rising on the white man's dominions, which meant that it was setting on the Iroquois, Shawnee, and all the other tribes. Nothing I have seen since that day has ever taken me to a different conclusion. We must be vigilant to preserve the practices of our people."

"I am ashamed of the white blood in me."

"You are wrong to be so. Childish, even," she scolded tersely. "If you punch an Iroquois comrade in the nose the spurting blood is red. Ojibwe blood, red. Shawnee blood, red. Punch an Englishman, Dutchman, or Frenchman in the nose, the blood is the same red color. Does not logic make clear to you that the difference between peoples is only skin deep?"

His brow furled, his jaw pushed out and his mouth puckered as he ruminated on her reasoning. He dropped onto his knees and twined his fingers together on his lap. "You have given me understanding that must alter my thoughts. I will think deeply on it, eh."

"You are to be proud of the two bloodlines in your veins," she said, sober-voiced. "Your father, Xavier Jondreau, had an eye and ear for the whys and ways of the Iroquois. I blessed his marriage to my daughter. His loyalty was to the Iroquois, not the French." She pointed a finger at him. "He respected all people, but bowed to no one. Live the same, Charley Jondreau."

"Do you have a best memory of him, Grandmere?"

"His laughter," she replied quickly. "His joy was an infection that affected everyone. He could not go even an hour without seeing something that required a funny remark, but he was not an addled joker. On matters of the heart he was serious-minded and shouldered much wisdom."

"Is any of him in me, Grandmere?"

"He *knew* things, Charley Jondreau."

"Like me, eh?"

"The Great Spirit's gift is more robust in you."

"It troubles me sometimes, Grandmere."

"That should not be," she said, eyes narrowing on him. "The Great Spirit knows of what you are made and would not have touched you with the *seeing* insight if you were incapable of carrying it. Remember Joseph the son of Jacob? The Great Spirit makes no mistakes."

"Why me, Grandmere?"

"Why not you? Are you wiser than the Great Spirit?"

"Of course not, eh."

"Where'd you ever get the idea that you could tell the Great Spirit what to do?" she asked, a mirthful challenge glimmering in her eyes. "The Great Spirit has knowledge from the beginning to the end. There are no mysteries that he did not write into creation. He gives gifts as he pleases, to whom he pleases. You must receive it in gratitude and honor it. Always."

"Oui, Grandmere."

Nekoma warmed him with a shiny smile. "When you rise each morning, give thanks for the breath in your body, for the light that is life. Give thanks for the Great Spirit's hand upon you. Give thanks for the birds of the air and the beasts of the field, for the food that you eat and the water that you drink. If you have no thanksgiving in your heart, you are the problem."

"I am thankful, eh. I will be thankful, Grandmere. Always."

"The hawk with the red tail is your kindred spirit," she said zealously. Her countenance became clouded and intensely severe. "You must follow the hawk. It will accompany you. Do not doubt. For you, the hawk is a messenger of the Great Spirit. Trust its guidance."

He lowered his eyes in reverence, seeking strength to *always* be spurred into obedience. The seeds planted by his grandmother would germinate as he practically applied the counsel. He checked on the rabbits and decided that their meal needed to cook awhile longer. Then, Charley Jondreau took a prolonged look at the distance and reflected on the man he was becoming.

Cheveyo was twelve years old when he eye-witnessed supernatural violence. It came in a roaring cyclone of fury and pain. The experience put his feet on a pathway that tapped into the proclivities of a sadistic nature and delved into every excess of evil. He would become a bloodthirsty scourge of terror on the western frontier known as Smoky Crowe.

The boy was on a journey with his father, Istaqa and his mother, Chumana. He had his mind on the destination for he was told that a ceremony of tremendous import awaited him; a rite of passage to manhood. Even so, he was bored and dragging his feet. Three sunrises had already passed. He led a knobby-horned goat on a leash and walked ten paces behind his parents.

"Father?"

"My son."

"How much farther?"

"We are here. Just over there," Istaqa said, tilting his head toward the entrance of an enclosed canyon off to the left. The eroded and barren landscape, dotted by sagebrush and scrub junipers, had been unvaried since yesterday—a network of gorges and gullies. In the distance, above all the ridges and cliffs, a pillar of uniquely shaped rock dominated the skyline.

Cheveyo followed them into the boxed in ravine. He smiled at the sunshine playing havoc with the colors on the steep walls. "What would you have me do, Father? Command me."

"Stake the goat," Istaqa replied, pointing to the far end, fifty or so yards away. "I will smoke, be in communion with the Master, and make preparations to present the sacrifice. Be vigilant and collect rocks to build an altar. Chumana will gather wood for the fire."

His wife, pride swelling in her dark eyes, placed a hand on her son's shoulder. "You are Cheveyo, a spirit warrior. The only fruit of my womb, a brother to the crow and coyote. My heart leaps within me, for you will be a priest of wickedness and the prophet of the dark one."

"Too much chatter, woman," Istaqa said nastily.

Chumana lowered her head and genuflected. "Forgive me."

Istaqa shooed her, sneering. "Be gone."

She hurried away. Cheveyo watched for a split-second, then went and put the goat on a short tether where he had been told to do so. He stretched, looked around and began picking up suitable rocks handily available. His task took him ranging and searching far and wide. He got sweaty and dirty. His mind was full of tales of the fame and greatness that was to be for him; from his earliest days, his mother had spun yarns that stimulated his imagination.

He lugged rocks nonstop for over an hour, accumulating a diverse collection of shapes and sizes. When Istaqa was satisfied as to the stockpile, he rose from his cross-legged position and scraped out the bowl of his pipe. The shards of burnt tobacco flittered off his leggings. He started to select and arrange the foundational stones. He was methodical; sacramental, even. His expression, stoic and reserved, illuminated his eyes and shone like a lantern.

While he worked, he chanted deep in his throat, and Chumana joined in singing low as she brought load after load of deadwood. She heaped the fuel at a spot designated by her husband, then as he verged on completion, she and her son carefully stacked the logs and sticks behind the three-foot high pyramidal monument, according to Istaqa's detailed say-so.

The patriarch inspected their handiwork and declared it good. He took a knee, placed his hands over his heart in worship and spoke a strident incantation. He then kindled a fire. It only took moments for the sparks to become tongues of fire licking at the base of the woodpile. The tinder rapidly became tumultuous flames leaping and snapping like horsewhips.

As the blaze raged hotter and higher, Istaqa stripped down to a loin cloth. Chumana loosened the shoulder straps and released the belt at her waist, and the doeskin dress dropped around her ankles. She was as she was on the day she was born. Her husband heeded her example and removed the diaper-like garment. The couple danced and swayed side by side. He sang loud and energetic, an ancient song to the cadence drummed out by their footsteps.

The mantra rose and fell in guttural notes until it came to an end in perfect unison. He went to where his belongings were and retrieved a steel blade. "Be naked, Cheveyo," his father ordered, knife in hand. "Bring the goat to me. Submit to it, surrender your will." He stood proud and as inflexible as a totem pole in front of the rock structure; the fire heated his backside.

The twelve-year-old's eyes were gaped open and there was no hesitation in him; he peeled off his clothes and laid them aside. He led the goat. Istaqa took hold of the scruff of its neck as Cheveyo knelt in front of it. The father screamed an undulating war-whoop that echoed along the canyon. Chumana wailed in shrill excitement, hitting discordant notes and rhythms. When her husband raised his voice again, he was singing a song of death.

Istaqa, his face furiously passionate, did the deed. He pressed the nose of the goat against his son's forehead, then with a flick of his wrist, slit the animal's jugular vein. Gushers of hot blood squirted all over Cheveyo's face and through his long black hair. The splashing crimson tide bathed his chest, dripped off his shoulders and spread down his back.

While his mother screeched an earsplitting yowl, his father swiftly hacked the goat's head off. Its body flopped and twitched on the sand, and Istaqa, with a profound reverence saturated in religious significance, placed its head at the top of the altar. Chumana fell prostate on the ground, and mesmerized by spiritual ecstasy, cried out a litany of words in an unknown language.

Istaqa lovingly cradled the beheaded corpse in his arms, took a step and threw the goat on the raging fire, ginning in sickly triumph. "It . . . is . . . finished!" Istaqa bellowed, eyes aglow.

A booming growl within the flames crackled. Despite the size and intensity of the inferno, the air prickled and took on a nippy chill. "Now you have your reward," a disembodied voice said, sounding as though it came from the underworld realm of a thousand graveyards.

Istaqa convulsed. A force seized him. Agony mashed his face into a horrid and misshapen clutch of knotted wrinkles. A rushing swirl of inflamed wind spiraled into a gruesome vortex around him. The high-pitched noise of a demonic choir battered the area in swooshing howls of madness; the deranged clamor was a spine-tingling disharmony.

Spasms roiled through Istaqa. His arms were locked over his chest. The earth quaked and shuddered beneath him; it suddenly erupted and heaved him upward. For a freakish instant he was suspended above the altar, then crumpled into the flames. Yammering snarls spewed from the conflagration, as though a pack of feral dogs were on a feeding frenzy.

Istaqa died shrieking and writhing, and his son, still on his knees never even blinked. The happenings intrigued his rabid fascination. He watched his father burn to death, emotionless. He began to rise to his feet, but then halted and gasped in awe as a jagged red finger of energy emerged from the flames. It wavered, then stretched forth and struck him in the left eye.

Cheveyo uttered a pain-racked groaning that tore at the lining of his lungs. He was thrown backwards a dozen yards or more, arms flailing and legs kicking as though he was in a wrestling match against fiends and fallen angels. He passed out and drifted through mystic realms; he saw himself high and exalted, wreathed in power and supremacy.

There was deathly stillness when he regained consciousness. Chumana was with him. She had his head resting on her lap. "All is as it should be," she crooned, smiling blissfully.

His hand was clasped over the seeping socket. Tremors quivered up his spine. His left eye was no more. His palm felt a vibrant pulsing; something was rising in the cavity. He took a large breath and gradually withdrew his hand. She held him tight. Her jaw dropped. A shimmering whiteness was growing in the hole; it seemed to be a living thing.

He sat up. "What is happening to me?"

"All is as it should be," Chumana reiterated boldly. She gestured at the towering hoodoo whose shadow embraced them. "Remember this location. Here is your sacred evil place."

Cheveyo cocked his head to a twisted angle and gawked at it—a sandstone formation that resembled an oversized archangel with hulking wings rounded forward. His chest fluttered and cramped as his heartbeat raced. Even then, though he had no true comprehension of what had just been sealed, he knew that he would repeatedly revisit the Angel Peak badlands.

Three years before the monster-man kidnapped and abused her, the Navajo girl who became Sally Twosongs was in her eighth summer. It had been hot and arid for months; the precipitation, always iffy in the high desert, was almost nonexistent. Her family had kept on the move since springtime, herding a flock of sheep from east of Santa Fe.

A week ago, north of *Naayízí*, they had encamped along the deeply cut banks of a winding arroyo referred to as Diablo Wash. While her parents and members of their clan grubbed and stayed busy providing sustenance and support, she was mostly left to fend for herself. She spent her days running and wandering, or sitting and inventing fanciful ideas.

Just now, while the sheep were being tended to on a knoll a half-mile away, the little girl with a lengthy tangle of hair was lying in a patch of shade beneath a gnarled old tree on the edge of the dry creek bed. The clouds were entertaining her; she had proficiency as a cloud-watcher. Her imagination soared to the heavens as thin wisps became tumblers of cottony-white that were going through a series of shape-shifter contortions that caused her to giggle.

"Sally."

"I am here." She sat up. Her head jerked side to side. She saw no one. She scrambled to her feet and spun around. Her eyes, dark and innocent, were sparkling with curiosity. She turned in a tiny circle. A warm breeze became a momentary gust that blew dust devils past her.

"Sally."

"I am here."

A tall, dark-skinned man with golden hair and flowing robes appeared in front of her. The pure white garment had a metallic sash that glittered like a starry necklace around his neck. His countenance was tranquil and full of grace. He stretched forth a hand and said, "Behold."

She shivered and looked. Diablo Wash was a flooded river of foaming waves coursing fast and furious. The coolness of it refreshed her. She had the urge to dive into the middle of it and splash in gleeful abandon, but instead, stood fixed and firm, hands fisted against her thighs. She gazed at the watercourse, then stepped toward the celestial visitor. "It's not real."

"It is imagery of the future, Sally."

"Who are you?"

"If I were to tell you, would you understand?"

"Only if you explain it."

"I cannot," he said, mild and pacifying. "At a time not of your choosing travails and trials will strike, then afterwards, hope and healing will be poured out according to your ability. As streams enrich desolate locales, you will be a reservoir of enlivening water for many souls. Be strong and fear not." He blinked and vanished, and in the same instant, Diablo Wash was exactly as it was before; parched and scorched to brownish clumps of distressed flora.

The eight-year-old, wobbly-legged and dizzy, teetered onto her posterior. She rubbed her eyes and shook her head in a sluggish and deliberate motion. Gripped by amazement, she ogled the waterless arroyo and wondered if she'd just had a dream, but then, certainty flared up, and she knew that she knew that she knew that the encounter had been real. She told no one.

Her flesh was clammy and goosepimply. She replayed the incident over and over. She treasured it and expected to have it always, but as weeks faded into months and years, it got buried in a dustbin of forgetfulness. The revelation, however, was destined to be vividly resurrected while Sally Twosongs was in a life and death spiritual battle.

∼ ∼ ∼

It was a place of sorrow and suffering. That fact sliced into Charley Jondreau as he entered the longhouse, stepping soft and nimbly. His eyes squinted and watered a bit because of the smoky haze hanging in the air from multiple firepots. The flames cast a bluish tint that veiled the faces of those milling around the bedside of the dying woman.

"Your grandson is here, Nekoma," someone said, strained and muted.

"I knew he would make it back," the old matriarch replied, eyelids flapping rapidly. She tried to lift her head, but her diminishing strength failed her. A sly grin tightened her mouth and she managed to turn her head to watch as he slipped past the dozens of kin gathered in clusters throughout the spacious dwelling. "He is who I have waited to see once more."

Jondreau knelt beside the pallet that was raised a foot or so off the floor. He took hold of her hand beneath the bulky fleece blanket. "I was traveling to Quebec City when I *saw* you like this, Grandmere. I turned and came quickly, eh. The Great Spirit soothed my heart with the knowledge that I would return in time to speak to you and hear your wisdom."

"I have no wisdom, Charley Jondreau."

"That in itself is wisdom, Grandmere."

"You are wise for one so young."

He bent low and kissed her icy cold forehead. "I was raised by a shrewd and intelligent woman whose eyes never missed taking note of the wherefores of nature and people."

"No need to flatter me, Charley Jondreau."

Those close and extended family members present kept vigil; most were stoically silent, but sporadic tears and stifled sobs overcame some of them. Male and female keepers of the faith made offerings of tobacco while singing and chanting prayers. Despite the activity surrounding them, it was as though Nekoma and Charley Jondreau were alone at their favorite campsite alongside of Chippawa Creek. Thick and heavy emotions churned between them.

She inhaled a rasp-ridden breath and began hacking; it sounded as though she was being strangled. Her pasty complexion drained of all color and dimness hooded her eyes. The coughing fit passed. "I must soon journey to the land of the dead in the sky world. We will not make our pemmican no more. It always tasted best when we worked together to mix the ingredients."

"So true, eh."

"I have sore teeth and everything tastes sour to me now."

"I will enjoy it for you, Grandmere."

"Many thanks."

"Fried or cold?"

"No matter. Your choice."

He exhaled a low whistle. "Fried it will be."

She winced and gulped a gurgle of air. "I am tired and worn down."

He squeezed her hand. "I do not want you to leave me, Grandmere."

"You have no say; neither do I." She cackled a burst of choked laughter. Her breathing was spotty and took exceptional effort. "When the Great Spirit beckons, I must go."

"I will be alone, eh."

"No. My stories are in your heart."

"You have many more to tell me."

"I am an old bag of bones."

"You're wrong, eh."

"Am I, Charley Jondreau?"

"You carry many years, but you are not old."

"You ought not bear false witness."

"Will you punish me, Grandmere?"

"I never have."

"Why not, eh? I got into mischief."

"Nothing serious. Ever."

"I just never got caught."

"I cannot be fooled, Charley Jondreau. Not then, not now."

"You always had cunning, Grandmere."

"And you, my grandson, are blessed by the Great Spirit. An eagle screamed as a herald of your birth," she said, pride rising in the fragility of her voice. "You were bent and shaped by a moral center that came from the ancient ones. An understanding has always been in you."

"You gave me interpretation and awareness, eh."

"I guided you here and there, is all," she replied modestly. "The gift is yours to use at the Great Spirit's bidding. You identify right and wrong, good and evil. More importantly, you see and grasp the shadows and shades that float in the nooks on either side of right and wrong; those prevailing areas where good and evil get confused as to which is good and which is evil."

"I *see* much of that, Grandmere."

"Yes, but you have no fear."

"Fear is in me, but I refuse it, eh."

"My husband, your grandfather, told me the same words." She applied determination to produce a smile. "You have the strength of nations in your blood. Do not ever forget."

"I will not, Grandmere."

"The Great Spirit has a path for you."

"Where will it lead?"

"I know not. You must find it."

"How, eh?"

"Follow the hawk," she said in a tone that had a hint of rebuke growing in it. "You shall go where you shall go, see what you shall *see*."

His face clenched and darkened—in tension, he lowered his head. "I did not seek the smell of the skunk, to know what I know, to see what I see. It can be a difficult burden."

"You want ease and comfort?" she scoffed, eyes almost closed. "You must be available and faithful to the Great Spirit. Always. In doing so, evil will hunt you, Charley Jondreau."

"It already has tried, eh."

"When? Where?"

"No reason to trouble you with it, Grandmere."

"I will pray for you."

"And I for you."

"The prayers of a dying woman are powerful."

"It would seem so, eh."

"When you come against evil, make a stand. Be light in darkness."

"Always, Grandmere. I will not fail."

"Evil is a bastard, Charley Jondreau."

"I will stay strong."

"The hawk will lead you to justice. Always."

"I trust your counsel, eh."

"Live courageously so that the fear of death will never be in your heart," she said weakly. She tilted her head toward him. "On the other side of death there is life. I will be with many who have gone before me, including your mother, Rozene, and your father, Xavier Jondreau."

"My heart will not say farewell."

"Nor should it. I will see you again, Charley Jondreau," she promised, her voice now nothing more than a whisper. "We will once more sit and visit by a riverside." She exhaled a sticky mist. Her head and shoulders sank, and she seemed to become smaller and smaller. A shudder went through her and she gave a herky-jerky gasp, then her spirit flew away.

The grandson was blank-faced. While others in the room sang or wept, he pressed his lips against her ear and wholeheartedly told her, "I'll catch you on the other side, Grandmere." He stroked her stringy white hair, his jaw taut and twitching. He stood and departed, having to push or shrug past many mourners who were crowded in the longhouse.

Outside, twilight hues colored the wintry sky. He ran and ran, sprinting for miles through the forest. He stopped when he was sure he was unaccompanied. Then Charley Jondreau, fifteen years old and struggling with grief, took his hunting knife from its sheaf, chopped off his hair and shaved his scalp clean for the first time. His head would remain so until his dying day.

Cheveyo had been a killer since he was six years old. He demonstrated an enthusiasm for it by preying on lizards and snakes—he dissected them with a delicate touch. He soon graduated to birds and larger animals, and it became about much more than simply ending life; the boy developed an innate affinity for torture by mercilessly skinning creatures to death.

He learned his lessons well. At seventeen, prompted by an unappeasable bloodlust, he ventured forth to test his prowess and apply his skills on a human being. Mounted on a savvy and fleet-footed cayuse, he spent weeks prowling the southern route of the Santa Fe Trail. The appaloosa was decorated in black and yellow streaks and circles. His face was blackened.

He was patient, passing up one opportunity after another until the perfect circumstances ripened. He carefully stayed hidden to silently stalk a man and woman in a crotchety conveyance pulled by a pair of boney oxen; they were falling farther and farther behind the protection of the wagon train. He stealthily kept them in his field of vision. When the distance separating the couple from the safety of guns and numbers became days, the young Ute went into action.

After a midnight ritual strangulation of a rattler, he crept into position and bided his time in expectancy. He then launched a predawn attack. The husband greeted death in his bedroll; he didn't even stir from sleep until a steel blade was plunged into his heart. His eyes bugged open as blood fountained over him. He fainted and drew his last breath shortly thereafter.

The wife, blonde and pregnant, came awake shrieking. She scratched and punched, but to no avail. He dominated her. His heart was inflamed and she would know the depravity of its fire by being subjected to gross indignities birthed inside a fuming cesspool of evil. She screamed and blubbered as he dragged her from under the ragged canopy of the wagon.

He tossed her around as though she were a sack of straw. She tried to scramble away, but each time her efforts were thwarted by a kick or a series of bludgeoning fists. He knocked her down, beat her bloody and ripped her clothes off. She crawled in the dirt, naked and bleeding from her mouth and nostrils. Her sobbing and whimpering had no end.

He flung her on her back and took a knee so that the full weight of his body rested on her throat. His head angled crookedly and his menacing left eye, whitish and sickly, pulsated at her. "Are you foolish enough to think you'll escape me? You do not have a chance against me, for I am strong and powerful and you are a weakling. I will have my way with you."

"Please let me go." Her voice was gagged and gurgling.

"Your man died like a dog."

"Oh, God. Please . . . please. Please don't hurt my baby."

"Aarg. I will do whatever *pleases* me."

"Help me, God. Please . . . somebody . . ."

"How long before your time?"

"Three months."

"Aarg. I slice your belly open it'll be today." He stood and dragged her to a patch of barrenness near the wagon. He proceeded to use rawhide straps to fasten her wrists to the spokes of a front wheel. He went to his horse and came back with two sharpened pegs. He used a rock as a mallet to drive them into the ground two yards from her feet. He yanked her legs and stretched her out spread-eagle, then tied her ankles to the wooden spikes.

She cried and begged for mercy, but Cheveyo knew not the meaning of the word. He responded to her pleading by tugging his loin cloth aside to urinate on her face, which he topped off with a generous gob of saliva. "Aaaaaaarg," he growled, sneering wickedly. He skipped and hopped to the appaloosa once more, and returned with a beaded leather pouch.

As she wept, whined and moaned, he got into a comfortable squat beside her. He packed a pipe with a blend of tobacco and peyote, and casually smoked. A crow cawed. It swooped back and forth over him twice, then landed on the bench seat of the wagon and squawked insistently. He nodded acknowledgement and spoke tender tidings as he puffed contentedly.

The blackbird raised a ruckus, screeching and hissing noisily. It was joined by another and another and another. And another. Soon a swarming flock of crows were perched on the wagon or walking all around it. The clucking gibberish became louder and louder. Some of the birds began pecking at the helpless woman; others approached Cheveyo in submission.

The morning passed as he smoked bowl after bowl; a cloud continuously encompassed his head. He yammered conversation with his feathered confederates, but said nothing to the woman. When the sun was at its apex he viciously raped her and ended the assault with a flurry of punches to her swollen midsection. Mucus and blood flowed from between her legs.

The horde of crows were crazed and ecstatic, taking flight as one in a deafening flapping of wings. He waved at them, then ran and leapt on the painted stallion. He leaned back, held his hands high above his head and released an exquisitely keen whoop that reverberated across the landscape's contours. He dug in his heels and reined the horse to a galloping exodus.

Just past sunrise of the next day, three scouts riding ahead of wagonloads of wayfarers bound for greener pastures came upon the repugnant scene. The men, peppery veterans of the western trails, were nauseated. Two of them spat blasphemies. Despite the degradations she had suffered, the befouled and dehydrated woman was still alive, though barely.

Her disorientation was in the stark raving mad category; she blathered hysterically as the men cut her loose. Her ranting told a tale about smoking crows and a savage who smoked with crows. She frantically alternated between the phrases again and again; smoking crows, smoked with crows—she died before her would-be rescuers could do anything to help her.

When reports of the attack reached the closest outpost, histrionics gave the news the properties of a wildfire. The smoking crows, smoked with crows repetition was disseminated and took on mythic dimensions. Telegrams were wired eastward. Within days of Cheveyo's ruthless brutality, a newspaper account dubbed the barbaric butcher Smoky Crowe.

It was a decade and numerous killings later before Cheveyo discovered the name his enemies in the white world called him. His first inclination was to reject it, but after a sojourn of fasting in the wilderness of the Angel Peak badlands, he decided to glorify the infamy. In doing so, he went on a slaughtering spree and wrote Smoky Crowe with the blood of his victims.

In December 1875 Sally Twosongs was eighteen years old and had been married for six months. Her heart was full of amazement. She sat cuddled and cozy in a quilted comforter at the bedroom window gazing through frosty designs on the glass. Moonlight danced across a layered dusting of newly fallen snow. The beauty of it was serene and warmed her from the inside out.

A clumpy wax candle burned on a nightstand; its flame pointed heavenward and its cinnamon scent saturated the room. Her mind was adrift in a free floating reverie that took her backwards and to the present and future in a seamless montage that flushed her cheeks. She sensed rather than heard her husband treading softly behind her.

"Good morning, Caleb."

"Morning? There's still plenty of night until daybreak," he said, touching her shoulder. He sat on the floor beside her and leaned against her legs. "Did you have a dream?"

"I guess, I suppose. I don't know."

"Not knowing is weird, isn't it, *lucero*?"

"Or maybe normal for me."

"What's wrong, Sally Twosongs?"

She shrugged half-heartedly. "Nothing. I have much excitement in me. Christmastime has me anxious because it's our first one together and I want to be sure that it's extra special."

"Christmas is still a week away," he replied, stifling a yawn. "The sled is ready. I finished the runners yesterday. We can go cut us a tree after sunup. I have my eye on a blue spruce."

"Wonderful! Where?"

"A mile or so to the east."

She ruffled his hair and bent down to plant a kiss on his forehead. "Christmas means so much to me, Caleb. Did I ever tell you about my first Christmas with Father and Mother?"

"The Christmas Eve dream, yes."

"Oh, my." She smiled, eyes sparkly and full of joy. "Jesus placed his healing hand on my heart and something marvelous and wondrous happened in my soul. I got up and sat on a stool at the window. Father came and we talked, then Mother. We shed many blissful tears."

"A few months later you and I met."

"The Creator shaped a path for us through hurt and hardships," she said earnestly. "We were made for each other. What will it be like when we share Christmas with our firstborn?"

He jerked and flipped onto his knees. His mouth was open and his eyes widened into deep pools of blue glowing excitedly in the reflection of candlelight. "Are you . . ."

"No," she cut in, "I'm not yet with child, Caleb."

"One day soon, I hope."

"Yes. The Creator will make it so."

"Are you telling me I must be patient?"

"Not me, Caleb. The Psalmist," she answered, hugging him tenderly against her bosom. "All through the poetry and praise we read over and over. *Be patient. Wait on the Lord.*"

"While we wait, we can do our part. Let's go back to bed."

She giggled pleasantly. "Yes, let's do." She held on tight as he picked her up and carried her across the room. There were no secrets hidden between them, and an easiness in their passion that was rooted in trust and reliance on each other. They were gentle and ardent, and in the sweet warmth afterwards, slept entwined in an embrace until long past dawn.

∽ ∽ ∽

A year and a half after Snow Maiden and Jean Pierre were buried, Charley Jondreau was a guest in the Welland County Jail. He had thrashed and smashed Jonesy Smith to a battered and wheezing pulp because the merchant had welched on a deal. He lay flat on his back on a saggy cot; the dusty burlap covered mattress was a collection of lumps. His hands were clasped together at his waistline and he was idly twiddling his thumbs.

It was a mid-January evening. An extensive warm spell had hit and settled in; the meltdown was transforming the countryside from white and frigid to mucky and downright balmy. He had been in the lockup for over two months, and just now came to a decision. His liberation date wasn't until June, but his sentence was about to come to its conclusion regardless of whether the authorities approved of his early release schedule.

The how of it would be a simple matter—the why of his escape had to do with the fact that in his mind the verdict was in; his account was paid in full for the alleged offense of procuring a measure of justice. He bounced to his feet, intending to stretch and do some calisthenics, but then, flopped onto the bed and twitched uncontrollably.

His eyes flickered and went white; his nostrils flared. Inside the smell of the skunk he saw terrain that was foreign to him. Surrounded by steep mountains, he stood on the edge of a plateau watching a monster masquerading as a man; he had nondescript features and paraded around in the style of a dandy with an ivory-handled pistol prominent on his left hip.

"Don't you know I'm the devil, little girl?" the smallish man droned, spinning a bowler hat in his hands. He cocked it onto his head and strutted like a rutting buck in front of a young girl with long black hair. She shied away from him, a jumble of defiance and fear etched on her face. Her hands were clenched more tightly than her teeth as she narrowly glowered at him.

There was creepy evil in the air. Jondreau could taste its coppery bitterness slinking up the back of his throat. His blood boiled. He had an irresistible need to go to the dirt-streaked girl. He tried to step toward her, but it was as though he was bound in chains; no matter his effort he couldn't move a muscle. He scrutinized her and noted that she was doing the same to him.

She was disheveled, arms folded over her chest as she sat on her heels in a cluster of bushes. Beneath a layer of grayish grime, she was a pretty child with a button-nose and darkly enigmatic eyes. She was staked and tethered like a dog, trembling in a threadbare buckskin shift, but she was not defeated. Neither the despicable outward circumstances nor the fright in her could extinguish a molten fire within; Jondreau could see pure iron in her veins.

His eyes dovetailed with hers and locked. He felt a jolt strike him. Shimmering waves of heat passed between them. She stood and reached a hand toward him. "I will help you."

Jondreau sat up, breathing hard and raspy as he reconnoitered the present reality. He put his feet on the floor and leaned forward. He pinched the bridge of his nose and blew to be free of the acidy stench clogging his nasal passages. What he had seen and experienced was vividly clear, but he was entirely perplexed because none of it made a lick of sense to him.

He got to his feet and began pacing around the twelve by twelve jail cell. His mind was beleaguered, but he forced it to sort through clues and meaning by applying a strict discipline. He grasped for comprehension, hands flexing at his sides. There was a brief instant when he thought he might have the capacity to understand, but that moment got swallowed by an all-consuming convulsion that made his legs rubbery and put him on his backside.

In the extrasensory phenomenon, he was on the edge of a long valley enclosed by a fortress of mountains. His attention was straight ahead and all he could see was a substantial barn and several corrals. He looked to the left and saw nothing but a misty haze; his head riveted rightward and his heart sprang into an astonished thump-thump-thumping.

A charming princess stood facing him. She was less than ten yards away, with a gnarled staff in her hand and a tote on a shoulder strap; the bag rested on her hip. A rough-coated tricolor dog sat attentively at her side. Her face was radiant and her eyes bored in on him. Her thick and luxuriant black hair was formed into a single braid. He was filled with awe; his mouth was working to speak, but not a sound emerged from his voice box.

She spun away and flipped her head so that the plaited ponytail dangled down the middle of her back as she walked away. The wonderment in him escalated off any known scale. He took stuttering steps in an attempt to catch her, but was stopped cold by an invisible barrier that held him fast. He shouted at the top of his lungs but all that swished out was a strained peep.

She moved like a whispery breeze heading toward the woods. Just before she entered the cover of a dense copse of aspens, she cast her eyes upon him and said, "I will help you."

Jondreau lurched in his footsteps. He gasped for air, and returned from the vision reaching and groping like a blind man as orientation came in stages. He was sprawled on the floor. His head throbbed. His eyes were blinking as though the lids had become unhinged in a windstorm. He cleared his nostrils once more and slowly mustered his senses. He shakily crawled onto the cot and sat, elbows on knees and head hanging down.

He remained in that posture of bewilderment for a contemplative interval. He determined that the straggly girl and beautiful maiden were one and the same. The disparate representations had him stumped; who could she be and how did she fit into the checkerboard of his life? Would he ever know, or would her presence be erased from the fabric of memory?

The questions rattled in him, then he squashed them and abruptly sat up. The hour had come for him to follow-through on his timetable. He held his breath and listened intently. The only sound heard was the snoring of the guard on night-watch. Satisfied, Jondreau retrieved a coil of snare wire from a slot stitched inside his moccasin leggings.

He bent off a foot of it, doubled it over and shaped it, then went to work. He picked the lock with an exceptional ease; it took all of thirty seconds and the barred door opened. He was silent, reaching the foyer and office area in the speed of a few heartbeats. He grinned at the snoozing officer, then crept outside into the exhilarating freedom of a moonlit night.

He hurried. By dawn, when his disappearance was discovered, he had gotten his dapple gray and yearling pinto, collected a handful of possessions and was well on his way to a hideout along the Grand River that he'd taken advantage of on more than one occasion; it would be a safe-haven for him to lay low and wait for a red-tailed hawk to lead him.

When springtime bloomed, he was heading west and south on a trail that would take him far from the territory of Chippawa Creek and the Great Lakes region. Charley Jondreau had no particular destination in mind. A loner and a pathfinder, he would savor the currents of whims and chance as he diligently followed the guidance of the hawk from place to place.

After acquiring a room at the Central Hotel, a block north of the railroad depot, Lucinda Enochelli was on a walking tour of Dodge City. The afternoon was bright and cheery, but had no impact at all on her attitude; she was in a lousy mood. Her stomach was queasy and her eyes itchy from smoking a few too many cigarettes on the train from Abilene.

To add to her cranky state of mind, she had yet to glean any useful information. She was disgusted by the difficulty that kept confronting her. The desk clerk at the hotel, a pimple-faced young adult, was of no help at all—she wondered why it was that everywhere she went those individuals in positions of responsibility seemed to be greener than grass.

She had been directed to the telegraph operator. Unbeknownst to her, she was nearing a destination where her grumpiness wouldn't even be noticed in comparison to what it was about to smack against. She strolled languidly, hips swaying and purse swinging at her side. The boardwalk had a squeaky plank or two, which irritated her all the more.

She arrived and brusquely entered the Western Union office. A cowbell clanked loudly above the door. "Jumping and stinking! You really need that noisemaker?"

"Huh." A roly-poly man glanced up from his desk and set aside some papers. The sleeves of a grungy white shirt were rolled above his elbows and he was chomping on the stub of a burnt out cigar. "Had it installed a week ago. Nothing like giving folks a good startle."

"Well, I for one, am not amused," she said sourly.

"Huh. You're who made it ring," he replied, jowls jiggling as he slumped lazily in the barrel-like chair. "If you don't like it, don't let the door hit your ass on the way out."

"Excuse me?"

"Are you deaf as well as ignorant?"

"I happen to be a customer."

"State your business. Huh."

"Aren't you supposed to be accommodating to the public?"

"Huh. Take a gun out and shoot me."

"You are beyond obnoxious, mister."

"Name's Butch Mackenzie," he said, removing his bifocals. He cleaned the lenses with a tissue, then put the spectacles on his nose in such a precarious balance that it was as if they were going to slide off. "Report me to the head office. I'm sure there's a stack of complaints against me a foot-high or more." He heaved to his feet and duck-waddled to her. He made no bones about checking out her front porch. He had a long gander down the neckline of her dress.

"Are you enjoying the view, Butch Mackenzie?"

"Cover 'em up if you don't want me looking. Huh."

"Who said I didn't want you to look? I asked if the view was enjoyable."

"Let me tell me you something, lady," he replied, ruddy-faced. "I'm old, I'm fat, and I got no sap left in me. You could pull those boobies out and play with them for all I care. My pod is shriveled up and dried out, so save your strumpet flirtations for someone else."

"By God, you're a miserable cuss."

"Huh. State your business."

"Do you know Deacon Coburn?"

"What? Huh? Have you got telegraph business or what?"

"Depending on your answer to my question, perhaps."

"Do I look like a social director to you? Huh?" He chewed the cigar from one corner of his mouth to the other. He was bulgy-eyed and snarly-voiced. "I am acquainted with the man. I was actually just reading a letter from his daughter when you so rudely interrupted me."

"He has a daughter?"

"Are you asinine? Huh."

She was flustered by his petulant crabbiness. She inhaled deeply, pressed the friendliest of smiles at him and sweetly asked, "Would you know where I could find Mr. Coburn?"

"He ain't in town, I can tell you that much."

"When will he be back?"

"How the tarnation would I know?"

"Pardon me all to hell for asking."

"Huh. You think it's my job to keep tabs on people?" he inquired, spitting the slime of tobacco in a garbage bucket. "He's on the trail, probably to Santa Fe would be my guess. He may or may not return to Dodge City. I wouldn't bet one way or the other. He's a wanderer."

"Then Santa Fe will be my next stop."

"Huh. Glory be. Ain't I pleased to know your plans?" He glared hotly and shook his head in dismissal. "If you ain't sending a telegram, leave me be." He returned to the desk. She exited and slammed the door so hard that the windows rattled louder than the clanging bell.

On the sunshiny boardwalk, she cursed a blue streak. She shielded her eyes and squinted in search of a bench in a shady spot, then hurried to it and took a seat. She dug the fixings out of her purse and built a ciggy. She mulled matters over, calming as she considered the next leg of her journey. Her belly growled a reminder that she had not eaten a bite since yesterday.

Lucinda Enochelli would remedy that soon enough.

April 21, 1888

Dear Diary: It is not yet five in the afternoon, but I am exhausted. I have been on the go nonstop since before dawn and I only had a few hours of restless sleep after Brenda went to be with Jesus last evening. It has been emotional and stressful, but I take some encouragement in the fact that I complied with my dear friend's request for quickness and simplicity.

Her funeral service was a grief-stricken celebration in the Cantina Room. Most of the Suncurl Café regulars attended, which was truly a blessing because everyone pulled together in support to honor her life. Mom's widespread contacts in the community took care of all the details and provided a clergyman to read Scripture and officiate. I said a few words of remembrance in eulogy. I was crying and sniffling the whole while.

Stace has been a trooper—stiff upper lip and all that, but I am concerned. There is an obvious tug of war in him. In his sorrow he has doubts and fears, but has clammed up and not uttered a word. His eyes have been moist and red all day, but I have not actually seen any tears. He's fighting to hold it all in; not sure if I know what to do or how to help him.

Mom is keeping him close to her. Just now they're downstairs chatting. She is telling him stories about his mother because she says that's the best way for all of us to keep her in our hearts. There are so many memories of Brenda that I treasure, but one particular experience with blood and chocolate had us laughing so hard we almost peed our pajamas.

It happened late one night when we had a hankering for brownies. There were none around, so we decided to turn our gabfest into a baking party. We lit all the oil lamps in the kitchen, then fired up the cookstove. We were barefoot and full of giddiness, cracking wise and gossiping about men and poking fun at each other.

We were just getting started, and all was fine and dandy, but then everything unraveled. Brenda dropped the crock of cocoa. It was on a top shelf, and when it slipped through her hands it ricocheted off the corner of a cupboard. From where I was standing it was as though the whole action slowed down. The lid flew up and she reached to try and catch it while the container dropped to the floor and shattered. Powdery brown dust exploded all over the place.

Brenda did a hipping hop backwards, but it was too late. A shard of the stoneware had slashed her big toe, and blood was spewing. She plumped onto her bum and started giggling like she'd gone berserk. I was afraid she was going into shock or something. I crouched beside her to ask what was so funny. She pointed at the gooey gobs of cocoa commingling with the flow from the cut and said, "Blood and chocolate looks like ketchup covered meatloaf."

It was then that I caught the infection of her hilarity and burst out laughing. I plopped onto my tush and we clung to each other, shaking as though we had palsy. When we got under control, we proceeded to list off all the ingredients for brownies and verified that blood didn't make the cut, which inaugurated another bout of boisterous laughter.

We finally got past the silliness. I found the first-aid kit and patched her up, then we cleaned our mess and went to bed minus any brownies. We told the tale the next morning to the breakfast crew, and they all chimed in with witty remarks and additions, which were colorful embellishments that caused Brenda and me to chortle all over again.

I am going to miss her so much. My heart has a heaviness that hurts. I pray that Deacon and Whitey will arrive soon because hashing things out with them will be beneficial in giving me a proper perspective. Mom and I have unloaded on each other, which I'm sure helped us and was healthy for our equilibrium, but we both need our Dodge City friends.

I told Mom of my plans to go on the trail with Deacon and Whitey whenever they head off from Santa Fe. She was hesitant about the idea, but when I explained that I intended to take Stace along whether he is of a mind to or not because I'm convinced it will be good for him, she enthusiastically agreed. She said that Deacon and Whitey would be positive influences and the best possible therapy for getting Stace to work through all his complicated feelings.

So now it's a matter of waiting for them to get here. I expect it will be any day, but perhaps that's wishful thinking. Since their travels are all about having fun, I'm sure they're plodding along with a "we'll get there when we get there" attitude. The good Lord knows that they are needed, so I will trust in his perfect timing, though I am anxious and out of sorts.

That's it. I have no more words in my head.

From an abundance of habit, Avis Lahay read all that she had written. A smile, pinched as tight as a miser's kisser, put a tiny sparkle in her eyes. She closed the journal with a thud and returned it to its compartment in the roll-top desk. After praying for an anointing of peace and courage, she fluffed her hair and headed downstairs to get a glass of ice tea.

The same hawk had led Charley Jondreau for most of the day. He was in Illinois, riding through a woodlot along the Rock River. Clouds were scudding across a pale afternoon sky. Rain was in the offing; its cleansing fragrance sweetened the air. He was relaxed and at ease, but then had an inkling of discord an instant before he heard a commotion in the distance. Goosepimples snuck up the nape of his neck as the red-tailed raptor dipped low ahead of him.

The shrill cry of a woman in distress pierced the stillness. His hands flicked the reins and the piebald pinto gathered speed in response to him shifting weight in the saddle as he directed it in a beeline toward the disturbance. The droopy brim of his hat flopped as he hunched low to avoid branches. He had to do zigs and zags to get past hedges of underbrush.

When he emerged from the cover of trees, he came into a grassy clearing and immediately surmised the situation; ruffians were harassing a sodbuster couple. One scoundrel had a gun at the wife's head while another gunman had tied up the husband—a third had a torch in hand, apparently prepared to toss it onto the porch of the farmhouse. Their crowbait horses, gaunt and skittish, were picketed in the shade of an oak tree.

Jondreau had the stallion gallop into the thick of it. He dismounted and strode toward the beefy tough guy holding the woman hostage. "Is there a problem here that needs fixing?"

"Ain't none of your business," the leader said, pressing his pistol harder against the woman's ribs. He had a scraggly beard and clumpy eyebrows overhanging eyes that were hot and oozing hate. "You best scram unless you intend to die. I ain't telling you again."

"Ain't no one going to die, eh." Jondreau set his feet shoulder width apart and calculated the way it would go. The other two men were scrawny and scared, with fraidy-cat eyes and trembling hands. He had no doubt of their weakness as chumps of a blowhard bully.

"You want me to kill this woman, jackass?"

Jondreau tilted his chin upward. His eyeballs disappeared for a moment. He smiled, as cold and hard as a block of ice. "I will put a bullet in you and a blade in your friend before your trigger finger flinches, eh." His hands were together above his belt, thumbs twiddling. "Then while the one with the fire is standing with his mouth open I'll put a slug in him."

"Your gun ain't even gonna clear leather."

"Test me, eh."

"A clean draw, Frenchie?"

"I have *seen* it." Jondreau erupted in a smooth blur of movement that was so fast as to be almost imperceptible; both hands whooshed in unison. His pistol flashed a bluish blaze while the glint of his knife caught a ray of sunlight as it struck its mark and another blast roared from his revolver. Shouts of shock blistered the air as he scampered to collect their weapons.

The leader was dancing a lunatic jig and cussing heaven and earth. A bullet had splintered the bones in his gun hand. The other two reprobates were on their knees crying; the one who'd been standing over the husband now had a knife sticking through the center of his right hand; the torchbearer's hand had been mangled by a gunshot.

Jondreau retrieved his throwing knife, then got eyeball to eyeball with the bigwig. "You will leave these folks alone, eh," he said, casually wiping off the blade on the shirtsleeve above the troublemaker's busted up hand. "I have *seen* you, hoss. If you ever seek to harm them again I will find you and you will die. I am Charley Jondreau. I only speak truth, eh."

A crackle of lightning flickered overhead followed by a rolling rumble. The wounded mischief-makers hurried to their horses. Not a word passed between them, but a spitting mad furor of swearwords curdled their wake. One by one the men got mounted and irritably took out their pain and anger on the animals by yanking the reins and digging in their heels.

Jondreau waited until the hoofbeats could no longer be heard, then holstered his pistol and slid the knife into its sheath. The woman, reddish-haired and pretty, had fainted and was beginning to stir. She was groaning. The man, ankles and wrists still bound by ropes, had scooted on his buttocks to her side, and was urgently attempting to assist her.

She let out a whimpering cry and started to sit up. Jondreau rushed to her and offered a hand, which she accepted. He lifted her to her feet and in doing so, his palm brushed against her abdomen. His eyelids flickered. She hitched in a gulp of breath, eyes gaping open in alarm and astonishment. Her frame, slender and willowy, went as rigid as an oak plank.

Jondreau gasped and recoiled in a chilling tic. "You will have two children, eh. A boy, Joseph, will be born before another year passes, then many moons from now, when you think you are old and barren, you will have a daughter named Sylvia. She will be *gifted*."

"How? What? Who are you?" she sputtered, fear tugging on her expression.

"Mr. Jondreau . . ." the man said, struggling to get up.

"I am Charley, eh." He knelt and nimbly unknotted the bindings with a few flicks of his fingers. "There will be no more conflict or trials for you from those halfwit browbeaters."

"I'm Edgar Bower, Charley," he told him, standing up and wrapping his arms around the woman. An eye was almost swollen shut, and welts and bruises were rising on his ruddy cheeks, which were fringed by wisps of peach-fuzz whiskers. He was a foot or so taller than her. "Edgar *Joseph* Bower. This is my wife Kathleen. Her middle name is *Sylvia*."

"Who are you?" she asked, clinging to her husband.

"What was that with you and Kathleen, Charley?"

"A promise of blessing, eh."

"Who are you?" she asked again, shaky-voiced.

"A friend, eh. How old are you two?"

"Eighteen," Edgar replied, somewhat apologetic.

"Young and strong. Brightness awaits you, eh."

"We love each other," Edgar said firmly. "We will make a go of it."

"I have *seen* much. You will more than make a go of it."

A sprinkling of rain misted them. Kathleen Bower glanced skyward, then took a tentative step away from her husband and reached out to take hold of their champion's hand. "Thank you. Will you join us at our table, Charley? I wish to hear more about who you are, please."

Jondreau nodded cordially. They went inside, where he doctored Edgar Bower while Kathleen put together a scrumptious meal. Charley Jondreau appreciated the connection and fellowship. So much so that he stayed with the Bowers for several months, sleeping in the loft of the barn and doing the work of a handyman in exchange for home cooking. Then, on a dark and dreary morning, a hawk screeched, and he obediently tracked its westerly trail.

"Let me ask you something."

"I reckon you can, but I ain't sure why you tell me you're going to ask me something before you ask me something," Deacon drawled, giving him a wrinkly-eyed grin.

"Don't be starting in on me," Whitey parried, click-clicking.

"I ain't starting nothing."

"You're being cantankerous."

"Ain't you a mite thin-skinned?" Deacon queried dryly. The pair were in Santa Fe, having just departed the livery on route to the Suncurl Café. Their saddlebags were in hand as they moved along at a leisurely gait. The sun was sinking and daylight was fading to wraithlike streaks of gray, which meant that traffic on the thoroughfares was diminishing.

"Can I ask you something or canst I?"

"Have at it."

"I'll have at it, alright."

"I ain't holding you back, my friend."

"Ain't you laying it on a bit thick, Deacon?"

"Are you going to ask me something or not?"

"How long have you known Delores?"

Coburn puckered his mouth. "Gotta be twenty years or more."

"In all that time, did you ever take a good look at the woman?"

"Of course."

"So what be wrong with you?"

"Nothing," Deacon answered, scowling at him.

"I was wondering if you was blind or something."

"What are you getting at, Whitey? You got a point or no?"

Fitzgerald gave him a click-click and the smile of a sage. "Well, I've known her for nigh onto that long, and I can tell you that's she's always had a touch of the gorgeous. To my way of thinking the question that comes up is, how come you two didn't ever became a couple?"

"There was never a chance of that, Whitey," Deacon said flatly. "When we met I was on the job at the *Double B Ranch* and extending care to Big Bull Wallace. She was known as Flora and was in the whoring business. I wasn't on the lookout for such doings, but tendered kindness whenever our paths crossed. She was a teaser, but even then, her heart was golden. Years later, when she relocated to Abilene, we became friends. More than friends. Family, really."

"Us, too. She be one fine lady."

"The finest."

Fitzgerald pushed the coachman hat up and crooked an eyebrow. "I be no silly busybody, but you know, it ain't too late for you two to jump the broom into the land of matrimony."

"A brother doesn't marry his sister, Whitey."

"It ain't exactly that, Deacon."

"You well know that's the true kinship between us."

"I be figuring I can't argue."

"Besides, I'm a tad old to be courting anyone."

They turned onto San Francisco Street. Fitzgerald took a glance at the multicolored sunset to judge the time, then grinned wider and wilder than the cat who swallowed a canary. His brown eyes came alive with sparkles. "Let's sneak down the alley and creep into the Suncurl Café via the backdoor. Catch Delores and maybe Avis by surprise. What say you?"

"A splendid idea," Deacon said, chuckling jauntily. He increased the length of his strides and the short statured barber rushed to keep pace. Their lighthearted expressions were identical. In the space of a dozen footsteps, Deacon Coburn and Whitey Fitzgerald, men toughened and tenderized by the crucible of experience, had converted to free as the wind pranksters.

Jesse Axler was scared. His palms were damp. His eyes had not strayed from the same thicket of shrubbery for more than twenty minutes. The waiting game was putting him to the test, and there was now a twinge cramping its way up the small of his back. He tried to relieve it, but had no chance to do so because the danger kept him tensed in a motionless position.

The bobcat was crouched in the undergrowth. He knew it was still there—he and the animal were entangled in a match of wills, which he had no intention of losing. It was bad enough that he had missed an opportunity to squeeze the trigger just before the prowler had bolted beneath the cover of hedging; he would set right that mistake by putting a bullet in its head the instant it showed itself in an attempt to make an escape.

He kept watch, patient and determined. He was on his belly in a shooter's stance with the Spencer at the ready. His mind was actively playing out a scenario in which his quarry gave him the smallest opening and the result would be that his aim was true and on the mark. He fancied taking the carcass to *WT Ranch* to skin it and make a rug or wall hanging from the hide.

That fantasy was in full blown mode when there was a rustle of movement. The tension in his back spread upward and became a bulging knot between his shoulder blades. He winced against it. A branch of brush flitted ever so slightly. All the saliva in his mouth dried out. Beads of perspiration formed on his forehead. His right index finger slid gently onto the trigger.

He waited and waited. And waited some more. Time seemed to be nothing more than a game that required him to outlast the wiles of a feline predator while enduring the physical test of overcoming the obstacles presented by weaknesses of the flesh. His teeth were clenched as he persevered and resisted the urge to flex his muscles in an attempt to release the discomfort across his shoulders, which was now akin to a hot poker twisting tighter and tighter.

The bobcat poked a paw out from under its hiding place. At that precise instant, a single droplet of sweat trickled over the bridge of his nose and into an eye. His vision was blurred by the salty sting, and it was then that Jesse Axler's eyelids contracted in a blink; his eyes shuttered for a mere fraction of a second, but it was enough to dramatically change the situation. He fought to achieve focus and when it cleared he saw the wildcat creeping toward him.

His hands were more than just moist; wetness made his grip on the Spencer's fore-end slippery. A lump the size of a fist formed in his throat and his heart was in a race that unleashed spasms in his chest which rapidly connected to those in his upper back. He held his breath and prudently lined the bobcat up in the rifle's rear and front sight. Crouched low, its eyes were cold slits and the whiskers of its muzzle were twitching as it steadily advanced.

Onward it came, step by methodical step. A contraction corkscrewed through his torso. His cheek was pressed against the stock as he stared down the barrel; he had it leveled so that the shot would be a dead-center strike in the wildcat's snout. He gradually increased pressure on the trigger, but then, at the compression point where a discharge should've occurred there was no blasting roar; instead the gun misfired and the only sound was a sick, hollow click.

He felt frozen and helpless; horrified, even. The bobcat let loose a meowing screech and pounced, paws spread wide and claws menacing. He shouted an exclamation and pulled the rifle up as if to use it as a defensive shield. He thrashed backwards, then Jesse Axler wrenched awake, smacking his head against a two-by-four stud. He muttered a complaint and grabbed fistfuls of air as though he was plummeting and grasping for something to break the fall.

It took many moments for him to recognize the surroundings of the chicken coop. He was sitting on the floor with his back against the framing and the Spencer resting on his lap. His skin had an iciness that made him shiver and he was gagging on lungfuls of air. The squawking and scratching of hens was muted compared to the panting of his noisy breathing.

Shadowy sunrays slanted through cracks and crevices of the dusty hutch. He found calmness. He unloaded the rifle and thoroughly checked each shell, then refilled the magazine. He was exhausted, yet determined to best the bobcat that haunted his imagination. Alertness prickled in him, and Jesse Axler settled in for an evening as a watchman on the hunt.

Sally Twosongs had spent much of the day in her usual sanctuary—a storage outbuilding nestled in an aspen grove. She was going through a well-honed process of seeking to be in alignment with the plans and purposes of the Creator for such a time as this; her heart was deeply inclined to the stuff of eternity and her yearning was to be faithful.

After entrusting Bethsuelo to her mother-in-law, she had packed a tote with canteens of water and a flute crafted by her father, and on an impulse, she also included a pouch of dried berries. She got a gnarled walking stick, then started out to learn and be in communion with the One who had called her to himself. Hank tagged along, acting as though it possessed the strength and energy of a carefree puppy, skipping and running circles around her.

By noontime she was cross-legged on the floor of her refuge, eyes closed and mind full of reverent passion as she played her prayers. She would do so for an hour or more, then pause to listen in silence and solitude. She repeated the pattern over and over while daylight dwindled away. The tricolor collie, ever watchful, lay nearby and never once disturbed her.

The notes rose and fell in melodies written by the secret groanings of her soul; the hush of hearkening to hear what she needed to receive had an exhilarating buoyancy. During one of those cycles of petition and stillness what unfolded provoked an urgent restlessness that made her skin clammy and cold. The distinct plainness of the vision could not be denied or evaded. She replayed it and keenly concentrated so as to categorize every detail.

What she saw was this: It was nighttime and Charley Jondreau was hatless. His freshly shaven scalp reflected glints of orange from the flames cast by a campfire. He was despondent and sullen. There was disarray and annoyance in his spirit that leeched from his pores. His partner, fuming and furious, sat across from him, unable to articulate her emotions.

The currents seething between them were saturated by disbelief and uncertainty. Then in a whirling tempest, Charley Jondreau was alone and on foot in a vast wasteland of arroyos and canyons walled in by steep and rocky bulwarks. He crept along stealthily. Now it was sunlight dancing upon the tawny skin of his head. His eyes were ever darting side to side.

The sky, bluer than blue from horizon to horizon, sputtered grumbles of thunder that came from the unseen world beyond the blue—it was the hope that follows lightning that was driving him onward. He slouched behind a boulder, paused and sent supplications for help heavenward, then took a dozen racing steps to confront an ancient enemy.

Charley Jondreau was face to face with Smoky Crowe. Ten yards separated them as they cautiously assessed possible frailties in each other. An enormous surge of volcanic power sizzled between them; the positive of good smashed and sparked against the negative of evil. The dead odor of singed ozone was an invisible fog that scorched the air. The one-eyed Ute witch had an arrow slotted in his bowstring which was drawn back and ready to be released.

"You are the dragon, eh."

"I am the great prophet."

"You are squadoosh," Charley said, bopping up on the balls of his feet. His hips were loose and relaxed, while his right hand held the knife poised to sling it. A smile, so subtle as to be undetectable, grazed his lips. "Nothing more than a counterfeit abracadabra artist."

"I am the messenger of death."

"The Great Spirit is the author of life and death."

"I am the herald of the dark one."

"I will kill you, eh"

"I am indestructible."

"You are a pillager. Pillagers die."

"I am indestructible," Smoky Crowe reiterated, head craning crookedly. The milky white sickness of his left eye roiled and pulsated incessantly. "I will ascend the mountains and walk upon the clouds. You have no power to stop me." He leered an exultant grin. "Your Navajo princess will not, cannot save you from the hellfires of damnation and victory."

"You will die here today, eh."

There was a flurry of activity that had the attributes of a sandstorm. Everything became unglued in a chaotic mishmash of blood and thunderbolts. A nightmarish roar, a scream, a shout, a shriek and the horrendous noise of crows cackling and flapping wings; then inside the stunning vividness of the scene, there was death and emptiness on the face of the earth.

Sally Twosongs was uneasy. The rerun of the foretelling did not result in a clearer perspective. She abruptly stood. Though her expression was downcast, she spoke reassurance to the dog as she put the tote over a shoulder and adjusted the strap. She would trek to Bulldog Mountain to pray and fast and seek the Creator's favor on behalf of Charley Jondreau.

She stepped outside and flipped the braid of her hair so that it dangled down the center of her back. The setting sun was halfway behind the craggy peaks of the western wall that bordered *WT Ranch*. Hank was whining and making an excited fuss. She responded with a profound sigh of resignation that served to steel the resolve of her backbone.

It made no sense for her to embark on the journey while twilight gathered into darkness, but she had heard from the Creator, and in the tests of time she'd learned to be obedient to those promptings. Therefore, Sally Twosongs put one foot in front of the other and used the staff to go forward in faith, believing that there was no turning back, nor any place for doubts to prevail.

An hour later, Caleb Weitzel came home and had a sense of loneliness. He immediately knew the house was empty. Anxiousness hastily tugged on his heart. He had spent the day on horseback checking the perimeter of *WT Ranch*. He flipped his hat onto the twelve-point mule deer rack mounted on a plaque centered above pegs for sweaters and outerwear.

He went to the kitchen, which was aglow and had the sweet aroma of the desert after a springtime sprinkling of rain. A large block candle scented with sage had burned down to almost nothing in its bowl on the table. Beside it was a sheet of paper weighted by a black-veined white stone. He recognized the artistic flow of his wife's handwriting. The unsettling disquiet in his heart increased as he sat and read what she had written for him.

> *My Dearest, Sweetest Caleb: You are my strength when I am weak, my joy when I am sad, my contentment when I am restless. Your heart is my heart, your destiny my destiny. There is no intrusion*

or pathway that can ever harm or separate us because we have a bond that existed from eternity past until way over yonder when time is no more. You are my hero, my lover, my friend. My heart never stops being aflame because of my love for you.

Bethsuelo is safe with your parents. She was laughing happily. She warmed me to my core when she told me that she would talk to Jesus about his good medicine for me. You will be tempted to be troubled, but as I have told you in the past, don't ever worry on me. I will be protected as I am faithful; guardian angels will be on watch over me.

I must do what I must do. I cannot explain or even glean any true knowledge of what transpires in the heavenlies, but am adamantly sure that the Creator compels me. I must help Charley Jondreau. I will be gone for a week or more. Do not come after me. I am secure in the mercy and compassion of the Creator. All my love, honor and respect belongs to you.

Lucero, your little bright star.

Weitzel had moisture on his cheeks. "Oh, Sally Twosongs," he murmured thickly. He exhaled a loud rush as he put the letter down. He planted his elbows on the table and fisted his hands under his chin. He harnessed the precepts of Scripture to his prayers for the woman who was the other half of who he was; his heartfelt appeals were brief and straightforward. When he said amen, he extinguished the candle and remained in the darkness for a long while.

"Heathen redskins ain't welcome here."

Charley Jondreau didn't even blink. He was in Missouri, at the Kingsley Tavern, a rambunctious roadhouse on the outskirts of Chillicothe. He touched the floppy brim of his hat as he calmly regarded the four rabble-rousers looming in an arc around his corner table. He leaned back and subdued a smirk. "I will tell you this once, eh. I don't chit and I don't chat."

"We got us a lynching rope."

"You're liquored up," Charley said dully. He dismissed them and tossed off the whiskey he had been nursing, then placed his palms down on either side of the glass. His fingers started drumming out a tattoo on the tabletop. Stagnant streamers of hazy smoke hung from the ceiling rafters, dense and cottony. He coolly measured his adversaries from left to right.

The one who had spoken was chunky and red-faced; braggadocio and nothing more. The middle two were obviously brothers; both bucktoothed and wiry, jittery and bobbing on their feet as if fiddles were playing a reel no one else could hear. Those three presented no peril to Jondreau. The fourth man, however, had the look of a lean and battle tested soldier, confident and savvy in close quarters combat. He wielded a bowie knife and was surly-eyed.

"Walkaway, eh."

"To the closest tall tree," the red-faced windbag replied, simpering.

"I'll cut his balls off first," the man brandishing the blade said stonily.

"Then let's dance." Jondreau's hands had never stopped tapping. Half a second before he exploded like a coiled spring his mouth took on its bulldog guise. The table went flying at the antagonists as though it was hurled from a catapult; the braggart demonstrated nimbleness and stepped aside, but the men with protruding front teeth were knocked onto their backsides. At the same time, Jondreau eliminated the dangerous one by sending his stiletto on a deadly course.

The knife struck the slim and sinewy man between the legs at an upward angle. His eyes bulged hugely and a bloodcurdling shriek poured forth from his lungs as he crumpled to the floor and writhed around like a beached catfish, gasping and sputtering cusswords. The Lord's name was repeatedly being squealed in vain. Other patrons were hurriedly scrambling to their feet, hooting and hollering, along with offering gales of derisive laughter.

Jondreau had never ceased or even slowed the assault. He stomped one brother in the groin and grabbed the other's right wrist, hoisted him up and twisted the arm around at the exact incline and force necessary for the shoulder to dislocate. The suction snapping noise was sickening, but was drowned out by a yelping that was similar to a newborn wailing.

The red-faced man was bug-eyed and in full-fledged backtracking form; fear leaked from him. Jondreau had placed mercy on a shelf in his heart. He delivered a sweeping left-hook to the solar plexus, which doubled the flabby man over and earned him a two-fisted clout to the back of his neck. His face smashed into the floor. His head bounced crazily and he flopped onto his back. Blood spurted from both nostrils as the tub of guts blubbered and slobbered.

"I ain't no heathen, eh," Charley said tersely. He withdrew his pistol and made clear he would use it on any bystander who might decide to make a move against him, though there was trifling chance of that occurrence since the onlookers were cowed and had retreated to give him a wide berth. He went to the slender man bleeding from his crotch and took a knee at his side.

"You maimed me," the man whimpered, grinding his teeth.

"Don't be a crybaby, eh," Charley chided, gentle and low-key. "You only got what you intended to give." He wiggled and yanked the knife free. "Your plumbing ain't gonna work."

The man cringed, swore vehemently and blacked out. Charley Jondreau cleaned his blade, stood and returned it to its leather casing high on his left hip. Blithe and undaunted, he strolled past gawkers and once outside, tanked up on chilly night air. The full moon was bright and high. He went to the hitching rail and swiftly untethered the piebald pinto.

There were no regrets or qualms troubling him. He mounted and rode westward through the moonlit night. It was past noon of the next day before he made camp. Then, a month later, on a stifling hot Kansas evening in June 1872, he meandered into Abilene for a taste of whiskey, and at the Alamo Saloon, became acquainted with a broad-shouldered preacher-man.

When Lucinda Enochelli breezed into Delmonico's Restaurant it was almost closing time, but she couldn't care less; a fact that she assertively made known to staff and customers alike. "I haven't eaten a morsel since yesterday," she said, standing in the doorway. "I want steak, eggs, and fried potatoes, along with a quart or so of cider to wash it all down."

A block-bodied man in a Panama hat rushed toward her and spoke cheerily to the solo waitress still on duty. "Whatever the lady wants put it on my bill. You will receive a more than princely gratuity." He grinned chummily at the newcomer as he attempted to sneak a furtive peek at what had brought him running to the front of the eatery. The low-cut neckline of her dress revealed much; he was noticeably intrigued by the valley of cleavage.

"Thank you, mister. Your kindness is welcome."

"Willy Phips. Will you join me and my friend at our table?"

"Why certainly, sir," the swarthy brunette answered, hooking a hand around his offered arm. She introduced herself as he ushered her to the back of the room. She gave his bicep a squeeze and was pleased that beneath his baggy suit there was a degree of hardness.

"This here tadpole is Jack Whistler," Willy said, holding a chair for her. "He's boyish and still wet behind the ears, but claims he's a globetrotter and has got some mystery about him. What the frig do I know? He may be a truth teller or full of crap, but he's entertaining."

She lightly bussed her escort's cheek, then swished her skirt and sat. "Glad to dine with such a fine pair of swanky gentlemen." She situated her purse on a vacant chair. "Willy, if you have any more of the whiskey that's on your breath I'll expect my cider to be fortified."

"That I can do, ma'am."

"Call me *ma'am* again and you'll be walking funny."

"Gotcha loud and clear, Lucinda."

"And as for you, tenderfoot," she said, directing her focus on the teenager. "If I ever hear you refer to me as a *ma'am* you can kiss your butt goodbye because I will take you out. And make no mistakes, I do mean *ever*. You understand where I'm coming from, Jack?"

"Indeed, I do, Lucinda."

The waitress, a dishwater-blonde in a plain blue dress and bib-apron with frills around its edges, interrupted them to deliver a pitcher of cider and a tall glass. "Please be patient. The cook promises that your meal will be out as soon as possible. I apologize for any delay, ma'am."

"What's with all the *ma'ams* around here?" Lucinda asked theatrically. "Just shake your buns and get it here before I die of starvation and all will be well." She promptly poured half a glass. When the server was out of earshot, she bent forward and remarked, "For what are you waiting, Willy? Top off my glass, then do the same to the pitcher, if you have enough."

"I do." Phips picked an opportune time, then pulled a silver flask from an inside slot and another from a side pocket. He discreetly emptied the first one in her tumbler, then filled the jug to the brim with the other. "How's that, young lady? The best rye money can buy."

She took a slow and satisfying sip. A sly smile crested on her lips, then she gulped the liquid refreshment down in three swallows. "Smooth and sweet, Willy. Drinks fine."

"A woman who enjoys whiskey is my kind of lady."

"I ain't no lady, Willy," she said, refilling her glass. She flaunted a come-hither look and twittered. "If you play your cards right you just might discover how unladylike I can be."

Phips guffawed and gave an emphatic handclap. "I bankroll my lifestyle by astutely reading the cards, so I expect to win the jackpot you speak of sooner rather than later."

"We shall see, shan't we?"

Whistler coughed, fake and exaggerated. "What's your story, Lucinda?"

"Are you a copper, Jack?"

"No, but I do have a healthy curiosity."

"I'm on the lookout for someone."

Whistler eyed her studiously. "Who, pray tell?"

"Have you ever heard of Deacon Coburn?"

"No."

"I have," Willy piped in as he boosted his coffee with a splash of rye. "He's a preacher or religious type. From what I gathered he had some connection to the outlaw Kid Greer."

"When and where, Willy?" Lucinda queried eagerly.

Phips slumped back and puckered his mouth. "When I got off the train here in October of '82 that Coburn fella seemed to be at the center of everything. He and a white-haired Negro were on the platform at the depot seeing three women and a lad off. I overheard bits of conversation. The older woman, a good-looking redhead, was a restaurateur in Santa Fe, I think."

"Delores Solrizo?" Jack asked, eyebrows crooking.

Phips scowled in surprise. "Yeah, now that you mention it, I think her name was Delores. I never caught her surname, or if I did, it's long forgotten. How'd you know that, Jack?"

"Data and facts."

"Data and facts," Willy mimicked scornfully. "Explain yourself."

"Life's all about information," the young man replied, arms outstretched in a disarming manner. "I file as much as possible in my head, never knowing what will be profitable."

"Spill what you know, Jack."

Whistler absentmindedly cracked one knuckle after another as he spoke. "In September of '82 I was in a stagecoach with Delores Solrizo out of Santa Fe. I got off in Las Vegas, where I met you, Slick Willy. Delores, as I recall, traveled on to Dodge City."

Lucinda giggled huskily. "Slick Willy?"

"A gambler's moniker," Willy answered, low and dispassionate.

"Isn't that charming?"

"It's what I do and who I am."

"Well, Slick Willy, how much of a gambler are you?"

"Whatever do you mean, Lucinda?"

"In a few days I will be on a train to Santa Fe," she said, polishing off her second glass. "Boredom is a drag and there's been plenty of it on my trip." She moistened her lips and lowered her voice to a whisper laced together by a promising smile. "I could use an occasional diversion, so would you like to accompany me on the chance you'd rake in a bosomy bonanza?"

"I will be at your side with bells on, young lady."

Whistler coughed again. "I'll gladly come along."

"We don't need a chaperon, Jack."

"He knows this Delores woman, Slick Willy."

Phips sneered thinly. "I suppose that could be helpful."

The waitress, her face flushed and harried, arrived and set a platter of food and a basket of biscuits on the table, then backed away and departed without a word. Lucinda Enochelli didn't waste a moment. She dug in with gusto, making the knife and fork clatter noisily. The two men simply watched as she devoured every last crumb, along with draining the pitcher of spiked cider. Then and only then, were plans discussed as to their upcoming excursion.

The kitchen of the Suncurl Café was warm and cozy, lit up by a dozen oil lamps and an equal number of candles. By the clock it was approaching midnight, and old friends were visiting and chatting about interests that mattered. Deacon Coburn, shaggy and bewhiskered, sat across from Delores Solrizo at the island bar in the center of the spacious room.

He had a mug of coffee and shot of whiskey in front of him. She had to rummage around a cubbyhole until she found a dusty bottle to accommodate his taste buds. Sorrow pooled in his eyes and compassion wrinkled the lines of his face as his hands fidgeted and he studied her. "We didn't know about Brenda's illness when Whitey invited Avis along via telegram."

"It all happened so fast. We're still in shock."

"All the more reason for us to stay put for a spell," he said, scratching at his beard. He let loose a drawn out sigh. "Given our travel plans I'm concerned about you being alone."

"Alone? I won't be alone, Deacon."

"How do you figure?" he asked mildly. "From what I heard, Avis is determined to bring Stace on the trail with us, which is fine, but honestly, I think Whitey and I got bit by some kind of bug or something. We're just riding to ride, taking some detours and side trails we ain't ever been on. We have toyed with the idea of going to Colorado to winter at *WT Ranch*."

"Avis would enjoy that," she said, eyes brightened by a spontaneous smile. "And it will all be good for Stace, though yes, I will miss them terribly, but they have to grow and do. I want no more complaints or protests, Deacon. I insist that you carry on exactly as proposed."

"You won't see Avis and Stace until next spring."

"When do you intend to saddle up?"

"A few days, I reckon."

"Sometime before then I'm setting a chair on the back-stoop and Whitey's going to put his scissors and razor to work." Her lips pursed as she shook her head and snappishly jabbed a finger at him. "I declare, every time you show up here you got that sheepdog look."

"I ain't had no reason to be pretty."

"Now you do."

"I suppose," he replied, chuckling. "Why aren't you going to be alone?"

"Nothing is as constant as change, correct?" she asked, folding her hands together. "The Suncurl Café has undergone a radical transformation, which has been beneficial for many."

"Tell me more."

"We're busy six days a week. People in and out from morning to night," she answered, joy and pride evident in her voice. "The place is no longer a money-making operation. We are a volunteer hub for churches in the community. My role is to coordinate workers with needs."

"That's impressive, Delores. Truly."

"It's fulfilling," she said with a nod. "My breakfast crew has changed in personnel over the years, but I still have a rotation of men to do odd jobs and the heavy lifting in exchange for a hearty meal. We also serve hot soup and such at noontime for everyone and anyone. Spring and autumn we do clothing drives, then distribute the apparel to those stricken by poverty."

"Do you have any funding issues?"

"Not at all," she replied, lips curling impishly. "My investment portfolio set in place from monies earned in the bad old days provides a fair to middling income, plus when necessary, I can be rather persuasive and have solicited regular contributions from a broad base."

"God redeems our bad old days, Delores."

"Amen, brother," she intoned, waving a hand over her head. "Our donations, mostly from businesses and churches fill in any financial gaps and serves to sustain the activities. There's no doubt in my mind that if a crisis occurred an emergency solicitation would have positive results because this ministry is entrenched and has developed a solid reputation in the city."

"You are an inspirational woman." He sipped his coffee, which was already cold, but that mattered not to him. "Take encouragement from a Proverb of Solomon: *He that hath pity upon the poor lendeth unto the Lord; and that which he hath given will he pay him again.*"

"Thank you, Deacon. You are always too kind."

"In this ofttimes cruel world, one can never be too kind."

"I don't disagree," she said, leaning forward as she pressed her hands upward in a prayerful posture. "Though one can be always watchful to the concerns of others and in doing so forget to tend to their own wellbeing. Something I've seen you be guilty of in the past."

"I guess I have difficulties in that area."

"Tell me, Deacon, how are you, really?"

"I've been nagged by headaches of late."

"Too much riding? Not enough rest?"

"Thinking too much, maybe," he speculated, thumbing aside his bushy moustache. "The older I get the more I find myself casting backward glances and trying to reconcile my past."

"Didn't you just tell me that God redeems our bad old days?"

"Ah-huh. I said and believe it, but my brain has been churning up sorrows that have me pondering mistakes and fragments of regret from a long ago time and place," he said dismally. "I grew up with two brothers and two sisters." He slammed back the whiskey and grimaced as he swallowed. "Naomi is the only one I've connected with since before the war, but it's weird." He flinched warily. "The other night I dreamt about my brother Josiah. It was a straight arrow true recollection, word for word as I remember it. He even brought up Lucy Elburt."

"Who's Lucy Elburt?"

"A girl from the River Brethren community of Conoy Creek," he answered, downing the coffee and shrugging offhandedly. "She had her hat set for me, but on my part, there was no attraction. She was overbearing, along with being wild and having a rebellious streak."

"An old girlfriend in Deacon Coburn's closet?" she jested, laughing joyfully.

"On that note I'm heading upstairs for some shuteye." He slid off the stool while the woolly-worm hiding his upper lip twitched as he tried to stifle a grin. His tired eyes perked up some and he nodded goodnight. He trotted up the steps, taking two at a time. Her mirthful teasing rang in his ears, but was soon silenced by slumber. Moments after hitting the sack, Deacon Coburn slept heavily, where once more, days gone by occupied his dreams.

Meanwhile in the *Cantina Room*, aglow from wall-mounted oil lamps, Avis Lahay was spiritedly schooling Whitey Fitzgerald at the pool table. Their friendship, forged in both bleak and congenial situations, had been reestablished in the swiftness of a lickety-split hug. She sank the final ball from their sixth game—Whitey had managed to be victorious in one.

"That's it," he said, grousing a click-click. "I be in one of those rockers admiring that cascading waterway when you be ready to just sit and chin-wag instead of beating on me."

She giggled as giddily as a wee child. "I will gladly join you."

"That be dandy." He had a hobble in his giddyup as he went to the painting of a waterfall that dominated one wall—it appeared as though the foamy spray of the river emerging from the lush green forest could be felt and tasted; a local artist had been commissioned to create the mural. He sat and got the chair moving at a rapid pace. "I sure has missed you, sweetie."

"I've longed for you to be here, Whitey."

"We ought to get wise and reside in the same town."

She settled in the bentwood rocker beside him. "What's with the limp?"

"I be saddle sore, is all," he replied, slackening the back and forth momentum. "Jezebel needed a rest from me as badly as I needed to do a bunch of walking on my owns two feet."

"Stretch out those kinks now because we'll soon be on the trail together and it will be wonderful," she said, eyes excited. "Hey, I never wrote you about my new horse, did I?"

"Nope, I ain't never heard word one about a new horse."

She sighed an expansive yawn as she adjusted sideward. "After Pumpkin spoiled me I had an extremely difficult time bonding with any mount. Then, at an auction six months ago, I found a three-year-old strawberry roan mare. We had an immediate attachment."

"You look fine on a strawberry roan."

"Cookie is affectionate and as smart as a fox."

"Smarter than you, sweetie?"

"Sometimes it seems that Cookie reads my mind."

"Then you got yourself a special horse."

"I'm pleased."

"You got any other tidings for me?"

"I have some mystery in my life."

He wiggled his eyebrows. "I be a connoisseur of mysteries."

"A connoisseur?"

"You ain't got one that'll fool an ole geezer like me."

"It's about money."

He stiffened and frowned. "I best hear it."

"A year ago January I received a substantial check sent from a law firm in Dallas," she said, studying him close to read his reaction. Then added almost as an afterthought: "The cover letter explained in vague and obtuse language that I would get a check every January."

"For how long?"

"*Every* January," she answered emphatically. "Sure enough this past January one came in the mail. Same law firm letterhead, same fancy legal *whereas this, forthwith that* phrasing."

He averted his eyes. "That be a stumper."

"Even for an ole geezer?"

"I'm guessing I ain't so clever after all."

"You don't have any knowledge or ideas about it?"

"I be a barber. I know nothing about highfalutin things."

"Mom thinks Big Bull Wallace set up a trust fund for me."

He click-clicked a staccato barrage of chuckles. He nodded and said, "I betcha she be right. Big Bull be a big-hearted man. And I be remembering that you and him hit it off. He got the riches of glory and he done right by you. He could have sneezing fits every day of the week for months at a time, blow his nose on hundred dollar bills and never miss a nickel of it."

Her jolly peal was musical. "Oh, Whitey!"

"I be saying truth, sweetie."

She shook her head, brow furrowed. "Mom told me that since I don't need the money just now that I should invest it. She set me up with a banker who helped me put together a plan."

"Delores be a first-class businesswoman."

"Yes," she said, pensive and fretful. "With Stace and this new responsibility I figure to let the money grow until it becomes a necessity to take a draw from the nest egg's earnings." The trenches on her forehead darkened. "There are worries and concerns because motherhood is all new to me. I have to raise Stace good for Brenda. I need to be tough and tender with him."

"Tender first, tough second," he advised, smiling subtly. "Love him, but hold him to a high standard. Make him accountable for his actions and choices. Bend him straight and he grow upright and honorable. Trust the Lord Almighty step by step, and you be finer than fine."

"I want to be third, Whitey."

"Third? Whatcha mean?"

"God first, others second, me third."

"You be a blessing to my heart, sweetie."

"Are we ever going to get wise and reside in the same town?" she asked, slouching back to enjoy the picturesque waterfall. He started to respond, but then, copied her bearing. Inside a shelter of silence, the emotional strings that bound Avis Lahay and Whitey Fitzgerald together were hemmed even tighter. Time ticked onward as they basked in each other's company.

chapter three

Chases

"He shall fly away as a dream, and shall not be found: yea, he shall be chased away as a vision of the night. The eye also which saw him shall see him no more; neither shall his place any more behold him."

~Zophar~

Five days later, early in the morning while pinkish glints of dawn were streaking to dullish grays and brilliant blues, Deacon Coburn was away from the campsite in a swatch of forest alongside the Rio Chama. He sat on a deadfall log, alternating his attention between reviewing Scripture and watching poufy clouds floating effortlessly.

He was excavating gems from a favorite Psalm—an action that was integrated into his daily devotional routine. Though he had studied the Bible since childhood, and across the years had memorized huge sections of it, he never ceased being amazed by the fact that it was an irresistible exposition that could always speak vital truth and exhortation to his soul.

A gentle breeze wafted through the trees, which were budding. He glanced up and caught stealthy movement off to his right. His mouth puckered, bottom lip pushing out as he pretended that he didn't see the nine-year-old poking around near the riverbank. After several minutes of waiting, he said in a soft voice, "You're up and at it mighty early, Stace."

"Just like you, Mr. Deacon."

"True enough."

"I ain't bothering you, am I?"

"No, sir," Deacon answered genially. "Appreciate your time if you got any to spare. In the quiet before the labors of the day begin is a great opportunity to share important stuff."

Stace frowned as he sidled closer. "Important stuff?"

"Man talk."

"I don't know if I'm any good at man talk."

"We can give it a try, don'tcha think?"

"Sure, Mr. Deacon," Stace replied, squatting comfortably on his haunches with his back against a cottonwood. "I ain't one who has lots of words running around my head."

Coburn smiled amusingly. "How do you like the trail?"

"I guess it's alright."

"It'll grow on you, I expect."

"Aunt Avis surely enjoys it."

"Yeah, she does. Like she was born to it," Deacon said, closing the Bible. He scrunched forward to rest his elbows on his knees. "I've admired your sorrel. It's a splendid horse."

"Aunt Avis bought it for me when she got Cookie." His expression was animated in a big grin. "We picked it out together, but she paid for it. I'm still working off what I owe her, though with all the extra chores she's got me doing now I should be free and clear soon enough."

"I've noticed she does keep you busy."

"Oh, I ain't complaining."

"Stating facts was all I heard."

"Where we going?"

"Everywhere, nowhere," Deacon answered wryly. "We're on a roundabout route toward Taos. I have an old friend there and I want to check in on him, if he's even in the area."

"Why wouldn't he be?"

"Daniel Twosongs is a wayfarer like me. Never stays put for long."

"Is a wayfarer like an explorer?"

Coburn squinted at him, head tilted oddly. "Kind of, I suppose, Stace. I ain't sure I ever thought of myself as an explorer. I'm just at home on horseback, a wandering cowboy wondering about what can be seen across the next river and on the other side of every mountain."

"That makes you an explorer, Mr. Deacon."

"I'll take your word for it, son."

"I'd like to be an explorer," Stace said, eyes lighting up excitedly. "Mom taught me that life was a big adventure so I want to see and do things that you always read about in books."

"You're doing so now, Stace."

"I guess I am, ain't I? Wow."

"Your mother would be proud."

"I don't want to talk about that, Mr. Deacon."

"Understandable. What's on your mind?"

"Why do you read the Bible every day?"

"That's an interesting question."

Stace shrugged as deep lines drew across his brow. "Mom did, too. *Every* evening. As far as I can tell, Grandmom and Aunt Avis never miss a day. I was thinking about it, is all."

"The Bible is God's story."

"God's story?"

"From the beginning of Genesis to the closing passage of Revelation it is God's story of redemption unfolding in creation and throughout history," Deacon explained plainly. "God is sovereign and constant in his interaction with individuals for the purpose of seeking and saving those who are lost. And since we all have the stain and stink of sin in us that means he is always actively drawing each one closer so everyone can receive and accept grace and mercy."

"Mom told me that we're all sinners."

"Your mother was correct, but be assured that she didn't come by that idea out of nothingness," Deacon said, a chuckle weaving its way into his words. "In the book of Romans a man named Paul wrote: *For all have sinned, and come short of the glory of God.*"

"*For the wages of sin is death; but the gift of God is eternal life through Jesus Christ our Lord,*" Stace quoted boldly. "Romans 6:23. Mom taught me those verses when I was littler."

"She was wise to do so. Do you understand them?"

"Of course. I've got Jesus in my heart."

"Me, too."

"So why read the Bible every day?"

"Life is about God, not us," Deacon replied, the rasp of his voice eased by persuasion. "Our lives are about what God desires to do in and through us, so I read it every day to be vigilant and keep discovering how or where I fit into the big picture of God's story."

"I ain't sure I can figure that, Mr. Deacon."

"I was just pondering Psalm 139." He flipped open the Good Book. "Listen to the first six verses: *O Lord, thou hast searched me, and known me. Thou knowest my downsitting and mine uprising, thou understandest my thought afar off. Thou compassest my path and my lying down, and art acquainted with all my ways. For there is not a word in my tongue, but, lo, O Lord, thou knowest it altogether. Thou hast beset me behind and before, and laid thine hand upon me. Such knowledge is too wonderful for me; it is high, I cannot attain unto it."*

"That's hard to get," Stace said, tapping his forehead.

Coburn nodded knowingly. "God's purposes and plans are being worked out in our lives, whether we grasp that or not. We are no mystery to the Creator. He knows us inside out, so we cannot ever fool him or cut a deal with him. All the seasons of our lives are laid in front of us by God, and it is our task to continually get our footsteps aligned on his pathway for us."

"And reading the Bible every day helps?"

"It's the only way I know, Stace," Deacon answered, succinct and sincere. "That's some heavy lifting for your brain, isn't it? What say we head back to camp and get breakfast started if someone hasn't beaten us to it?" He stood, as did his young friend. Then Deacon Coburn and Stace Hawkins strolled side by side through the woods and into the clearing where Whitey Fitzgerald and Avis Lahay were still snoozing, and the campfire needed to be rekindled.

For Jesse Axler, dawn was breaking in the shadows of towering crags and peaks north of Wagon Wheel Gap. The gleaming orange blades stirred whitecaps of excitement in him. He was determined to accomplish what was in his heart to do. He had written a note of explanation, packed gear in anticipation of possible variables, and departed in full dark.

He was along a westerly bend of the Rio Grande, mounted on a soot-gray mare that used to belong to Max Dawson. The bridle-wise mustang had some age and miles, but remained savvy and intuitive, and he trusted its fleet-footedness. There were no tracks or signs to indicate the trail he should take; he was operating entirely on instinct and a patchwork of memories. He intended to cut a hard right at the Willow Creek tributary and follow its northerly route.

He was considering the challenge ahead, and though the mission was foggy and unclear, he knew that he had to be true to what was inside him—no matter the hazard or consequences he had to do what he had to do. No obstacles or difficulties could be allowed to distract or deter him because any semblance of failure would not be tolerated.

All those thoughts took him far into the future. He enjoyed being alone—his mother told him that he inherited that trait from his Uncle Deacon, which gave him a sense of pride and belonging. The horse beneath him trotted spryly as it picked its way over a path of least resistance, and his mind daydreamed about where life would take him.

Of all the open doors of opportunity set before him, there was only one that he absolutely knew he had no yearning or compulsion to go through, and that was to be in the military. Uncle Deacon had been a sharpshooter in the Civil War, and late one night while he was visiting *WT Ranch* a few winters ago, Jesse had sat quietly in a corner of the living room and listened to his uncle talk sorrowfully to his mother and father about soldiering and war.

According to Uncle Deacon, armed men in uniform were mere pawns and cannon fodder for politicians who didn't have the intestinal fortitude or wherewithal to solve boundary disputes or diplomatic differences. There was no logical reason for anyone to choose war and slaughter over common sense and peace-making, but due to the self-absorbed nature of man, humankind would never come to that conclusion until the end of history.

Jesse Axler had no desire to be trapped on any bloody battlefield. He had read *Moby Dick*, which fascinated him and put his imagination on course to become a seafarer. He wanted to see the world—as much as he enjoyed ranching and horses, he contemplated that in not too many years he'd travel to San Francisco and get hired on as a deckhand on a merchant ship that would take him to various exotic ports of call and give him a wide range of experiences.

He'd learned about Francis Drake, and other daring men of action who had sailed up and down the Barbary Coast, around the southern tip of Africa, onto India and beyond. Drake was the buccaneer who got inside his skin; Drake circumnavigated the world, and the expedition was all so real and amazing to him. Sir Francis Drake churned up a desire to confront danger and reach for the impossible, and he fully expected to become a maritime adventurer.

The sun crested above the mountaintop and the low-laying terrain was awash in brightness. He glanced over a shoulder and had to shield his eyes against the blazing sunshine. The sheer beauty of the surroundings caused his breath to get stuck in his throat; the fresh and brilliant greens of springtime filled his senses with wonder.

He roused around in the saddle and in doing so felt hardness pressing against his left thigh. A smile, faint and thin, momentarily graced his lips. He stooped his back and shoulders, and dug into a front pocket of his dungarees to retrieve a special souvenir. It was the carved oak medallion his father had created especially for him. It usually sat on the dresser in his bedroom, but on this journey he felt compelled to bring it for good luck.

He examined the wooden keepsake, turning it over and over in his hand. Perfectly round and about the dimension of a pocket watch, its backside was flat and as smooth as glossy brass, while the front was an intricate work of art; a seamless replica of a horse's head, with the plume of its mane abundant and flowing, its eyes deep-set and lifelike.

He remembered his mother showing him the piece that his father had whittled for her in Abilene when they'd started courting. The two were near exact reproductions—as was the third ornament his father had fashioned for his sister. The exquisite detail and dedicated craftsmanship never failed to spur him ever onward to excellence. He held it tight in his palm, then securely tucked it away. He pulled his hat low and spoke kindly to the mare.

Just then, it whinnied and began acting skittish. He patted its neck, but the animal would not be placated. A rustle of movement on the other side of the river arrested his attention. He stiffened as he looked and saw a bobcat skulking in the tall grass, padding step for step with the mustang—he became convinced that it was the same cat he had been pursuing.

He withdrew the Spencer from its scabbard, but the wildcat snarled once, then scampered out of sight and was gone before he could even shoulder the weapon. Urgency heightened his awareness. He stood in the stirrups and studied the lengthy grass in an effort to determine where the feline would reappear, but there were no riffles or fluttering to give its position away.

The pestering notion that the bobcat was now stalking him reared up inside his head. He strictly evaluated the likelihood of that, and concluded it was a genuine possibility. The roof of his mouth got dry and a lump solidified in his windpipe. He bent forward and encouraged the horse, then Jesse Axler rode cautiously, alert and on the lookout, with the rifle at the ready.

In the Dakota Territory, a pair of soon to be six-year-olds were on a hillock that sloped to the bank of Wounded Knee Creek. Langton Beadle and Yaz were not alone. A mangy bluetick heeler had assumed their position, pressed flat on its belly between them. The inseparable trio were currently on an exciting undertaking for the ages.

The sun was low in the east, the sky speckled by dots of clouds that were as still as still could be—the scent of woodsmoke hung in the shiftless air. Though the encampment was less than a half-mile away, from the point of view of the boys it may as well be nonexistent. Their focus was on a horde of butterflies clustering together on the backside of the hill.

"What's happening?" Langton asked, face crunched in puzzlement.
"Strange."
"Listen to their wings."
"Much flapping."

"Have they gone batty, Yaz?"

"Don't know, *Hé Tuwá Oyúmni.*"

"What?"

"Nothing, Beadle."

"What?" Langton made his fingers move rapidly as the frown deepened into a scowl. The friends communicated in a mix of English, Lakota and sign language. "Those are words I do not yet know. I must learn them, so say again slowly and tell me the meaning."

"It is not right for me to do so, Beadle."

"Are you being difficult, Yaz?"

"I overheard Standing Wolf call you that," the Sioux boy replied, hands motioning in a fluid gesture. "I should not have said those words. It was wrong to speak for an elder."

"He will tell me?"

"I cannot say what another will do, Beadle."

"You are not helpful today."

Yaz shrugged and draped an arm over the dog's neck. "I am as I always am. We are here to chase and catch butterflies, not to chatter. Boxy is ready to run. Are you?"

The heeler cocked its ears up and muffled an exuberant whine. Langton smirked in such a way that one eyebrow dipped while the other arched lopsidedly. "I will be the wind."

"You cannot be the wind. I will be the wind."

Then, like jumping grasshoppers, the three comrades leapt in unison and burst down the hillside. The dog easily raced ahead of them, despite the fact that their legs were chugging and arms pumping like pistons. The airborne butterflies thronged into an even tighter flock, hovered for several seconds, then fluttered upward and flew off in a southerly pattern.

Boxy zigged after the winged insects—both boys were exerting every effort to be the wind and stay on pace with their four-legged dasher, but were lagging farther and farther behind. The persistent drone of the swarming myriad of butterflies in flight hummed loudly, but lessened as the distance separating the youngsters from the flock grew more and more.

The dog had not barked at all, but then, it stopped and yapped thrice as it flattened onto the ground. Langton and Yaz dove forward as one and skidded onto their bellies because they saw what had startled the bluetick heeler. A hundred or so yards away, a detachment of U.S. Cavalry were in twin columns riding westward at a hurried clip.

"Bluecoats," Langton whispered edgily.

"Trouble."

"Just passing by, Yaz."

"Trouble, probably."

"Let's get back."

"Wait, Beadle."

Langton made a terse clucking noise by sucking against his cheek. Boxy perked up its ears and slouched back, tail wagging erratically as it hunkered almost atop them. The threesome remained stationary against the grass until the swirling billows of dust generated by the squadron of horse soldiers dispersed. Then, with Boxy taking the lead, Langton Beadle and Yaz sprinted back to the community of tepees with news about the movement of troops.

At *WT Ranch*, Naomi Axler was flummoxed. Breakfast was cleared and though she had called him, she still had not seen her firstborn. Agitation dominated her outlook. She moved down the hallway like a woman possessed. She gave the door a cursory knock, then opened it and entered his bedroom, and came to a sudden halt two steps away from the doorframe.

Her heart sank. His bed was newly made; every crease and wrinkle had been smoothed exactly how he had been taught, which shouldn't have surprised her, but it did. She had expected and truly hoped to find him beneath the covers. The sinking feeling in her chest became a jagged weight when she spotted a single sheet of paper propped against the pillow. Her legs carried her to the bedside. She grabbed the note and read it, weakening as she did so.

> *Mom and Dad – I want you to know that I am safe. There is no reason for you to worry or anything like that because you raised me to think matters through and be responsible. I will take every precaution necessary, but I must do what must be done. Sally Twosongs has been heavy on my mind. I am going to find her. She may be in peril. I will be back soon. Your son, Jesse.*

Naomi wobbled, gasping a teary breath as she plumped onto the edge of the bed. She let out a cry and slumped forward. "Pete!" she hollered, scared and angry. "Pete, come quick!" She heard his dawdling footsteps in the corridor, which distressed her all the more. "Pete!"

"What is it?" her husband asked, ambling into the room.

"Look at this."

He stepped to the bedside, took what was offered, then spent a minute or more perusing it. He gave a perfunctory shrug and handed the message back to her. "What's the problem?"

His relaxed demeanor infuriated her. She straightened and stiffened her posture. "What's the problem?" she parodied, waggling the paper at him. "Is that all you have to say?"

"It is." The ever-present frown lines on his forehead and around his eyes were dug into furrows deeper than usual. "I don't understand, Naomi. What's gotten into you?"

"What's gotten into me?"

"Tell me what you need me to say."

"Tell me what you need to say?" she blurted, moisture pooling in her smoldering eyes. She fixed a withering glare on him. "What kind of response is that, may I ask?"

"It's all I got, Naomi."

"You best get something better, Pete."

"What's the problem?" he queried again, perplexed and faltering. The air in the room seemed to be heated and prickly. He took a knee in front of her. "I must be dense, Naomi. I'm not getting it. Make allowances for my thick skull and explain what's got you so upset."

"Jesse has gone missing."

"That's an unreasonable conclusion, Naomi."

"I'm afraid it's not, Pete."

"You're afraid, I'll grant you that, but it's an unfounded fear," he said, gently taking hold of her hands. "This is life and life only, Naomi. All is as it should be as far as I can see. Letting Jesse grow and go may not be easy, but life ain't providing no other option. He has a good head on his shoulders. You're making a mountain here where there's not even a molehill."

"Am I?" she asked hotly. She jerked her hands away from his grasp. "Our son has ridden off to who knows where on a bootless errand that has disaster written all over it, and evidently you expect me to thoughtlessly sit here and do or say nothing about the situation."

"One, it's not a bootless errand, or a merry chase," he told her, holding his hands up in half-mast surrender. His tone was calm and unflustered. "And two, Jesse is doing what's in his heart to do, so in my opinion, the expectation is for us to support his decision. I have no doubt that he has thought the details through and put together a plan to succeed."

"How is that even possible, Pete? He's a boy."

"He's a man, Naomi."

"A man? In October he'll be thirteen years old."

"When I was his age I was doing a man's job," he replied, head shaking. "I had a man's freedom and responsibility. It's the way it is, and I'll not take that away from our son."

"He's becoming a man, but he's still a child."

"I beg to differ, dear."

"You can beg to differ for all you're worth. It's not at all relevant," she answered, jabbing a finger at him. "Your protests cannot change the fact that a twelve-year-old is just a child."

"That's where you're mistaken."

"I am not!"

"I ain't arguing no more."

"You have to go after him, Pete."

"No, can't do it, Naomi."

"Why the dickens not?"

"I don't want to embarrass him . . ."

"That's lame," she interrupted, tears spilling down her cheeks.

". . . or make him think I don't trust his judgment," he finished, brusquely scratching at his chin-whiskers. "If Jesse was off hunting to put meat on the table would that bother you?"

"That's different."

"Not really, dear."

"It's altogether different," she insisted, eyes widened and steaming.

"I ain't arguing no more," he restated, firmness sutured into his words. He knelt forward to reach over and take a strong hold of her hands again. "What's really wrong, Naomi?"

She stared at him in disbelief, as though he had made an intimate inquiry that shocked her sensibilities. Her lips quivered and she shuddered several hefty breaths. "What do you mean?"

"Come on now, Naomi," he replied, gradually squeezing her hands. "I'd have to be blind and deaf not to have noticed that you haven't been your customary buoyant self of late."

She suffocated a sob. "I'm sorry. I'm unsure and frightened."

"Give it time. Everything always works itself out," he said, bending at the waist to kiss her brow. He stood, then cupped his hand around the nape of her neck and peered lovingly into her big brown eyes. "Remember your verse from Romans: *For I reckon that the sufferings of this present time are not worthy to be compared with the glory which shall be revealed in us.*"

She rose and smiled bravely. "Thank you, Pete."

"I have to go to South Fork. Mail, banking and such. If I get to it soon I can be back before sunset." He fingered her hair, which was loose on her shoulders. He traced a hand down her side and rested it on her hip. "Amanda went over to visit with Eliza and Bethsuelo. Please ask her to bake ginger snaps this afternoon. I've had a taste for them since yesterday."

"Will do. Be careful." She hugged him fiercely—he returned the embrace with the same enthusiasm. She smooched his lips, then he was out the door and gone. Her cheeks were wet and shiny. There remained an intense chafing in her heart, but she determinedly clenched her teeth in an effort to shoo it away. She dropped onto the bed and folded her hands on her lap.

A shivery whimper escaped her throat, which was the prelude for a crying deluge. She didn't know why her perspective was skewed toward fretting and apprehension, but she yearned to quell the fickle emotions. Naomi Axler sniffled and hushed the weeping; she audibly recited the Lord's Prayer over and over until the unsteady trembling disappeared from her voice.

Avis Lahay had found an isolated spot to be alone. The sun had risen over the treetops and glinting beams glistened on the choppy currents of the Rio Chama. She sat on a triangular boulder that jutted over the river's edge. A pleasant breeze rustled the branches above her as a counterpoint to the medley of water rippling past.

She toyed with the gray metallic fountain pen. Her head was full of thoughts that were bits and pieces in an untidy swirl, which she was attempting to pacify so as to collect them into a cohesive arrangement. She opened the maroon leather journal, adjusted her position and crossed her left leg over her right to prop the book in the knee's nook. A cheery smile made her eyes sparkle as the wondrous serenity of nature inspired her, and she put pen to paper.

April 27, 1888

Dear Diary: Our third morning on the trail and it's gorgeous. So peaceful that it makes me wish I could live far away from the hustle and bustle of the city. I don't know. I guess that's a smattering of selfishness, though maybe it's just me reacting to the joys of the great outdoors. The air is fresher and sweeter, the songbirds prettier and more abundant.

Of course, getting away now is therapeutic and healing. The aching in my heart has me unnerved. I miss Brenda and continue to shed tears whenever I think of her, which I suppose will be a regular occurrence for quite some time. I try not to get weepy when Stace is around, but I'm not sure if that's wise, or perchance a false sense of pride on my part.

Perhaps it would be helpful if Stace actually saw me grieving—there's no way for me to know how best to proceed. Trial and error seems to be the only choice available to me, which can be maddening because it feels like guesswork. Stace shuts up, and acts all standoffish and withdrawn around me. It's difficult for me to know what to do or say. He seems to be getting more and more relaxed around Deacon and Whitey, which has to be good for him.

I'm worried. Even as I admit that, aloud as it were, I realize that I am misguided. No amount of me indulging anxiety will change anything about the circumstances that have come about for me. Worry is such a useless emotion. I am responsible to raise a young gentleman, so instead of wasting energy stewing over what or how to do so, I should trust God and my instincts, and set forth to be the best surrogate mother I can possibly be.

Writing all that encourages me, but there remains nagging doubts. Lord, I believe in your grace and protection; I believe that nothing happening now has taken you by surprise; I believe in your all-powerful provision. Please grant me strength and faith in those moments when the task ahead threatens to overwhelm me. I stand in constant need of your mercy; give me an anointing of wisdom to be available to all that you desire to pour into me.

Earlier, a few minutes before I started my entry, a mommy goose swam by with eight goslings mobilized behind her. It was a lovely scene that made my heart swell in happiness. How wonderful is creation? The newness of springtime reminds me of the hope of salvation; how God is alongside us through all the difficult vagaries that we must pass through on the journey. And that the good work God began in me will be completed for his purposes.

How wonderful? How marvelous? How unexplainable is the mystery of God? Day after day creation speaks of his majesty and supremacy, yet we can be blinded to the language of nature because of the hardness of the world. I do not know what the future holds, but am grateful beyond measure that I do know the One who holds my future in his redeeming and sovereign hands. I am thankful for so much; I should concentrate on expressing gratitude.

There's talk that we are going to winter at WT Ranch and not return to Santa Fe until next April or May. Mom told me before we departed that option could be in the by and by. She was not at all disapproving of the idea. In fact, was quite supportive, which is reassuring. Speaking entirely from my heart and on my behalf, that outcome would be fine with me.

I have only been to WT Ranch once; three years ago Mom and I took the train and spent a month visiting and site-seeing. It was all quite exhilarating. Mom and Naomi were thrilled to be together; they have faithfully kept in touch over the years by corresponding, and it was evident that their friendship had an abiding tenderness.

The social dynamics were enlightening. I finally got to meet and know all the folks that are so much a part of Deacon and

Mom's history. I felt real kinship with everyone, but had a special connection to Sally Twosongs. I long to see and spend more time with her. I suspect there is much that I can learn from her. The prospect of being at WT Ranch for the wintertime is an exciting opportunity that I will lobby for the next time the topic arises.

That is all for now. I best get on the move.

She closed the notebook and pocketed the pen. She stretched her legs and surveyed the sky, catching a glimpse of a large bird soaring high above, which yielded a lively sigh. She tilted the brim of her skimmer lower over her eyes and squinted. Sunspots hampered her sightline, but she concentrated and focus cleared so she could see that it was a golden eagle.

There was a swish of leaves behind her. She spun around as her adopted child piped up. "Aunt Avis, our horses are saddled. Mr. Deacon and Mr. Whitey are ready to go."

"Then we ought not to keep them waiting." She slid her derriere across the surface of the rock and hopped to the ground, giggling softly. "Whitey might turn into a grumpy grumbler."

Stace had his hands jammed into his pockets. He sidled in beside her. "*Dillydallying be just fine with me*, is what Mr. Whitey said," he reported, big-eyed and grinning.

"He's a lovable character." They walked along together. She gently placed a hand on his shoulder and felt tension tighten in him, so promptly removed it. "I appreciate you caring for Cookie. You're doing a great job, and I'd say that you have an aptitude with horses."

"An aptitude is good, right?"

"Indeed," she replied solemnly. She waited a few moments, then cautiously expressed her sentiments. "You know that I'm available whenever you want or need to yak about stuff."

"Sure I do, Aunt Avis," Stace said, sounding exasperated. His head was ducked and his shoulders hunched into a shrug as his attention remained locked on his footsteps. "I ain't stupid. I just got lots of junk to work out in my head. Feelings, you know. Mostly yucky feelings."

"I understand, Stace."

"Aunt Avis."

"Yes."

"Thanks for bringing me. I like the quietness."

"You're with me wherever I go from here on out, Stace."

They came to the campsite. The fire had been extinguished and all was packed. Their horses were standing side by side. Deacon Coburn was sitting relaxed on Gilgal twenty yards away, his right leg hooked over the saddle horn. His eyes were wrinkled and his moustache twitched in a broad smile. "Stace, many thanks for tracking down the lollygagger."

"Lollygagger?" Avis laughed, eyes vivacious and delighted. She slipped the journal in her saddlebags, then mounted Cookie. "I was gathering wisdom from all this beauty."

"Always a productive endeavor," Deacon said, nodding.

Whitey Fitzgerald stepped into the saddle. Jezebel hee-hawed a trivial protest, and he click-clicked. "I was gonna say we ain't got all day, but then, I 'membered that actually, we ain't got no deadlines, so I just shut my yapper. And besides dillydallying be just fine with me."

Stace snickered cheerily. "See, Aunt Avis, I told you so."

His amusement beget a surge of hope that gladdened her core. She watched him clamber onto the sorrel, waited for him to slip in behind the molly mule, then gave the strawberry roan a nudge. As was the usual pattern, the silver-dappled buckskin took the lead. The day promised sweetness, and Avis Lahay rode in easy anticipation of the wonders in the miles ahead.

Abbey Langton sat on a short stool in front of a tepee, listening to her son talk so speedily that his words slurred together. The golden tints in her auburn hair had become more prominent over the years, and just now, were emphasized by the morning sunshine. Her elbows rested on a lap-desk, and she was intentionally giving him her full concentration.

When he finished his tale, he inhaled a chest-swelling breath. He took a step back and his eyebrows raised seriously as he said, "That's the whole caboodle, Mom. You can ask Yaz."

"Do you have anything else to report, Yaz?"

The Sioux lad stiffened under her scrutiny, but didn't flinch or avert his eyes. His brow darkened and he nodded, hands pressed against his thighs. "No, ma'am. Beadle told it all."

Standing Wolf sat cross-legged near a small campfire. "How many horsemen?"

"Looked like many," Yaz answered curtly.

"What do you say, Langton?" she asked, setting the lap-desk on the ground.

"Yaz is correct. Many horsemen."

"Many to young eyes not the same as many to older eyes," Standing Wolf said, smiling thinly. Six decades had blown away like mist since the day of his birth, but his shoulder-length hair was still black and retained thick vibrancy. "Cavalry riders come and go at will."

Abbey got to her feet and reached for the sky, wiggling her fingers. She wore a colorful poncho-like dress that flowed to her ankles and had a wide cloth belt at the waist. She glanced around at the peaceful efficiency. The settlement of a dozen tepees was engrossed in living and doing. Family units were clustered together, eating or doling out the allotment of tasks.

She returned her bottom to the stool. "Butterflies and soldiers, huh."

Yaz squatted. "Hundreds of butterflies."

"Thousands, maybe," Langton opined, kneeling beside him. The bluetick heeler started spinning around, rambunctiously attempting to catch its tail as it yelped and whined. It got going faster and faster, kicking up dirt that bombarded the area like a rain of pellets. The boys were laughing and making sport, which incited the pooch to increase its noisy rollicking.

"Shush, Boxy!" Abbey ordered sternly. She clapped her hands twice. The dog stopped and plunged downward in submission, ears laying back and eyes emitting sorrowful humility. She shook a finger at it. "The entertainment is over. You got it, Boxy? Behave, or else."

"Or else what, Mom?"

"Wait and see, Langton. Wait and see."

"It's only important that the dog knows," Standing Wolf said, as he used a stick to stir the coals. "Look at it. Do you think there is any misunderstanding about who's the boss?"

"No, sir," Langton answered, chuckling.

"Let that be a lesson to both of you." Standing Wolf tossed the stick into the embers and altered his position so as to put his gaze directly on them. "Speaks With A Quill is not a woman to cross. She possesses strength and is wise. Her words have honor and power and truth."

"Too kind, Standing Wolf."

"Straight utterances are not kindness."

"Whatever it is called, thank you."

"I have seen much, lived much, done much," Standing Wolf intoned, hands gesturing expressively. "There is sadness in me because change has overtaken the Sioux people. The great herds of buffalo are no more. Our past is forever gone. We Sioux have lost our homeland and pride, and must find peace and harmony with the whites. I have enormous respect for Speaks With A Quill. Honesty and truthfulness are in her. She can help us make our way."

"What about the bluecoats?" Yaz asked aggressively.

Standing Wolf shrugged. "Some good, some bad."

"Soldiers are instruments of empire, Yaz," Abbey said in a restrained and solemn voice. "Standing Wolf is accurate when he talks about some being good, some being bad."

Langton balked. "Why are the bluecoats so cruel to our friends?"

"Soldiers follow orders, that's all, son. Policy is set by lawmakers."

"It's not fair, Mom."

"Fairness seldom happens, Langton."

"That's just wrong."

"It's how it is, son." Her countenance was marked by stern and ominous lines. "The world is full of hard and thorny soil where the bitter fruits of sin and corruption flourish, and we must do the good works of weeding and cultivating. It's up to each of us, including you and Yaz, to right wrongs and do whatever is possible to transform injustice into justice."

"I'm gonna right wrongs, Mom. I promise," he said forcefully. Silence fell over them for a minute or more. Langton scooped and squished several handfuls of dirt, then unexpectedly turned to the old man. "Yaz called me some words he said he heard from you, sir."

Standing Wolf pursed his lips and bowed his head for a moment, then sat upright to regard the white boy. "*Hé Tuwá Oyúmni.*" His dark eyes flashed indignant displeasure at his nephew. "Yaz should not have spoken it. The name I have given is inside you."

"What's it mean, Standing Wolf?" Langton asked sharply.

The venerable and fervently spiritual medicine man held his hands up and grinned. "I can tell you, but that would be like throwing smoke into the wind. Gone. No understanding."

"How can I understand?"

"Time, years, miles," Standing Wolf answered, strict and somber. "You will grow, you will learn, you will become the name. I see how you are and what is in your heart. You *are* a righter of wrongs, and boundaries are merely suggestions to you." He abruptly waved in a dismissive manner. "That's enough blabbing for now. You boys have chores."

"Yes," she agreed briskly. "First off, the goatskins need rinsed and filled with fresh water." She refrained from further instructions because the youths were immediately up and at it. The bluetick heeler pranced dependably alongside them. She returned the lap-desk to its place, lifted the lid, and fetched a feather pen and numerous sheets of stationery. Then, as the sun ascended the eastern sky, Abbey Langton proceeded to proof-read her latest manuscript.

∽ ∽ ∽

For Daniel Twosongs, the dream that had him on a southerly trail would not give him any release. It'd first startled him awake a month ago, after his wintertime houseguests had departed on their quest to pursue and punish Smoky Crowe for his heinous crimes. Twosongs had bid Charley Jondreau and Max Dawson farewell in the morning, then after a day of chopping and stacking wood, slept until slumber was snatched away by an assault of tangible images.

The night-vision hassled his imagination—interpreting it was akin to putting together a jigsaw puzzle that was missing dozens of key pieces. What he could distinguish troubled him: He saw a wounded schoolboy in agony, but the half-pint kept it all stuffed down inside him; he saw a woman at odds with doubts and fears; he saw a wise companion from his past suffering as he met the needs of others while mostly ignoring an inner alarm that required attention.

He also saw a diminutive black man full of grumbly joy, which appeared unusual and out of place. Twosongs wrestled mightily to capture the meaning of the snippets, and was tempted to let them go, but was not one to shy away from a mystery or allow it to mystify him. Plus, the persistent visitation returned twice more—three times he saw the same moving pictures flutter through his head and he could clearly recognize the landscape.

Then, true to his disposition, he welcomed solitude and consecrated it by smudging sage and other dried botanicals. He humbly invested days on end in solemn prayer and meditation because according to his discernment, all things had spiritual roots interweaved around them. There were no time constraints on his seeking; only reverent patience as he worshipped.

Daniel was an old soul, a man of no country, but of many lands—much of his life had been spent on horseback scouting history and basking in the diversity of the Creator's artistic genius. He had sprung from the loins of a Navajo brave, born out of wedlock in scandalous circumstances. His mother, a white woman from a respectable missionary family, placed the baby in a basket on the doorsteps of a Franciscan mission near Albuquerque.

A note was attached, in which she provided relevant information and requested that the child be named Daniel, out of the Bible. The order took to their task with sacred diligence, seeing to his care and education. He exhibited an eager mind that absorbed knowledge. He became fluent in English and Spanish. He also had a fondness and affinity for music, acquiring proficiency on a pair of instruments, the violin and wooden flute.

When he learned of his parentage, he was a serious and sensitive young man of fifteen years. The news didn't disturb him, but instead, enthused a latent curiosity. Without a word or warning to anyone, he disappeared from the countryside to wander where the wind would take him, and in a burst of impulsive pride, added the surname of Twosongs, to remind him that the rhythms of two cultures flowed in his veins.

He made his way to a Navajo village, where a holy man befriended him. The wizened healer, who understood that to achieve a degree of tranquility meant narrowing the gap between the physical and spiritual spheres, took the teen into his hogan. For three valuable years Daniel Twosongs served his mentor as he garnered wisdom passed down from the ancients.

The training was grueling. He had to be immersed in the language and oral traditions of the Diné. He tackled the commitment and developed a strict discipline that became a lifelong trait. He never slacked off as he memorized a multitude of supplication chants in word-perfect precision. There were taboos to be avoided, along with ceremonies of cleansing if a prohibition was violated. The rituals and procedures were treasures that totally resonated.

He noted with contentment that the common theme in them was to bring an individual back into alignment, to restore health and balance—the Navajo concept of *hozhó*, which roughly translated meant being in harmony or walking in life with beauty. The principle vibrated in him like a stringed instrument being strummed; he sought to apply every note of *hozhó*.

The methods to maintain *hozhó* were steeped in the mythologies of antiquity. The pupil found it fascinating—he could easily identify various crossroads where bits of Catholicism came into agreement with pieces of Navajo spirituality. Those junctions were fated to be the places where his interest would always be aroused. When he bid farewell to the medicine man, Daniel Twosongs was a man tutored in the humanities of two civilizations.

Now, as a woodpecker tapped out an insistent cadence, he emerged from a dense thicket of forest into bright sunshine dancing on the reddish rocks and soil of a craggy escarpment overtop the Rio Chama. The panoramic vista that spread before him was spectacular in its beauty; a rush went through him and he had a desire to study its delineations.

His pony, mountain-bred and sure-footed, sensed his mood and halted a jiffy before he actually gave the reins a slight tug. Twosongs chuckled and gave the chestnut's neck an affectionate pat. "We've got time to have us a good long gander," he said quietly. "I don't know where or when we'll find him, but in the glimpses I've grasped, I'm persuaded we are on course. It's just a matter of plodding along and enjoying the pleasurable scenery."

The stallion pranced in place as it snorted rowdily. Daniel Twosongs flicked its mane. He sat restful in the saddle, a squat and bow-legged man who reveled in isolation as much as the preacher he expected to find somewhere on the trail ahead; a kindred spirit he'd met two decades earlier on a December night in Nebraska, at a tent-town of the continental railroad.

The train clattered over the tracks through the Raton Pass. Jack Whistler had his face pressed against the windowpane, eyes upward and neck craned sideward as he strained to see all that could be seen. Sudden-like, he flung the window open wide and thrust head and shoulders outside. The sun was straight up in crystalline stillness, but the air had an frosty chill.

"Jumping crimany, Jack!" Lucinda exclaimed from the bench seat across from him. "Are you a frigging Eskimo? Shut that damn window or else I'll toss you out and slam it myself."

Whistler complied with her wishes, sheepish and surprised by her reaction. He gave her an off-center smirk and held his hands up in a shrug. "Not sure what your problem is, Lucinda."

"*My* problem?" she snapped haughtily.

"You're the one complaining."

"What's *your* problem, Jack?"

"None whatsoever from my perspective."

"Then perhaps you can tell me what can be so interesting for you to be gawking?" she asked, eyes churlish and narrowed on him. "Why were you hanging out the window?"

"Making an observation." Whistler leaned back and crossed his arms over his chest. "The snow on the mountaintop. Got to still be six or eight feet of it up there. Amazing."

"Amazing?" Slick Willy queried tersely. He sat beside the buxomy brunette with an arm snuggled comfortably around her shoulder. "It's stinking snow, for pity's sake."

"And it can damn well stay up there," she added in a huff. "I swear, Jack. Have you got bats in your belfry? You have to be the most curious human being I've ever known. What possible fascination can you have with a snow-capped mountain peak?"

"Everything is fascinating in its own way," Jack answered as his expression became contemplative. "Mountains and deserts. Jungles and swamps. The open sea, an underground cavern. Winchester Cathedral. A lightning storm, a rainbow, a sunrise." He regarded them directly, a smile enlightening his eyes as though a lamp had been lit behind the lenses.

"When I was in Kathmandu," he continued as his hands dropped to his lap and folded together. "I traveled for months with a Buddhist Sherpa. A lovely gentleman with a generous personality and a chirpy laugh that rang with contentment. There was kindness in Manju. The man had a delightful aura of intelligence and knowledge. Once we hiked for several days, then camped on a remote plateau because he wanted me to see something magnificent.

"I bundled in the sleeping bag and was straightway asleep. Manju woke me in full dark. We sat side by side facing eastward on a blanket woven from the woolly hair of a yak and waited in utter silence. Then when the first sliver of sunlight sliced over the Himalaya Mountains, he heard my gulp of awe and astonishment and simply nodded perceptive approval."

"A sunrise?" Slick Willy mocked, almost spitting laughter.

"Yes, a sunrise," Jack replied seriously. "The spectrum of colors were beyond anything imagination could generate. No artist will ever mix paint or blend chalk to duplicate the splendor of what I witnessed on that pristine morning. It made my heart swell and put me in mind of peaceful places where prettiness is ours to enjoy or disregard as we so choose."

"You are a weirdo, Jack," Lucinda exclaimed, glibly slapping his thigh.

Whistler ignored her. He remained pensive and preoccupied. "Manju and I took our sweet time on our return to Kathmandu. He told me stories of his childhood and his monastic training in the meditative path that leads to nirvana. I soaked it all in as best I could, but the richness of his words had such depth and significance I likely only retained odds and ends of sagacity."

Phips scrunched his face into a scowl. "Nirvana? Sagacity?"

"Nirvana is a state of peace and freedom from suffering. It's achieved by blowing out or quenching inner struggles," Jack explained in a deadpan monotone. "Sagacity means wisdom."

"Why not just say wisdom?" Slick Willy wondered heatedly.

Whistler brushed him off with a backhanded wave. "In my treks with Manju, we spent many afternoons in restaurants and marketplaces interacting with locals and sampling delicious cuisine that was often an explosion of flavor. At one particular hole in the wall tearoom, I was introduced to various recipes of chai, a spiced milk tea that is a matchless beverage. Full-bodied black tea and creamy milk, along with a mouthwatering combination of countless spices."

"You are definitely a certifiable weirdo, Jack," Lucinda announced, loud enough for other passengers to shift around to eyeball the threesome. "What is it with you anyway?"

"A superb inquiry, Lucinda," Slick Willy said, stuttering a chuckle.

Whistler humped his shoulders up as a blush of red colored his cheeks. "I read, I travel, I observe, I listen, I learn. Everything is fascinating in its own way. For example, it fascinates me that you are making this cross-country excursion to find a man who by your own admission you have not seen or had any contact with since before the unfortunate hostilities between the

North and South. Will you be forthcoming concerning your reasons and motivation?"

"Not to you I won't," Lucinda fired back as she lunged forward at the waist and thrust a half-bent forefinger at him. "Nor to any other busybody interloper for that matter. You hear me, Jack? My business is personal and private, so poke your snotty nose elsewhere, you whelp."

"No offense intended."

"Offense was taken, Jack."

"Sorry for the insult, Lucinda."

"Tend to your p's and q's, you pup."

Whistler raised his eyebrows. "Proper manners from here on. I promise."

"Don't sweat it, Jack," Slick Willy interjected, giving her a demonstrative squeeze. "The lady is miffed because this trip has been riddled by delays and breakdowns. One cannot fault her for tipping over and being agitated. She'll be in a gentler temper once we get to Santa Fe."

"Mr. Phips," Lucinda drawled, forcefully removing his arm from around her. "You've not yet accompanied me to my boudoir to be tantalized beyond your wildest dreams. If you hope to ever partake in the raptures of joining me in my sleeping compartment for a romp, you'd be wise to never again make excuses or project on my behalf. Are we understood, buster?"

Phips distractedly fiddled with the lapels of his frock coat. "Delays and breakdowns, my dear. I await your good pleasure," he said, sing-songy voice striking a flattering pitch.

"You best *be* my good pleasure, Slick Willy."

"I'll leave you two to your flirtations," Jack said, standing. "Fresh air awaits me." He slipped into the aisle and strolled to the back of the car. He had to jiggle the handle and slam a shoulder against the door before it creaked open. He stepped onto the platform and held onto the railing cage around the stoop to stay balanced against the rickety rocking.

Alone, he breathed deeply and thought through matters. His mind, always exact and demanding in its workings, began processing plans for the future. After Santa Fe he intended to hightail it to the west coast and get a job on any available ship heading to the orient. There was so much more of the world for him to see and experience—so much more information to compile. That settled, Jack Whistler relaxed and truly appreciated the passing scenery.

~ ~ ~

Something evil lurked nearby. Sally Twosongs could feel its creepiness—clammy coldness crawled over her forearms, electrifying the downy peach-fuzz. Coppery bitterness thickened her tongue and made it cling to the roof of her mouth, but she was unafraid. Engrossed, yes; watchful, indeed—fear, however, was hogtied by steely faith.

She had reached her destination two days ago and set up camp along the edge of the tree line on a gravelly patch of barren terrain. Her spirits were good; her heart and mind focused on what the Creator had for her as she waited in patient hope. Her devotional rigor and dedicated adherence to an interior toughness had prepared her for this challenge.

There were physical tests built-in to the spiritual vision quest. She was already rationing essentials as she engaged in a carefully modified fast; a mouthful or two of water morning, noon and night, which was supplemented by a few dried berries time to time. Weakness was beginning to make itself known, but she stuck to her dietary routine with a religious fervor.

The fire, fueled by sticks and shards of deadwood, was sparse and stunted, contained in a pit she had dug and shaped. She sat across from it, hands clasped together and eyes on a guest that had arrived at sunup. A mature red-tailed hawk, thick-chested and noble, was perched on a branch of the closest tree, a stumpy evergreen.

Hank was curled in its shade, regarding the bird with a mixture of relief and wariness. At regular intervals the raptor swiveled its head to the left and right as it kept silent vigil. The sun was midway across the western sky, but the hawk had not yet made a peep; neither had she spoken to it, but her desire to do so was a swollen yearning climbing up her throat.

A smile skimmed over her lips as she shifted her derriere. She stared determinedly. "So, Mr. Hawk, are you a messenger from Charley Jondreau? Or my guardian angel?"

The raptor bobbed its head and screeched, then waggled its wings.

"Yes, that'd be too easy, wouldn't it, Mr. Hawk?" she asked, studying it. "Affirmation to both questions, but what of another possibility? Could you be the fiendish enemy of my soul disguised as an angel of light? There is evil afoot. Are you its source?"

The red-tailed bird of prey swooped to the ground, landing between her and the tricolored collie; the dog didn't stand or make any move in tension or surprise—instead its tail thumped happily and stirred up bits of dust. The bird took several steps closer to Sally Twosongs. She remained unmoved as it probed her eyes, then bent its head upward and released a shrill cry before flying back to roost on the same branch at the same angle.

"Is one of your brethren with Charley Jondreau?"

The hawk nodded as it stretched its wings and flapped vigorously.

"Then evil will have its comeuppance," she declared, certain and courageous. "Our prayers will be armor around Charley Jondreau. He will prevail and sing a song of triumph amongst a great cloud of ancestral witnesses. There will be a grand celebration in the heavenlies." Her dark eyes brightened, sparkly and enthusiastic. "I have seen it."

Sally Twosongs didn't shift an inch, but just then, in the flicker of a blink she was transported back in time. A warm breeze gusted and battered her eardrums for several unruly seconds, then was gone and all was calm; a soothing stillness encompassed her. She was a daydreaming girl watching clouds, lying on her back beside a waterless Diablo Wash.

"Sally."

"I am here." She sat up. Her head jerked side to side, but she saw no one. Curiosity gripped her as she scrambled to her feet and spun around, turning in a tiny circle.

"Sally."

"I am here."

"Do you remember?" a dark-skinned man with golden hair asked in a comforting voice. The tall stranger's flowing garments were pure white and had a metallic sash that glittered like a starry necklace around his neck. His countenance was tranquil and full of grace.

"I am unsure."

"A long ago place."

"This isn't real."

"My dear child, do not question the destiny of your purpose. The hour of your testing is upon you. As streams enrich desolate locales, you are a reservoir of enlivening water for many souls. Be strong and fear not." He stretched forth a hand and said, "Behold."

She shivered and looked. The dry creek bed became a flooded river of foaming waves coursing fast and furious. The coolness of it refreshed her. She stood fixed and firm, hands fisted against her thighs. She gazed at the watercourse. "This is about me? This is who I am?"

"Truth dwells in your soul."

"Who are you?" she asked, dizzy and spongy-legged.

"Your heart understands."

"Only if you explain it."

"I will not," he said, smiling mildly. He tipped her a wink and within that instant, the past was no more as the present became reality—she was no longer a child at an arroyo; she was a woman on a mountaintop and the golden-haired celestial visitor was nearby. He stood, serene and in command, next to the stubby evergreen in which the red-tailed hawk resided.

"Why are you here?" she asked, absorbed by amazement.

"I was sent."

"To help me?"

"No," he replied bluntly. "To remind you that there is much required of you because you are Sally Twosongs. You were touched by the One who sits at the right hand of the Creator."

"I have not forgotten. I will never forget."

He held his arms apart in a blessing. "You are in a life and death struggle. The battle is against malignant principalities belonging to the evil one, but flesh and blood must pay the price. You have heard the trumpet and answered the call. Do not waver or falter. Be encouraged."

"My flesh is weak."

"Your spirit is iron. Be strong and fear not," he said, then vanished.

The Navajo woman suffered a convulsive shudder as she returned from the waking vision, shaking and sweaty. Her muscles complained because her hands were locked so tightly in her lap that spastic contractions struck the biceps and across her shoulders. Gritty confidence surged in her veins, and then, she thought she heard the cawing of many crows.

Her ears perked up. The grating caterwauling sounded somewhere far off. She listened and concluded that the racket seemed to be getting louder and closer, a strident cacophony strumming the air with notes of disdainful contempt. The red-tailed hawk shrieked. She was blanketed by a frigid shivering of goosebumps—she sensed huge and oppressive evil.

Sally Twosongs bolstered the intensity of her prayers.

Hank watched her with a vigilance that bordered on obsessive. Its ears were twitchy, its nose sniffing the air in every direction. The collie, bred to herd sheep and other livestock, was now on its feet pacing, as antsy as though its paws were in contact with crushed glass instead of pebbly stones. Every few seconds it uttered a tinny whine so low as to be unheard.

The flute-playing woman had been in its life since it was eight weeks old. There could be no denying its natural protective instincts or its abiding affection for her. As much as any human, or perhaps even more so, Hank loved Sally Twosongs; she had an inner essence that made a deep connection to its heart, which was enough to keep it attentive and ready to be her defender, but there were other factors that motivated it.

Since puppyhood, the tricolor shepherd had repeatedly heard that its primary responsibility was to take care of and protect Sally Twosongs. Her husband had been a gentle and firm taskmaster in its training, and absolutely unyielding as to its sole mission. Even now, with its hackles raised because of an unknown danger it detected in the air, Hank could hear the assertive tenacity in Caleb's directives and feel the confidence of the man.

There was also another voice that compelled the bush-tailed dog. It came from a bald man who had passed through *WT Ranch* some time ago, but the resilient bond remained woven into the dog's memory. He had a unique lilt in his voice, and the collie never forgot him, or failed to keep his strict instruction: *"You must always protect Sally Twosongs, eh."*

To that end, Hank never cowed or wavered one iota. Its bones and joints ached all the time; its eyesight and sniffer were not as trustworthy as they were once, and the strength and stamina of youth had become wishful thinking, but the heart contained within its ribcage was as stalwart and fiercely obedient as ever. There would be no abandoning the call on its life—though the scent of trouble was thick and heavy in its nostrils, Hank stayed alert and prepared.

Less than a half-mile below, sequestered in a thicket of underbrush, the bobcat bided its time. The gyrations of wickedness had found a worthy but unwitting vessel to succumb to its dictates. The feline predator, bewitched and driven by a demented impulse that had no meaning or frame of reference, was fixated on the woman with a single braid of glossy black hair.

The big male's juices were jacked up, which put it in an angry and aggressive mental state. A violent wildness filled up its senses with a bloodlust that was maddening. Hate inflamed its heart, while turmoil was a foggy murk in its skull. The animal had no comprehension of the crazed compulsions to be on the hunt for its current banquet. It intended to attack and claw the woman to death; it'd never tasted human flesh, but had an itching hunger to feast on it.

A demonic presence had crawled up inside and latched on like a leech; the bobcat's primal instincts were darkened and distorted—it was being twisted and cajoled to be a slayer of innocence. Its intelligence, compromised and overpowered, was possessed; the dog would die first, then the woman. There was no reasoning that could take it off the path it was on.

The wildcat licked its lips, which were puckered in an evil grin. Its coat had a variable grayish-brown spotted pattern, with streaks of black on its torso and inky bars on the forelegs and tail. In appearance it was typical, except for the greenish circles of its eyes; a dull and unreadable deadness had blackened the normal inquisitive brightness.

Camouflaged in the scrubland undergrowth, the bobcat skulked even tighter against the ground and waited. A chronology for action had not yet formed in its befuddled thinking, so there was no particular hurry. The timetable for a murderous rampage was in the future—an appointment set by the sinister force that scratched at its brain to kill, kill, kill the woman.

Dusk was stretching bone-gray fingers over a bluff above the Rio Chama, pushing the violet colors of twilight ever eastward. Deacon Coburn was enjoying the day's end. It had been some lazy riding, but there was much satisfaction with the company, mostly because of long stretches of silence interspersed by short spurts of verbal exchanges.

The fresh and sweet air had him feeling content and at ease. He sat on an improvised seat a fair piece away from the campfire that'd been kindled and stoked by Stace Hawkins, who was now off gathering more wood. Meanwhile, Whitey Fitzgerald went through some idiosyncratic quirks fixing a pot of black Darjeeling tea, which kept Coburn highly entertained.

The exaggerated theatrics never changed. Each step of the process had to be precisely to the letter of fussiness. Avis Lahay, ever attentive and disposed to assist or even take charge, could not edge her way in or interrupt the steps no matter her best intentions to be helpful. She would be rebuffed in the most genial manner, but rebuffed all the same.

She had recently began egging him on with bantering suggestions, which for Coburn, increased the amusement factor tenfold. "Are you sure you have the tea measured?" she asked tartly. "Looks to me like the water's about to boil, Whitey. You best have those leaves ready."

"Let me tell you something, sweetie," he replied, a tin scoop of tea leaves in hand. "The water has to boil for a full thirty seconds, then the tea goes in and immediately . . ." He halted briefly for dramatic emphasis, took a quick breath and click-clicked excitedly. "Immediately, I say: The kettle must be removed from the fire so as the leaves can steep and breathe proper. To gets the full flavor out of the leaves that's the way it must be done, sweetie."

"Thirty seconds on the boil?" she queried, serious-faced.

"That be the only appropriate way it can be done."

"Not twenty-five, and certainly not forty?"

"Heavens, no, Avis," Deacon said in a grim and somber tone. "Emphatically not forty seconds. That'd overcook and perhaps even destroy those longsuffering black leaves."

Fitzgerald ignored the remarks, grinning as he waited. At the prescribed moment, he went into action with a panache and flourish. He dumped the leaves in, dropped the lid in the slot and placed the pot on a flat surface he'd prepared for it, then stepped back and put his hands on his hips. "I know you two be just heckling me, but I ain't in no mood for such silliness."

Coburn scratched his whiskery chin. "Truthfulness ain't heckling."

"Nope," Avis agreed, giggling. "We're appreciating you."

"Appreciating me? Then let me tell you something else," Whitey said firmly. His shallow chest puffed up and he strutted like a sage grouse performing a courtship ritual. "Queen Victoria herself would take one sip of tea brewed by this here nigger barber and she'd declare in a highfalutin voice that it be fit to serve to the crown princes and princesses of Europe."

"Ah-huh." Deacon sat up straight, back stiff and hands clasped at his beltline. "And you'd be the one hobnobbing with them on account of being the maestro brewmaster."

"You ain't telling no lie, Deacon."

"Whitey, can I come along with you to those palaces?" Avis inquired, glib and gleeful. "I can clean up and put on fancy duds and preen at your side like a fashionable society lady. We'd make a nifty pair. We might even get to dance for Queen Victoria and her court."

"Been a coon's age since we danced, sweetie."

"Too many years, Whitey."

Fitzgerald tweeted a happy click-click. "We ought to get to a town with a dance hall and cut the rug for old time's sake before I turn into a crotchety old fogy who can just hobble."

"Turn into a crotchety old fogy?" Deacon remarked in a burst of chuckles. "You've been infected by flare-ups of the crotchety since the day we first met way back in Abilene."

"You be getting more cantankerous by the mile," Whitey said, pursing his lips. Just then, Stace Hawkins entered the campsite from the cover of trees. He had a double armload of wood and was struggling to keep it balanced. Fitzgerald quickly rushed to his aid. "Pile it right here. You done just fine, boss. Enough for tonight and to fry some bacon for breakfast."

"Thanks, Mr. Whitey," Stace answered, dropping to a knee to unload his haul. "There's plenty of sticks and deadwood around if we need more." He brushed dirt and bark chips off his shirt as he stood. "I hurried back because a man in a flat-brimmed hat is riding our way."

Coburn leaned forward. "A lone rider?"

"Yessir."

"Nothing to fret over," Whitey said, arranging the firewood in a neat stack. "It ain't like we got dibs on this real estate and besides, we has extra grub if his belly's a-growling."

A few minutes later there was a rustle of branches in the shadows of the surrounding foliage, followed by a low-voiced inquiry. "Hello the fire. Is there a preacher in camp?"

The River Brethren man from Conoy Creek leapt to his feet and a smile cracked his face as wide as the splintered divot from the strike of a razor sharp hatchet. "Daniel Twosongs?"

Twosongs rode in and dismounted. "I've come a-calling."

"Ain't this Providential? We're heading to Taos."

"To see me? That'd be a waste of traveling, preacher," Daniel said, and the old friends locked hands in a greeting that was saturated with respect. "I've been on the lookout for you."

"For what reason?"

"A dream," Daniel replied pithily. "Three times, same images."

"Prophetic? A forewarning?"

"Disconnected jots and tittles."

Coburn frowned doubtfully. "Could be nothing."

"I've got no interpretation. That much I know, Deacon."

"It's a burr under your skin, ain't it?"

"Somewhat troublesome because it sparked my curiosity."

"No matter. All is well now," Deacon said, giving him a clap on the back. "You have found me and I wasn't even lost. Perhaps that in itself is the dream's purpose and meaning."

"Possibly. Seems unlikely though."

"Don't dismiss the prospect too quickly."

Twosongs squatted on his heels near the fire. "Jondreau and Dawson spent the winter with me. We discussed much theology and philosophy. His oracle skills would come in handy just now. He had a rather cryptic message for me to deliver whenever our paths crossed."

"Here we be, Daniel, so give it to me straight."

"Be not overcome of evil, but overcome evil with good."

"Romans 12:21," Deacon said, scowly-faced.

Fitzgerald click-clicked nervously. "I ain't liking the implication."

The puckers around Coburn's eyes deepened. "Don't overthink it, Whitey."

"I be sipping tea and getting supper is what I be doing."

"Deacon," Daniel said, rising. "I also have something in my saddlebags for you, but that must wait until morning." He sidled over to the chestnut stallion. "If I'm going to throw my lot in with you folks it'd be best to start pulling my weight by seeing to the needs of our mounts."

"I'd be happy to help, sir," Stace spoke up eagerly.

"Glad for it, lad." The two went off and got the job done quickly. Afterwards, a meal of biscuits and beans was devoured by all; what came next was Whitey, Avis and Stace sitting rapt as the longtime comrades reminisced. A far-reaching gamut of places and topics were covered, while the moon, bone-white and fringed in yellow, provided pleasant ambience.

There was laughter and smart-alecky comments now and again, but for Deacon Coburn, it was a façade. His heart was burdened. He appeared earnest and cheerful, but was distracted by Romans 12:21. There was something ominous in the words that nagged at him: *Be not overcome of evil, but overcome evil with good.* He kept the concerns tied down in an inner niche.

Early the next morning, Deacon Coburn sat on the stump of a log, eyes closed and head uplifted as he consciously meditated on the ramifications of Romans 12:21. That the verse had come to him as a tiding from Charley Jondreau put him in an extremely speculative frame of mind. What did it mean in the context of the current circumstances? How could he know?

He was alone. Daniel Twosongs was tending to the horses while the others were on a hike to the bank of the Rio Chama. Dawn was breezy and blue skies, scented by various strains of budding wildflowers. Birds were chirping and conversing in a tuneful dialog that filled the copse of trees forming a half-circle around the campsite. The peaceful setting had Coburn burrowing through ideas and opinions in an effort to unearth plausible answers.

When Twosongs returned, he had a jaunty bounce in his steps and was humming a peppy tune. He slowed, smiling perceptively. He had a Harper's Magazine under an arm, which he took and handed over to his friend. "The latest edition hot off the press, preacher. An excellent piece written by a young woman with whom you are well acquainted. Page thirty-five."

Coburn thumbed to the designated page and exhaled a hearty chuckle that had delight rippling through it. "*Bandit and the Outlaw* by Abbey Langton," he read, eyes glinting in pride. He hunched forward and savored every word as he perused the tale, which was a fictionalized account of a factual episode he had seen transpire up close.

The names had been changed, but as he remembered it, the narrative was authentic and spot on perfect. The hero was Bandit, a steadfast and gallant red mottled cattledog that possessed the attributes of a gregarious lion, along with the reasoning powers of a human. The intelligent herder had chosen to take over guardianship of a headstrong young woman who'd ridden the rails from the east to experience firsthand the untamed streets of Abilene.

He was swept back sixteen years as the account put him in the middle of the action. The antagonist was a hard-case punk with the character and aspirations of a desperado. He was an unlikable fellow who had delusions about the woman. In his mind, she was sweet on him and their future would be linked together. He went about the undertaking of winning her heart by using bullying tactics, which resulted in a climatic confrontation with Bandit.

It was a compelling story. His cheeks were shiny and eyes moist as he studied the editor's footnote; it promised that this was the first chapter of an ongoing serial featuring the exploits of *Bandit, Champion of the Western Trails*. He flipped back to the beginning and started reading *Bandit and the Outlaw* again, but then, a ruckus in the woods interrupted him.

Whitey Fitzgerald limped into view using a crooked stick as a cane. "Whew doggies!" he blustered, rasping air into his wheezing lungs. "I ain't no spry spring chicken no more. That trip was farther down and steeper up than I figured. Way doggone steeper." He shambled along and groaned as he plopped onto his bedroll. "Lord Almighty, I may be done in for the day."

"We'll see to your care and feeding, old-timer," Deacon said slyly.

"You best not be starting up with me."

Stace Hawkins and Avis Lahay were on either side of Fitzgerald, looking a lot like matching bookends as both attempted to squelch grins. She cleared her throat. "If you two get to bickering, Daniel may pack his gear and take off," she said, moseying over to the campfire.

Twosongs rumbled a stammer of snickers. "I'll be sticking around for a spell. Especially since in our confab last night the possibility of heading to *WT Ranch* was touched upon."

"It better be more than just a possibility," Avis insisted as she fed fuel into the fire in anticipation of preparing breakfast. "If my vote counts it's already a foregone conclusion."

"Of course your vote counts, sweetie," Whitey blurted, rolling his eyes in an embellished manner. "Mine, too. And I say we quit jabbering about our destination and just go."

"Me, too," Stace said, accompanied by an enthusiastic nod.

Fitzgerald winced a grunting click-click. "That be three solid votes."

"Avis," Deacon cut in, fingering aside the flanks of his moustache. "This will interest you." He reached over and stretched the Harper's Magazine toward her. After she took hold of it, his voice thickened and cracked with emotion as he made an announcement. "Gather around and get comfortable while Avis reads *Bandit and the Outlaw* by Abbey Langton."

Everyone did so. Avis took a seat on a patch of grass in front of Deacon, then she waited until Whitey quit making moaning noises as he readied to listen. She began, and her audience was immediately drawn in and captivated. It was as though she had practiced reading it aloud several times because the inflection of her voice was expressive, pausing at specific junctures to allow the word pictures to linger. When she concluded, she murmured a pleased sigh.

"Golly!" Stace exclaimed, bright-eyed and energized. He nearly tripped jumping up to take a quick glimpse at the magazine. "I'd surely like to have a dog like that someday."

Coburn wrinkled his eyes. "A good dog is worth having because it will give much more than it ever gets. One can never out-give a dog. God created them with a servant's heart."

"How do you train a dog, Mr. Deacon?"

"Be consistent and kind. Gentle and firm."

"Could a dog really do what Bandit did?"

"Could and did, Stace," Deacon replied dryly. "What Avis read ain't no made-up story. I was there in Abilene when it truly happened in June of '72. The dog's real name was Old Blue. It slammed into that palomino and herded it to a standstill just like Abbey described it."

"Really?"

"You betcha," Whitey said, laughing a click-click despite his tenderized muscles. "Miss Abbey is a memorable and feisty lady. She be your Aunt Avis's sister, don'tcha know?"

"What? Really?"

Coburn bent forward and rested both hands on the boy's shoulders. "Family is deeper than blood, Stace. That's a fact you need to put in your noggin and apply at every opportunity. This world is sweet and lovely, but it also has difficult misfortunes that are harsh and bitter. No one ever gets through the dry and desolate seasons alone. We all have need of each other."

Stace lowered his eyes and his shoulders drooped. The words seemed to weigh on him. His brow took on shadows as he knelt. "Aunt Avis, is Miss Abbey really your sister?"

"Yes," Avis answered, closing the magazine. "Which is just one more reason to go to *WT Ranch*. That'll be the likely place to get an update on where Abbey and my nephew are now."

"It's settled as far as I'm concerned," Deacon said, standing and arching his back as he waggled his arms. "The five of us are bound for Wagon Wheel Gap in Colorado."

Fitzgerald bobbed his head. "Are we still in the stalling mode?"

"I suppose we are since no one has yet started breakfast," Deacon quipped, wrapping a yawn around a widening smile. "Daylight's a-burning so let's get to what needs doing."

The crew found tasks and worked as a team, jocularity amongst them. Soon the greasy aroma of bacon sizzling overpowered the tingly fragrance of nature. They packed the gear and filled their bellies. Then, drenched in shimmering sunshine, all were mounted and ready. Deacon Coburn took the lead as the sojourning family rode single file on a northerly route.

At *WT Ranch*, raving hysteria clutched at Naomi Axler. Her breathing was rapid, her cheeks flushed and ruddy. She kept her legs moving, but was not going anywhere. Her nerves were leapfrogging from one extreme to another, and palpitations had her heart beating out a manic tattoo that reverberated against her eardrums.

Ugly bugs were feeding on an increasing fear that constricted her lungs and caused hot flashes of perspiration which almost instantaneously beaded into icy bits on her forehead. She was convinced she was losing her mind. She could not restrain or tame the frenzy of panic that had its hooks sunk deep into her psyche. It was as though she was standing outside herself watching a mad woman pace in a frantic circular pattern around the barnyard.

Eliza Weitzel and her granddaughter were nearby, their attention on Caleb as he stepped into the saddle to ride off and scout for Sally Twosongs and Jesse Axler. He doffed his hat, then gave Shadrach the go-ahead. The still muscular steeldust neighed a snort, and though age and miles were gathering in its bones, it loped forward and broke into a stately canter.

"Thank you, Caleb!" Naomi yelled at the top of her lungs, tears streaming freely. Despite the warmth of the morning and the strength of the sun-rays she was shivering. She felt a tug on her hand and jerked away as if she'd been bitten by a snake. She blinked and shuddered in a gulp of air, then bleary-eyed and frightened, she saw the little girl staring up at her.

"Don't be afraid, Aunt Naomi."

"You are such a dear, Bethsuelo."

"The bobcat won't hurt Jesse."

"Bobcat? What bobcat?"

"The bobcat won't hurt Jesse," Bethsuelo repeated, eyes focused in a glassy stare—her voice was a reedy falsetto. "He will be with Mommy soon and heaven will be happy."

Naomi grabbed her skirt aside and dropped to her knees. She took hold of the child's shoulders. "Heaven will be happy? I don't understand, Bethsuelo. What do you mean?"

Bethsuelo stepped back and shook her head in surprise. Her eyes cleared. She had a look around, acting as though she'd just arrived. Her button nose got all wrinkly and she produced an uninterested shrug. "I don't know. I forgot, I guess," she replied, flashing an innocent smile. She abruptly turned on her heels and ran off as giggles of laughter filled the air in her wake.

Naomi bolted to her feet, ramrod stiff. Shocked and sickened, her stomach did a queasy flip-flop. Her hands locked together at her waist. "Heaven will be happy? Land sakes alive! What on earth is she talking about, Eliza? Do you have any idea what she means?"

"How could I?" Eliza asked poignantly.

"She's *your* granddaughter!"

"Naomi, that is so unbecoming. Do you hear yourself?"

"I do. I am going loopy."

"Not loopy," Eliza said sympathetically. "Going through a rough patch, is all." She pressed a reassuring smile at her. "A better answer to your question would be that Bethsuelo is a profound and spiritual little girl with a big imagination. Heaven will be happy? I'd take those words as encouragement and not extend any effort second guessing or worrying over it."

"Maybe so."

"Come home with me," Eliza suggested, brow crinkling. "I have something I need to chat over with you. We can do so as we stroll, then I'll brew a fresh pot of coffee at the house."

"I suppose," Naomi replied, shrugging as she stuffed her hands into the pockets of her homespun dress. "Amanda is immersed in knitting so she'll not want to be disturbed."

The women walked side by side. A rock-bordered path led up a gradual incline to the snug and efficient one-bedroom cabin situated on a level clearing along a slope several hundred yards from the laneway that ran between the two main houses. The ponderosa pine home had a broad front porch that presented a bird's-eye view of sunsets.

While Bethsuelo alternated between lagging behind them to racing far ahead, the ladies kept a leisurely pace. The aspens, which appeared to be battalions of sentinels at the base of the San Juan Mountains encircling the ranchland, were blooming bright green leaves. The woods were serene and inviting, conducive for a heart to heart discourse.

"I have an understanding as to what's troubling you, Naomi."

"Jesse is missing is what's troubling me."

"Yes, I'd not argue against that viewpoint," Eliza said in a tone that perfectly mixed compassion and sternness. "However, I surmise that your angst over Jesse being off on what might be seen as a wild goose chase is a symptom, not the root of the underlying issue."

Naomi got huffy. "Whatever do you mean?"

"When did you last have your monthlies?"

"That's a strange and personal question, Eliza."

"Nonetheless, it's what I'm asking."

Naomi remained silent for twenty yards or more. Her mind raced erratically. Deep lines plowed grooves in her forehead as she pondered the ebb and flow of her menstrual cycle. "I used to be as regular as clockwork, but six months or so ago it became spotty and sporadic." She took her hands out of her pockets and counted on her fingers. "Now that you raised the subject, it's probably been three months or more since the crimson caller made an appearance."

"How old are you?"

"I'll be forty-six in October. What are you getting at, Eliza?"

"You're going through the change, menopause."

"You think?"

"I'm no doctor, Naomi, but I'm not stupid."

"Menopause? Oh, my."

"Night sweats? Anxiety? Irritability? Mood swings? Fatigue?"

"Yes to all, Eliza."

"With the diagnosis, you should take a breath and relax some," Eliza said, smiling thinly. "Give yourself a break. I've been exactly where you are right now. Your emotions are off-kilter because of simple biology. The fact that the natural ailment coincided with Jesse's coming of age only made matters worse. By Christmastime you'll be your cheerful self and in fine fettle."

"Menopause? Oh, my," Naomi said again. "*That* never occurred to me."

"Me, neither. Not for me and not for you until this morning."

"Did you get all out of sorts?"

"Be assured, Naomi. I had my flaky moments."

"And on the other side of it?"

"Life is richer and more precious."

"Good to hear."

No other words were spoken as they completed the walk. Bethsuelo was sitting on the top step waiting for them. Eliza went inside to fix a pot of Arbuckle's, and the little girl tagged along to help. Naomi Axler settled in a rocker on the porch and drank in the brightness of the day. Her head was swimming, but beneath that sensation, a tentative peace made itself known.

It was the first time in longer than she even realized that she felt a measure of hopefulness.

Max Dawson had a bad feeling; it stabbed at her gullet like a darning needle handled by a perverse goblin. The irritant was an annoying distraction that she attempted to ignore, but could not. She was crouched sideways against a boulder, Stetson low on her head and eyes squinted against the sun, which was at high noon in a blue sky that had no end.

Though her palms were damp and sticky, she had her Winchester held loose and ready. Her partner had assumed essentially the same posture a mere ten yards away, but his frame was crunched tighter because the sandstone outcropping he had for cover was much shorter. Their concentration was on the Ute witch who had eluded them for so long.

Smoky Crowe was in a ravine below them, squatted in the middle of a sea of sagebrush, seemingly unaware of their presence. A rattlesnake was coiled in his lap and he was petting it as he sang a song with bass notes that were abnormally soothing; mesmerizing, even. His straggly hair, white and wispy, rested on his shoulders like a frayed cape of flimsy cotton.

The rattler was not his only companion. A pair of crows flew in a seesaw formation above him, gliding soundlessly on currents that kept them close to the one-eyed necromancer. Another member of the animal kingdom filled out the entourage; a lone coyote stood watch a few feet from its master, eyes fastened on him.

Dawson made a hand signal to Jondreau. He flinched his eyes and adjusted his hat, then held up one finger, signifying they would proceed and attack in sixty seconds. He had his pistol in his right hand, the blade in his left. His breathing was calm and steady. There was no fear at all between them; only a vigilance and determination for this to be the final showdown.

He nodded strongly. An expectation connected them; the end of their hallowed, almost religious crusade was imminent and would soon be realized. She puckered her lips and tried to manufacture saliva to moisten her mouth, but that was not to be. Reflexive spasms twitched and knotted her neck muscles—her tongue was a swollen and furry clump.

Beads of perspiration trickled down her spine, causing occasional shivers. Despite the tension and her alert status, she couldn't turn off the thoughts flashing through her head. She kept seeing her mother, bloodied and bruised, fighting against grievous abominations; bound on a chair by rawhide thongs and subjected to the knife-blade artistry of Smoky Crowe. A grotesque crisscross pattern of lacerations mutilated her upper body, front and back.

That horror remained at the edge of her brain as the memory of sitting at the deathbed of her father pierced her. He was a hardnosed and principled man, and died as a result of a poison-tipped arrow from the bow of the same butcher who had tortured her mother. She had made a vow to the corpse of her father; whatever it took to see Smoky Crowe dead, she would do it. *You can bet your money on me, Daddy.* The words—her words—galvanized her resolve.

Her jaw slammed shut and clamped as tight as a steel-trap. The flames of tenacity were a wildfire blistering through her veins, hot and outrageously formidable. Crowe had slaughtered her mother and murdered her father. She slid a hand under her left breast and felt the outline of her leather wallet in an inside pocket of the jacket. Her jawline hardened into a dauntless smile. What she kept in the billfold had an almost talismanic influence on her mindset.

In her own tenuous way she was a believer, and though she had much skepticism about the stuff of faith, just now she persistently prayed for victory. She petitioned heaven in phrasing that was heartfelt, but the booming purrs of Crowe's mantra disturbed and distracted her. She strenuously tried not to listen to the chant, but it was irresistible—the haunting and hypnotic melody drew her in and caressed her senses into beguiled numbness.

Her eyes bent around the stone barrier just as Smoky Crowe's voice shrieked. He was on his feet glowering straight at her as he strangled the rattlesnake; it flopped and writhed in its death throes. He held it high above his head, then brought it down to chomp off its tail and swallow the rattles whole. Her muscles bulged, her arms flexed to shoulder the rifle, but she was frozen; she could not move. She saw that Jondreau was in the same predicament.

Crowe began to dance and spin—faster and looser he twirled until he became a whirling blur. The crows squawked, the coyote howled and yapped. A shrill incantation tore from the bloodthirsty villain's throat, roaring like a mighty rushing wind from the innards of a tornado. He kept spinning until he was on top of Charley Jondreau, then stopped dead in his tracks.

"Aaaarg!" Crowe's face mutated into a grisly, death-soaked smile. He towered over Jondreau, who remained motionless; helpless; paralyzed. Bellows of mad laughter erupted from Crowe's lungs as he counted coup by swiping the floppy-brimmed hat. Then, Smoky Crowe was gone—just gone; as was the coyote, but the crows circled and cawed contemptuously. The temperature plummeted; the air was soured and tainted by the burnt stench of evil.

Dawson pressed a hand over her chest. Iciness encased her and she was struggling to breathe; the frigid air felt like gooey sludge clogging up her lungs. She wheezed and spat and plunked onto her backside. It took several panting moments until she found her voice, and when she did, the words were uttered in an asphyxiated gasp. "What was that, Charley?"

"The wily serpent, eh," he replied as he dealt with his own physical issues. He was on his hands and knees crawling to get a handhold on a rugged rock to use as leverage to get to his feet. He did so and wobbly-walked a half-dozen steps. His eyes seeped disbelief. He scuffed a palm over his shaven scalp. His mouth compressed in disgust and shame. "The thief of life."

Anger raged in her. "Crappola. I want Crowe dead."

"Fear not. I will kill the dragon, eh."

The sun was dipping past noontime. Jesse Axler finally had a sense of satisfaction. The tracking had kept him alert, though there'd been little success; one dead end trail led to another and another—he never got discouraged because each futility led to the next possibility. He followed every memory he had gleaned from listening to Sally Twosongs, but none of his instinctive riding had paid off; until now.

He sat upright in the saddle on a ridge a mile or so from Bulldog Mountain. Binoculars provided a close-up scrutiny of the peak's reliefs and curves. He methodically examined and probed one section, then moved onto the next, ever observant of details and peculiarities. There were several bare swatches of rocky soil fringed by scrubby foliage near the tree line—he thought the areas of barren topography resembled the thumbprints of a giant.

An indistinct wisp of smoke had his attention. He kept the area under surveillance while the tick-tock of seconds accumulated into a pile. It was then that a fleeting glimpse of black and white thrilled him. He stiffened and hitched in a breath as a ghost of a smile flittered over his lips. "Hank," he murmured, dropping the field glasses to his waist.

He measured the amount of daylight remaining and gauged the distance of the descent from his current position and the ascent through the aspens and evergreens to where he spotted the tricolor collie, then without much effort calculated the time factor. "Be strong, Hank. I'll be there before nightfall." He returned the binoculars to the saddlebags.

The soot-gray mare tilted its head back and snorted, sounding derisive. He tweaked its right ear. "I ain't gonna argue with you because you're right." He hesitantly pulled a canteen off the saddle horn, took a careful swig of tepid water and swallowed in stages so the wetness trickled down his throat. He indulged in another short sip, then hung the container and swiped a shirtsleeve across his face. "Yep, I should've known." He urged his mount forward.

While the horse picked its way down a winding trail through the trees, Jesse Axler proceeded to give himself a thorough inner thrashing; on more than one occasion he'd heard Sally Twosongs say that Bulldog Mountain would be an excellent setting to seek the Creator, yet the urgency of that knowledge had gotten misplaced in a nook inside his head. Bulldog Mountain should have been the primary site to check instead of just an optional prospect.

The twelve-year-old had already learned that getting bogged down in regrets was a useless waste of thinking, so he put the error in judgment behind him and pushed on. He rode decisively, eyes flicking in all directions to comprise a steady flow of information about the surroundings. A gusty breeze came up strong enough to ruffle the aspen branches.

His thighs tightened, as did his hands on the reins. The horse stopped. He listened. His breathing stilled as an icy creeper pitter-pattered down his spine. There seemed to be something moving rapidly to his left; a swishing movement that had nothing to do with the riffling leaves. He quickly withdrew the Spencer from the scabbard and cradled it.

The wind died, and at that moment, he was troubled by a presence—the realness was palpable, which increased his wariness, but try as he might, he couldn't identify its location. He lifted the rifle to his shoulder. A twig cracked. *The bobcat*, he thought, alarmed and vigilant. His eyes squished into slits. Standing in the stirrups, he surveyed the forest down the barrel of the gun, probing any likely recesses where the wildcat could be concealed.

His heartrate increased as his imagination went crazy—the feline was between clusters of trees; no, it was lurking at the fringe of a grassy knoll in the distance; no, it was crouched in the bushes ahead. He bit down on his bottom lip. He spied the bobcat stealthily sneaking here or there, but then, as his finger stiffened to pull the trigger it disappeared.

Truth was, he never actually saw it anywhere. The bobcat had gotten inside his head and was doing deceitful tricks that worried and wore on him. After many false sightings, he cuddled the weapon in a crook of his arm and prodded the mare forward. For several hours, Jesse Axler sat in the saddle in such amplified rigidity that every muscle in his body tensed into knots.

∽ ∽ ∽

Midway through that afternoon, Smoky Crowe was euphoric, but that feeling would soon be snatched away and replaced by seething anger. He crouched in a sliver of a cave, smoking peyote-laced tobacco and muttering a growl of a song low in his throat. The skull-shaped bowl was never empty for long; the only time the Ute sorcerer breathed air was in those jiffies it took him to dig out the cinders and repack the pipe with another load.

The floppy-brimmed hat belonging to Charley Jondreau was crunched in his lap; it would be used to cast a spell over its owner, which is what Crowe was purposefully preparing to do. He valued the ritual that would formulate a display of monumental power. These matters were not to be rushed into, but rather, every part of the process of drawing magic out of the darkness was to be cherished and done with a delicate touch of respect.

Smoky Crowe appreciated it all. He lived to be a sword of evil that delivered slashing blows against good. He would not be hurried—the voice of his long dead mother spoke instructions of protocol that he followed with a humble obedience which bordered on docile servitude. Chumana's words rang through him and he listened reverentially.

She had schooled him in all the ways that led into the maze of corridors where the mysteries of ancient secrets were unveiled. Command of those black arts was entrusted to him for as long as he bowed down to the beast that had been present in the garden disguised as a wily serpent; in the time before time that cloaked serpent was a silver-voiced archangel singing praise and honor to the One enthroned in the heavenlies for whom the earth is a footstool.

Evil flowed in Smoky Crowe's veins like the tar inhaled into his lungs with every contented puff on his pipe. Stealing and killing thrilled him from the inside out; wreaking terror and destruction awakened frenzied flames that crackled through his loins to the top of his head. Demons yelped in delight when he was conceived on an altar of death; hell rejoiced as he was immersed in the choppy currents of evil while he grew in his mother's womb.

At birth, as he suckled at her breast, a debased ceremony of consecration to the master of the netherworld stole whatever remnant of innocence remained. Cheveyo, the name given at that despoiled dedication, was the offspring of six generations of those who willfully dwelt beside dark streams and gloried in opening doors to realms where flagrant depravity flourished; where blackhearted wizardry and satanic runes were exposed and unraveled.

Now, in the depths of preparation to confront instruments wielded for good, Crowe saw visions of his triumphant entry into a labyrinthine canyon where men and women were on fire, but their flesh was not consumed. Soot and noxious gases hung in the combustible air as bonfires blazed from the sky to nourish molten rivers that overflowed their channels.

He grinned and cried out in ecstasy to see thousands upon thousands of tortured souls bawling and pleading for mercy from the miserable agony. Crowe's deranged satisfaction soared as he danced with carefree imps capering and carrying on while a choir of gargoyles, encamped along a ridgeline of sulfur and brimstone, sang a maniacal refrain of victory.

Wailing and gnashing of teeth was an endless litany tearing from the throats of those in horrifying pain who reached and grabbed at Smoky Crowe, seeking solace or release. He strode forward in a pompous strut, naked except for a diaper loincloth. His left eye—milky and pulsing—reflected a sinister sickness; his right eye dripped blood.

Crowe chanted a chorus as his feet began shuffling in fluid skips and hops. In an explosion of blackness, he lifted his knees high and kicked up his heels, whooping louder and louder. He elevated his velocity until he sped past a jutting crag and came face to face with the red-skinned devil brandishing a three-pronged pitchfork. The subservient Ute reeled backwards and fell on his buttocks, but hastily flipped over and stretched prostrate.

"Welcome, my son," the archfiend said, reptilian eyes slit-like and jaundiced. His lengthy arrowhead tail intermittently slithered around his shoulders as he spoke in a domineering voice, crafty and cunning. "Exult in this foretaste of evil because of your famous exploits."

"I pledge my life to you," Crowe said squeakily.

"Rise to your knees, my son. Bow before me."

Crowe obeyed, genuflecting humbly. "Command me."

"You are mine and I am yours, my child," he answered, smiling broadly. The pointy tops of his ears inclined in such a way as to nearly touch the curved horns protruding from the peak of his hairline. "Your infamy precedes you. The riches of my kingdom are yours for the taking."

Crowe wept genuine tears. "I am unworthy to be in your presence."

"You are a favored son," the devil said, entwining the barbed whiskers of his goatee around his curled fingernails. "You have inflicted havoc and reveled in anarchy. I have savored the plunders and rewards of your vengeance, but there is more for you to do on my behalf. Death to a pair of do-gooder nuisances. You have been prepared and set aside for such a time as this."

"I fear I will fail."

"You cannot fail, my son."

Crowe groveled fecklessly. "Yet doubt and fear are in me."

"You shrink when you should stand strong."

"He has power. She is blessed by the alleged anointed one."

"Jesus!" the diabolical prince cursed irately. He hoisted the pitchfork in a threatening manner, then clip-clopped forward on cloven hooves and gnawed the air, exposing sharpened dagger-teeth. His eyes gaped wide and shot fiery darts. Grimy smoke and orange flames gushed from his pores. "I will destroy and devour the crucified one. Failure will not be tolerated."

"I will do as I am told."

"Jondreau and the princess shall die."

"I am your killer. You are my master."

"My will must be done as dictated."

"I will do as I am told," Crowe restated confidently. Then, he blinked and all was as it had been. He was alone in the cave, unnerved and startled by the appearance of an apparition. The imagery, a prophetic hallucination, raked through him. A gasp whimpered from his craw and his jaw dropped to his chest; the stem of his pipe was released and it toppled to the ground.

Boldness evaporated and he cringed inwardly. As clear as if it was happening five feet away, he could see the bronze-skinned princess bathed in shimmering light and beauty; a shelter of brightness shone around her like a celestial halo. A single thickly woven braid lay over her shoulder and across her left breast akin to a chain-mail shield over her heart.

Smoky Crowe erupted in primeval rage. He pounded his fists against his thighs uttering foul blasphemies. He cursed God with a visceral hatred, stood and stomped. He unleashed an unholy screech of madness that bounced off the walls of the narrow cavern and reverberated along the canyon and across the dips and twisty bends of the Angel Peak badlands.

Meanwhile, at her campsite on Bulldog Mountain, Sally Twosongs had her eyes closed as she sat cross-legged, with the flute on her lap and her palms pressed together. For the better part of the last hour she had played prayers and now, she endeavored to hear the Creator, but there was only stillness in her soul and a longing to be faithful thumping in her heart.

Hank was flattened on its belly beside her, while the red-tailed hawk remained on its perch, head ever on the move as it kept vigil. She was unaware of her guardians for she was fully attuned to an interior sphere where tranquility waited in anticipation. Her responsibility was to block out all diversions and concentrate on listening. She had developed much patience and strength in waiting upon the Creator in expectation of his astonishing deliverance.

Dehydration was beginning to set in. She could taste the bitter badness of her breath for it was a foul sourness that clung to her tongue like gummy slime. Her vigor was being replaced by an increasingly powerful weakness that radiated from the pit of her stomach, and produced a plethora of cramping muscles in her legs and across the small of her back.

Her blood pressure was plunging. A low-grade headache had taken up residence between her temples, vacillating between outward and inward trauma. The pain wasn't incapacitating, but rather, a monotonous tingling that rang in her ears. She also had to deal with chills and kept trembling because she was feverish. She denied and defied all the symptoms.

Her body quivered—waves roiled through her. She was caught up inside a chimera and from her perspective she was no longer on Bulldog Mountain. She stood at the entrance of a cave. Bitter and rancid smoke, cloying in its sweetness, permeated the roughhewn chamber. Fear was absent; what assaulted her senses did not frighten her in any way.

Smoky Crowe was squatting like a gigantic frog on a flat stone. He was nearly stripped bare, wearing only a chiffon-like loincloth. His blotchy skin was a mass of crumply folds that gathered in bunches over the knobby protrusions of his elbows and knees. His lips were kinked upward in a threatening grin that revealed grossly yellowed teeth stippled by streaky blackish stains. His freakish left eye enlarged and pulsated malevolently at her.

He was surrounded by demonic minions—aroused imps pirouetted and pranced around him. He glared viciously—hate flared from his normal eye. "Aaaarg! I will destroy you."

"I think not," Sally Twosongs replied, bold and absolute.

"You shall die, missy."

"Not at your behest."

"I will cut out your heart. It'll pleasure my coyotes and crows to feed on it," he said, smugly brutish. "You think because you're Sally Twosongs you can thwart my will?"

"The Creator is my strong tower and refuge."

"Towers crumble and fall. Satan will triumph."

"You are delusional, Mr. Crowe."

"I will kill you. Who will be delusional then?"

"Not I, to be certain."

"Why not?"

"Whether I live or die, Jesus is good medicine."

Crowe shouted laughter and wagged a heavily knuckled finger at her. "Jesus is a liar and usurper. The hour of his reckoning will come when the skies are blackened and the moon blood red. He will be drawn and quartered, and his body cast on the winds of the four directions."

"Every tongue will confess that Jesus is Lord. All of creation will bow and worship Jesus Christ," she said, an avid vibration in her voice. "You cannot come against the Almighty."

Crowe's head angled rightward. The sickly white orb distended and throbbed as it fixed on her. Sally Twosongs defiantly opposed him, locking her eyes in unflinching moral gravity. Her face became radiant and full of a transcendental intensity; her smile glowed at him. The fiend attendants were rabid and out of control, spinning and screeching in fear.

Crowe convulsed and groaned as he broke free from her gaze. He teeter-tottered side to side and almost tumbled over. "Bitch!" he snarled through gritted teeth. He spewed a blistery smear of expletives in a profane rant that repeatedly accused her of unnatural acts.

Then Sally Twosongs was liberated and returned from the trance, or whatever it was that had carried her away. Her arms and legs were jumping and jittering. She shuddered, jerking and twitching as she gasped a massive breath and garnered control. Her eyes opened. She prudently scrutinized the mountaintop sanctuary, eyelids flickering against bright blades of sunlight.

Her lips curled in a subtle grin. "Greater is Jesus in me, than the Evil One who prowls around in imitation of a hungry lion." An incomprehensible peace came over her as comforting as a beloved shawl. She wiped her sweated brow. Sally Twosongs glanced approvingly at Hank and nodded to the red-tailed hawk. She calmed her breathing, picked up her flute and began playing soft notes that soon became a conquering song of freedom and victory.

The afternoon had some age on it. Stace Hawkins, sorting through yucky debris inside his head and heart, was by himself fantasizing that his mother was still alive. He hadn't even noticed how far from the others he had ridden. There were upsetting feelings preoccupying him—he wanted to holler or scream or cry to set them loose, but instead, he attempted to force all the troublesome questions and emotions to stay corralled within.

Some Bible words kept getting in the middle of his jumbled thoughts; a verse he'd first heard from a reverend in a pulpit, but then more recently, his grandmother had referred to it. The man in the clerical collar had been fiery and flamboyant, but Grandmom Delores was sincerely calm and persuasive. His understanding of the exact chapter and verse wording was foggy at best, but in the middle of his drifting thoughts, he tried and tried to grab hold of it.

The meaning was vexing and illusive, but he hoped that if he persevered, comprehension or consolation or some insight would come to help clarify it for him. He concentrated so hard that his eyes squeezed shut and stayed that way for an extended period. Hoofbeats came alongside him, jarring him out of his reverie. His head jerked up and sideward.

"How goes it?" Deacon asked, smiling gently.

"What? Not sure?" the boy replied in a puzzled tone.

"I thought you were snoozing in the saddle."

"Nope. Just woolgathering."

"I imagine there's much murkiness in your head," Deacon said, adjusting his hat up his forehead. "Losing your mother at such a tender age has got to be hurtful and confusing."

"I ain't real clearheaded."

"You'll make your peace with it, Stace."

"Doesn't feel like I will."

Coburn gave him a flint-eyed stare. "You plug away and one day, way off in a future you cannot imagine hereabouts, the gloom will lift and you'll have a sharper perspective."

"I'll trust your word, I guess."

"I ain't one to put powdery sugar on bitter pain," Deacon said offhandedly. He sloped his shoulders in a down-to-earth shrug. "All I can really tell you is that you're not alone. You got a family that loves you and are your biggest supporters. We're cheering you on, Stace."

"Thanks, Mr. Deacon."

"Make it Uncle Deacon."

The boy beamed. "That'd be swell."

"So what's on your mind?"

"A Bible verse," Stace answered wistfully. "I ain't sure about it, Uncle Deacon. Do you know that one that says something about God making everything work out for good?"

"As a matter of fact I do, young man," Deacon replied, eyebrows arched and moustache squirming to contain a satisfied smile. "Romans 8:28. *And we know that all things work together for good to them that love God, to them who are the called according to his purpose.*"

"That's it! What do you think of that one?"

Coburn took a peek at the western sky to estimate how long until dusk, then clasped a hand over his chin and nodded. "We got us some time to do this right and proper," he said candidly. "First off, preachers and laity regularly do it, but in my consideration, it ain't usually helpful to pluck a single verse out of a passage without thinking through its context. To get the full impact of God's Word we need to put our brains to work and apply basic facts."

"I enjoy thinking my way around problems."

"Then you're halfway there, Stace." Deacon loosened his hold on the reins. "Paul, the writer of Romans, was a highly educated man, and after many experiences and much learning, he concluded that yes, God works for our good and his purposes through all circumstances, but before he came to that declaration he wrote: *There is therefore now no condemnation to them which are in Christ Jesus, who walk not after the flesh, but after the Spirit.*

"That's Romans 8:1, the first verse after Romans 7, where Paul drills down to the bedrock and puts forth considerable honesty struggling through the reality of what it means to be trapped inside human skin and be in constant conflict with our failings and the sin nature; *what I want to do I don't do, what I don't want to do I do, oh what a wretched man am I.*"

Coburn raised a hand to express the point. "Yet it is within this framework of the human dilemma he resolves that God has made provision for our frail, fallible, sinful condition. *There is therefore now no condemnation to them which are in Christ Jesus, who walk not after the flesh, but after the Spirit*. Connect Romans 8:1 directly to Romans 8:28 and what do you have? No condemnation is forevermore linked to God being at work for our good and his purposes."

"It ain't easy, Uncle Deacon."

"No, it ain't, son."

"I can't make sense of the ugly junk."

"Not a simple proposition," Deacon said frankly. "Hard times come and hard times go in life. We persevere and grow through the difficulties by putting faith in action and leaning on those who, because of their own journey, can relate to our being bruised and battered. No one ever gets through the cruddy garbage alone. We desperately need to help each other."

"Do you really believe Romans 8:28, Uncle Deacon?"

"My belief far exceeds my comprehension, Stace."

"What's that mean?"

"We humans have vast limitations," Deacon answered dourly. "More often than not we can only come to terms with the heartaches and junk in hindsight, but we take heart because of God's love. In the closing handful of verses in the eighth chapter of Romans, Paul sheds light on his viewpoint by painting an extraordinary word portrait that illuminates the love of God. The crux of truth is that *nothing* in all creation can ever separate us from the love of God.

"Do we get it, Stace?" he asked, eyes brightening. "To put Romans 8:28 in complete context we must note that it is squarely in the middle with no condemnation on one side and the everlasting, forgiving, relentless, unconditional love of God on the other side—Romans 8:28 is a precious jewel set between the twin wonders of no condemnation and the love of God."

Coburn leaned back in the saddle. "So yes, Stace, when push comes to shove I truly do believe the Creator's plans and intentions are being worked out in our lives. Whether we grasp it or not, we must stand firm and have confidence in the realization *that all things work together for good to them that love God, to them who are the called according to his purpose.*"

"I like the way you explain things, Uncle Deacon."

"Comes from a lifetime of thinking about eternity."

The lad frowned and rubbed his chin as he pondered the response. He had a gander at the sky which was taking on dull shades of gray. The messy rubble in his head and heart could now be sifted through a sieve of Scripture that gave him opportunity for fresh insights. As his sorrel plodded onward, Stace Hawkins relaxed and quietly ruminated on all of it.

At dusk the train broke down, which prompted a rash of grumbles and complaints. A mechanical problem had plagued the engine for the entire trip, causing one delay after another. The passengers were assured that for this latest issue the engineer had the complications under control, but it'd be midnight or later before the glitch was repaired good enough for the locomotive to proceed to the Santa Fe depot, a mere hour away.

Lucinda Enochelli responded to the announcement in a burst of randy anger. She spat out a vulgarity and wasted no time in taking the bull by the horns to satisfy her desires. She grabbed Willy Phips by the hand and led him to her sleeping compartment, where she gave him a taste of carnal knowledge, which was unbridled and as promised, surpassed his loftiest imaginings.

The vigor of their passion caused the narrow berth to squeak and the floorboards to creak. Those noises, however, were muffled by groaning moans, of which the lecherous participants were oblivious. Unknown to them, their hot and heavy antics gathered a hushed listening audience in the outer passageway, many of whom were red-faced and goggle-eyed.

Twilight colors were streaming through the windows when they began shedding their clothes; it was full dark as they boisterously cried out in unison and collapsed in a heap, sweating and breathing hard. In the afterglow, they shifted around to achieve a level of comfort that had them lying partially entwined with a tangle of sheets covering their nakedness.

"I've had better," she told him, laughing brashly.

"Not me, dear lady."

"You did fine by me."

"Glad to hear it."

"It weren't bad for a couple old farts past their prime."

"No it tweren't, sweet lady."

"I'll do you again, Slick Willy."

"And I'll be happily done."

She gave him a squeeze as she snuggled downward to rest her head on his chest. "I'll tell you this once and once only, mister. Don't be clutching and grabbing at me, or latching on like a damn puppy dog. I ain't no one-man woman and I certainly ain't the settling down kind. If you know and keep your place, then perchance we'll travel along together for a fair distance."

"I've already learned that if I get too lippy you'll give my toes a verbal stomp," he said, chuckling heartily. "I sort of like you, my dear, so I shall dependably abide by your prescribed desires and be at your beck and call for such times you require my mannish attentions."

"Then we understand each other."

"Enlighten me, if you would."

"On what subject?"

"Who's Deacon Coburn to you?"

"A mystery man."

"Come now, Lucinda. Give me something."

She giggled, sounding like an innocent schoolgirl. "A handsome and upstanding man from days of old, which among other things, means that it's none of your business."

"If you find him in Santa Fe, what'll you do?"

"Not what I just done with you. He's likely still too straitlaced for such doings," she said, fingering strands of her thick tresses. She then placed a hand on his belly. "The answer remains to be seen and to be plainly unequivocal once more, it's none of your business. If you continue on that trajectory, I will crush your balls until you shriek like a hog getting its throat slit."

"Mercy sakes," he said, protest in his tone. "I was just making conversation."

"Choose another topic, mister."

"As you wish, dear lady. Have you ever been to San Francisco?"

"Nope," she answered, pressing her back against the wall. "Laying here, wherever here is, is as far west as I've gotten. I'm an easterner through and through. Until a few years ago I never dreamt of ever seeing the Mississippi River, let alone crossing it on a westward expedition."

"What changed your mind?"

"That'd be none of your business, too."

"Ain't you a bundle of riddles?"

"Is it not a charming bundle, Mr. Phips?"

"Indubitably," he replied in a hoarse and throaty grumble. "My suspicion is that it'll be great fun hanging close to you and pulling a fiber periodically just to see what unravels."

"Careful not to tug on the wrong thread."

"Why is that, sweet lady?"

"If you do so, you'll be the sorriest individual alive."

"That is beyond possible, my dear."

"Test me not, Slick Willy."

"My dear Lucy..."

Her body went rigid and she slapped his chest so hard he squealed like a child. "My name is Lucinda!" she exclaimed hotly. "Make that mistake again and I'll tear you a new arsehole."

"Now listen here, Lucinda. I'll not..."

"You'll not what, buster?" she countered, jabbing him. "You will do as you're told. My terms are nonnegotiable. Deviate from them again, and you and I will go our separate ways."

"That'd be a disagreeable development."

"Walk my line and we'll have us a spree."

"Dang, your sass excites a fire in my privates."

She pecked his cheek. "Have *you* been to San Francisco?"

"Hell, yeah," he replied cheerily. "On many occasions. It used to have a helluva nightlife and from reports it remains my kind of town. Gambling emporiums, dance halls, theaters..."

"Theaters?" she sliced in, sitting up in such abruptness that it elicited a startled cussword from him. She pulled the sheet over her topside, staring doe-eyed at him. "Theaters?"

"Definitely. Plenty of concert halls and playhouses."

"Depending on happenings in Santa Fe, I'd like to go to San Francisco and see it for myself," she said fancifully. "I would, of course, appreciate being escorted by a gentleman who knew his way around the avenues and byways, and around me, for that matter."

"A proposal that is distinctly appropriate, my sweet Lucinda." He licked his chops and flinched a ridiculously obvious leer. He adjusted his posture and tugged her down to plant a wet one on her lips. She reciprocated, then they crunched around for several seconds. She spooned against him, resting an arm over his chest. They settled in and soon drifted off to sleep.

Smoky Crowe skulked through the darkness as silently as mist. It was as though his footsteps never even touched the ground. His limbs were stress-free, as was his breathing. He was not alone. A sizable crow stood regally on his left shoulder, eyes attentive and darting nonstop. Its head never dipped or bobbed, and not even a trill issued from its beak.

The sky was dim and unwelcoming; the moon and stars were imprisoned behind thickened layers of clouds. He kept at an unvarying pace, stealing ever closer to the glow of a smallish campfire and the occasional sound of muted voices. The diabolic sadist could hear defeat and discouragement, which pleased him immensely because those emotions were conducive to his schemes. Success was at his fingertips to be seized and secured.

He came to a cluster of scrub cedars close enough to the campsite that he could see the pair who had been a pestering thorn in his flesh and were now about to have their world turned upside down. He sat on his haunches and bided his time, ears quickened. His blackbird disciple remained still and soundless. Crowe grinned, all smarmy and repulsive teeth, lips slinked back in eerie gratification as he paid mind to the whispered, almost inaudible conversation.

"I'm as empty as the shaft of an abandoned mine, Charley. I got nothing left," the woman said, anger popping in her tone. "What do we do now? Where do we go from here?"

"Wherever we must, eh."

"Why?"

"Surrender is not an option, Max."

"I'm close to being done, I swear."

"No chance, Max. We finish what we started, eh."

"Which is what? I don't even know anymore."

"We kill Smoky Crowe."

"That bastard's not human," she replied fiercely. "We can't kill him because his magic is invincible. He won't die, Charley. Not now, not ever. Evil has no end and no grave."

"He will die. I will kill him, eh."

In the bushes, Smoky Crowe quashed the expanding smirk, murmured the final evocative watchwords of an incantation that cast a slumbering spell over Charley Jondreau, then dispatched his feathered accomplice. He was on his feet and racing wraithlike—almost floating. The crow swooped out of the night and launched a ferocious pecking attack on the woman.

There were shouts and caws. And harmless gunshots; each flare of lead from the pistol's muzzle struck nothing but air. Jondreau was immobilized, flat on his back and bound by invisible forces and dominions that smothered him in a crippling coma. His hands, usually so quick and nimble, were cramped into arthritic claws, arms stretched out and pinned to the ground. He was as useless as a capon; he saw all that transpired, but could not move.

Max Dawson emptied her Colt Peacemaker at the flapping monstrosity that kept up a barrage of assaults. She reached for another weapon, but then, Smoky Crowe was upon her. He snatched her to her feet as though she were a lifeless bundle of blankets. He locked her head and neck in the vise-grip of his forearms and snapped her into unconscious submission. Her body went limp in his arms and he hurrahed high-pitched cries of maniacal laughter.

"Aaaarg!" He gleefully dragged his captive over to the hatless man who was still powerless. "You will kill me, eh?" the Ute mocked, proud and gloating. "I will take pleasure with your woman. Cut her, peel off her skin, make sport, rape her and leave her to be eaten by my crows and coyotes. Then I will come and you will die. I will kill you, eh."

Charley Jondreau was helpless. He tried and tried to heave his body at the savage, but all those stressed attempts were foiled and made impossible by the hocus-pocus jinx that engulfed him. His mouth, clenched in the guise of a bulldog, was unable to vent any grievance or plea. His throat was swollen shut, his muscles incapacitated. He gaped at his adversary, fearless.

Creepy silence, as prickly and cold as a subzero wind, draped the air in a bitter shroud of breathlessness. Smoky Crowe was jubilant. He did a preening hop and skip, swaggering like a show-off as he groped the woman crudely against his body. He crooked his head to its odd angle, which underscored the pulsing ugliness of the left eye socket, then in a shock of movement, spun into a blinding whirligig dance and vanished, along with the strawberry-blonde prisoner.

A smattering of seconds later, Charley Jondreau escaped the hexing. The inertia and numbness sluggishly departed. His head throbbed as though the tiny capillaries inside his skull had been twisted into a mat of knots and were now returning to their proper channels. His lungs came under control as he rationally evaluated all that had played out in front of him.

Though the state of affairs was dire and inching precipitously close to despair, he refused to give in to defeat. With his back against a metaphorical wall, he summoned virtuous courage so as to shed any and all thoughts of hopelessness. He then proceeded to pack and prepare to go on a rescue mission. The calm resolve that empowered him was encased by a simmering righteous indignation: *How dare that scum-sucking maggot put his hands on his partner?*

There was no fluster or dread in him. He knew what he knew; Smoky Crowe would surely die at his hand—he had *seen* it time and again. What was entirely unknown to him was a foretelling to illuminate the trials and travails of Max Dawson; what vile atrocities would she suffer at the hands of the mad barbarian before Charley Jondreau delivered death?

Caleb Weitzel felt the futile emptiness of midnight. A web of tension that originated in his heart had gotten entangled between his shoulder blades in a mesh of loops and lumps. He made camp in the dark without much thinking about what he was doing. He got a fire started and fed it enough twigs and sticks to keep it burning while he tended to his mount.

Shadrach was now twenty-two years old, as perceptive and intelligent as ever, yet age was evident in its diminishing grit and resilience. He stripped off the gear, then retrieved a brush from the saddlebags and began grooming its coat. His thinker was elsewhere. He paused frequently, which was not the normal procedure; usually the rubdown was continuous motion until finished. During one protracted break the steeldust whinnied an objection.

"Sorry, Shadrach," he said, patting its neck. "Sally Twosongs has got me bedeviled with concerns and apprehensions. The trail's colder than a tombstone, but I have one more idea as to where she could be. We'll get a few hours rest, then be on our way at the crack of dawn."

The stallion stomped a hoof in agreement. There were no further hesitations or stoppages and it was content to remain poised and unmoving until Weitzel completed the task. He picketed the horse on a generous tether where there was plenty of grass for its feed. Then got his bedroll and a hunk of beef jerky. He munched on the dried meat while collecting a mixed bag assortment of firewood. He stretched and exhaled a weary gripe as he bedded down for the night.

Flat on his back, with his hands linked behind his head, he stared at the roof of the world, which had numerous widespread swatches of bleak clouds that concealed the moon and obscured starlight. There were blotches of twinkles peering through in sporadic spots, but mostly the sky was dismal and forsaken, which accentuated the hollowness inside him.

He tried to relax, but could not. He tossed and turned for a dozen minutes or more, mumbling terse grumbles that were out of character for him. Upsets, chaotic and irrational, were running breakneck through him. His insistent struggles to quell or even slow the turmoil down were good-for-nothing. His mind jumped to an unbidden and unwanted scenario; a glimpse of his life without Sally Twosongs became saw-toothed emotions that hacked at him.

Loneliness oppressed him. He missed her. Their souls were connected in ways that he seldom understood. There were no secrets between them.

The meaning of contentment was to simply be with her—not having to be doing anything or going anywhere, but to simply sit side by side, and more often than not, converse in silence. A merciless skewer of anxieties bore to his marrow and he cringed as despicable fears of losing his wife became too awful to be real.

His eyes were wet. He tightened his jaw and ratcheted down steadfastness; he repressed all the tormenting anguish by force of will. It took much purposeful breathing for composure and reason to prevail. He prayed for guidance and protection, and while he was doing so, slipped into restful slumber assured that sunup would bring all the hopes and promises of a new day.

It was the third watch of the night, and Avis Lahay had been bulgy-eyed awake for over an hour. She sat alone beside the campfire, frightened by all the wondering ambiguities of the future. She was unable to terminate the endless questions agitating her imagination—each one demanded an answer, but all she could provide was another layer of barbed queries that promptly broke open to reveal a deeper dimension of insecurity and apprehension.

The stars were playing peek-a-boo with banks of clouds scudding along like cargo ships on a vast blue-black sea. She fluctuated between watching the slow moving game and studying her hands which were fidgety on her lap. A rustling breeze sporadically swept off the Rio Chama and eased a hush-hush jest to the trees; the leaves responded with fluttering giggles.

She took it all in while attempting to prioritize the mishmash of thoughts by putting them into supplications, but couldn't get past the salutation, which frustrated her immensely. A bevy of pangs woven into misgivings had falsified her true north outlook. The origins for her disarray of thinking was that she had come to wholeheartedly doubt her mettle to properly raise Stace Hawkins. She was in a taxing spot where her pledge to do so met callous reality.

"Care for a visitor?"

A dry lump hurdled up her throat as her head twitched toward the voice. A smile slipped over her lips. "That might be best, yes. I'm not making any headway here by myself."

Daniel Twosongs emerged from the murk and came into the firelight, his footsteps as soft and noiseless as a cat. He took a knee on the other side of the fire, picked up a good-sized stick and poked at the coals. "You are worried. I see it in your face and in the way you walk."

"Is it really that obvious?"

"My eyes are sensitized by discernment."

"Not sure how to be free from worry, Daniel."

"Worry has no good end."

"It's like I'm on a mean-spirited carousel."

He smiled sympathetically. "Round and round you go."

"Yes. It aggravates me."

"Worry is useless and accomplishes nothing."

She changed her position and clasped her hands together. "My head has been telling my heart similar facts for quite some time, but evidently my heart is not in a listening mood."

"Are you so sure it is the heart that has grown deaf?" he asked, low and quiet. "Could it not be that too much moping and fussing has become a smokescreen that misleads you?"

"Does spinning in circles qualify as being misled?"

He sat on his backside and pulled his knees up. He removed his flat-brimmed hat and dragged his fingers through his hair for several seconds before returning the headgear. "Your heart is good and brave. It knows much. You ought to be wise and trust it. Your head and heart must be aligned to one purpose, then worry cannot get a foothold to wedge its way in."

"What if worry has already dug a trench?"

"Root it out and toss it on the burn pile."

"How, Daniel?"

"Your heart has the key," he replied, leaning back to regard the sky. "The winds blow, the seasons change, life goes on. I was once just where you are now. Grief and responsibility have teamed together to sidetrack you away from faith, which allowed worry to dig that trench."

"What can I do?"

"Faith and hope. Search your heart."

"Of late my faith can't get any traction."

He chuckled knowingly. "Faith can be tricky and elusive. The experiential evidence of my life tells me as much. When my sweet Consuelo died faith was not my first response; nor my second or third, for that matter. I went into a funk that carried me to the darkest of places. Worry did not take its spade to my heart, but rather, anger and bitterness got buried in me.

"What I learned when I went through all the emotional wreckage was this: To get to the other side where faith and hope and redemption resides one must muck it out and arrive at the awe-inspiring knowledge that God is God. This is the Creator's world." He casually put some brushwood on the fire. "God is the author of our lives and the One who perfects our faith."

Her eyes narrowed. "God is God?"

He chuckled. "A profound simplicity. The wrongness and hardships of life ofttimes feel and appear to be too severe for us to persevere against and overcome, but the Creator is still on the throne of the universe. He is the ruler and commander of all from history past through the currents of the present and into eternity future. He is God, he changes not."

"And I must exercise faith and hope to banish worry."

"Yes, but do not pretend that it will be easy," he said sternly. "It's step by step, precept upon precept. Affirm the truth in your heart, pray the truth in your head and aloud, work out the truth in your life. As you do so, faith and hope will grow stronger and stronger to demolish the strongholds of worry in you; faith and hope will become a bulwark against worry."

"I appreciate your wisdom, Daniel."

"I'm glad. I pray it will be helpful."

"I'll take all the prayer I can get just now."

"Know this, Avis." He made eye-contact and maintained it as he spoke in a sensitive and potent tone interlaced with elements of steel and velvet. "That boy Stace respects and trusts you. Build on those foundational stones and he will become a man who will make you proud."

She sniffled and wiped tears off her cheeks. "Thank you. Now you must excuse me." She got to her feet and walked off into the woods. At first her gait was hurried, but then she slowed and made it a cautious climb down to the river's edge. The water was glassy smooth, the air brisk and refreshing. She roamed and sidled agilely until finding a stool-like rock to sit on.

Despite a revitalized confidence from getting her attitude recalibrated, tiny rivulets of moisture continued trickling down her face. She blinked the filmy blur away and contemplated the relearned lessons in the ever idyllic hues of daybreak. As an orange streak formed on the eastern horizon, Avis Lahay articulated appeals enveloped in praise and thanksgiving.

chapter four

Judgments

"For now we see through a glass, darkly; but then face to face: now I know in part; but then shall I know even as also I am known. And now abideth faith, hope, charity, these three; but the greatest of these is charity."

~Paul of Tarsus~

At first light, Deacon Coburn was entombed in a deep, but restless sleep. The synapses of his brain were sparking and misfiring fitfully, and a wild-eyed nightmare inhabited his dreams. The madman was as vivid and imposing as vivid and imposing could be; he had a towering frame and employed a shepherd's staff, the hook of which was a foot above his head.

"I am the Prophet Eliezer," he proclaimed in a croaky voice that cracked and snapped with the authority of a bullwhip. "I saw the bloodletting retribution of God at Antietam. It 'twas a glorious day that caused angels in the throne room of God to sing triumphant songs of praise. I was there at Fredericksburg and Chancellorsville when God poured out his wrath. Holy, holy, holy is the Lord Almighty. His scales are weighed in the balance of his prevailing right hand and there is no escaping the reach of his judgments, which are altogether straight and true."

"Preach it, Prophet Eliezer, preach it!" a woman shrilled, and other faithful ones in the crowd of sycophants shouted bellows of agreement. The tabernacle was a circus-type tent with a littering of straw and sawdust for a carpet. Torches burned at strategic locations, giving the sanctuary a mercurial glow and an oily stench that was chokingly overbearing.

The Prophet Eliezer moved back and forth on a raised wooden platform. He wore a robe of animal skins. His hair was a crusty crown of matted ringlets that shook and shuddered on his shoulders with every step he took. "Blood and sacrifice; sacrifice and blood. I was there to see great and terrible days of the Lord. What has been will be again. The Almighty, for whom I speak, is once more readying the double-edged sword of penalty and punishment.

"Be warned. Be not deceived. God is not mocked." He went to the edge of the stage and paused dramatically. He waited in holier-than-thou piety, cheeks ruddy and lips flattened. "God is pretty smart, you know. He cannot be fooled by false believers who pretend to worship him with their tongues while their hearts are hard and bitter stones as cold as the ice of death.

"Liars, gossipers, idolaters, drinkers of demon spirits, lovers of money and power, deviants and sexual sinners will not escape the scorching flames God has prepared for them." He veered forward, grinning and slobbering in livid excitement. "All transgressors and reprobates who dare to defy Almighty God will burn . . . burn . . . BURN in the fires of hell!"

The Prophet Eliezer pounded the wooden staff on the plank floorboards. "Glory, glory, glory, GLORY HALLELUJAH," he hollered, swaying like a lofty cedar in a stormy gale. Gobs of thickish spittle clung to the straggly whiskers of his full red beard, appearing to be yellowish burrs and briars. "Jesus . . . Jesus . . . Jesus! Glory, glory, glory, GLORY to God!"

The swarming mob was ecstatic. Some were cavorting and throwing their arms up and waving; others were slain in the spirit, writhing and quaking on the straw-strewn ground. The long-limbed zealot's face radiated power as he consumed the churning emotions of adulation. "A stark and harrowing day of reckoning cometh. The chastising rod of God will break the backs of the stiff-necked. Mercy has been pruned and purged from the vineyard in a blazing verdict.

"Woe to those who rebel against the dictates poured forth from God," the sermonizer intoned, pop-eyed in arrogance. "Blood and sacrifice; sacrifice and blood is required. A deluge is nigh upon us. The rivers of blood will flow as high as a horse's bridle to wash sinners away in the tide to the gates of hell, which will swing open to welcome them to damnation.

"I am the Prophet Eliezer. I have spoken it, so shall it be." Then, in a blast of hot breath, the captivated throng was gone, the tent was no more. The frenzied messenger stood alone in an uninhabited wilderness. He leered a scheming smile as he beckoned Deacon Coburn and belched apocalyptic language directly at him. "Death is coming to you. Destruction awaits.

There is no place for you or yours to hide, preacher. God speaks through me. I am God's vessel.

"Death will have its tithe. You will not know it, but death will strike soon." His voice became the cannonade of a colossal kettle drum as he transfigured into Smoky Crowe. The Ute stalked Coburn as if he was readying to do violence. He sneered, his baleful left eye discharging a seepage of glutinous mucus. "Trifle not with me for I am the harbinger of death, the herald of carnage. The Navajo princess Sally Twosongs will feel the lethal sting of my victory."

In that instant Deacon Coburn lurched awake. His lungs were ragged and raspy, billowing air in and out as he labored to shake off the haunted slumber. His joints were aflame, as though he had been overextended and tortured on a rack. He fought to gain a rational equilibrium, but the whitish orb of vibrating evil that was Smoky Crowe's deformed eye terrorized him.

He had an unending headache—splitting pressure behind his eyes that was currently so penetrating that he was nauseated. A queasy bile in his belly was gurgling upward and he could taste the putrid acid in the back of his throat. He swallowed and had to forcefully stymy the gag reflex. His eyes opened in a hesitant squint that slowly broadened.

He propped up on his elbows and had a look around. Pinkish dawn was spreading across the sky in streaks. He was tucked in on a rise twenty yards from the campsite, which was quiet and still. He laid back down, fingers interlocked at his beltline as he thought through matters. Sally Twosongs burdened his mind. He was unsure of any feasible connection, but recalled the message from Charley Jondreau: *Be not overcome of evil, but overcome evil with good.*

"Alright, Lord. Help me," he said in a scratchy mumble. He closed his eyes and went about the meditative business of enumerating the instances of God's faithfulness. To his way of thinking the list was limitless, and that conviction spurred him to be deliberate and specific. He remembered the wormwood and gall of his past, and how God had delivered him from plights that could've swallowed him whole. Those reflections put him in a place of humility.

Then, without prompting or desire to replay what had invaded his sleep, the Prophet Eliezer rushed to prominence in his mind. Muscles across his shoulders clenched in tension. The shock factor of the wild-eyed nightmare assailed his senses, disturbing him to his core. He drew a hefty breath and took a stab at relaxing, but that was not to be. The self-righteous diatribe of hate mongering theology sickened him even more. His stomach somersaulted.

There was a seed germinating in him that caused the discomfort in his head to flare into hectic pounding—his intuition and instinct told him that the Prophet Eliezer was not a figment of his imagination, but rather, a flesh and blood man, and somewhere further on up the trail he would meet him face to face. Coburn knew that as sure as he knew the sun was rising.

"*Why art thou cast down, O my soul? And why art thou disquieted within me?*" he asked, grousing somewhat in jest as he voiced questions originally penned by a king of Israel. He had a weariness in his bones. "*Hope thou in God: for I shall yet praise him, who is the health of my countenance, and my God.*" He clambered to his feet. With the valiant assertion of Scripture fortifying his guts and doggedness, Deacon Coburn got a start on the duties of the day.

In the ashen gray of dawn, Charley Jondreau was on horseback tracking Smoky Crowe across a familiar section of the Angel Peak badlands. Dim echoes from previous travels past the ravines and snaking curvatures of the canyons were in the air. His palms were moist on the reins. He felt and *heard* the vestiges of earlier pursuits of the treacherous occultist.

The dapple gray, spirited and robust, strode confidently without any reluctance, while the rider-less red dun kept pace on the lead-line. High above and slightly ahead, a majestic red-tailed hawk was swerving and turning in expansive circles, its wings flexing in minor adjustments as needed. It unfettered a full-throated shriek that was akin to a shrill steam whistle.

Jondreau minded its call. The thin follicles of hair on the nape of his neck became as erect as quills. He stopped his mount and sat back in the saddle to observe the raptor's flight. It sailed effortlessly in a spherical pattern that led in a general southwesterly direction. He hoisted his right leg up and slid to the ground to monitor the bird on foot for a dozen paces. A whiff of smoke nipped at his nostrils. He mused on from whence the trace of tobacco had come.

Then, in a dart of glimmering sunshine, it didn't matter—nothing mattered except the acute smell of the skunk that blistered him. His lungs slammed shut. He doubled over and fell forward, arms and legs akimbo, and face crunched in the pebbly sand. Frenetic convulsions made it appear as though spasms of electricity were surging through him.

What he *saw* riveted him. Max Dawson embodied defiance. There was no surrender or compliance in her; no flagging or dithering in confronting her captor. Her clothes remained on, but were shabby and sullied as if she had been dragged. Her durable trousers had rips and slashes shredded at the knees, and the left side of her waist length jacket was torn and tattered.

She was thoroughly secured to the knotty trunk of a juniper tree, arms yanked back and bound by leather thongs. Her wrists were raw and bleeding. Finger shaped welts disfigured her face, and blood was clotted below both nostrils and splattered on her cheeks. Battered and bruised, she kept her eyes focused on the Ute warrior, flashing raging anger.

Smoky Crowe strutted and skip-hopped in front of her, singing and grinning. His wispy white hair was tied back. He was barefoot and naked from the waist up, wearing fringed leggings over a loincloth. The slack and saggy skin on his torso jiggled with every step he took. In one hand was a curved blade knife and in the other, a frilled and beaded pouch.

He squatted in front of her and opened the decorated sack to remove his skull-bowl pipe. He packed in his distinctive mix of tobacco and peyote, all the while licking his lips and ogling her. "My crows will join us soon, but for now, it's just you and me," he said, inclining his healthy eye at the sun. "I have much time to be gladdened and feed on your agony."

"If you expect me to scream or beg, you'll be disappointed."

"You will scream. You will beg. You will die."

"I intend to see buzzards feasting on your corpse, Mr. Crowe."

The episode ended in blackness. Charley Jondreau gasped and in doing so sucked a mouthful of dirt halfway down his throat. He choked and hacked as he pushed up to his hands and knees, upper body heaving. His lungs were in flames and runners of watery snot were dripping from his nose. He blew it out and backhanded it away, flopping onto his buttocks.

He wiped grime out of his mouth, then his hands came together over his belly and automatically, his thumbs began twiddling. The stench was departing from his sniffer; as it did, his lungs cleared and started to function normally. He brooded over all that he had *seen*. Nothing in the affair had dodged out of his sight or been lost from his memory; he retained everything. The terrain was not unknown—he identified the precise details of the location.

He lifted his head, eyes closed as he uttered prayers. The supplication was brief and concise. He got to his feet, and noted that the red-tailed hawk had dropped close and was now swooping back and forth ten yards off the ground in front of him. He regarded it, and a breaker of awe and respect splashed over his heart. He went to the dapple gray stallion and leapt into the saddle, and though Charley Jondreau knew his destination, he followed the bird of prey.

∼∼∼

"That be the way of it."

"Are you being truthful?" the boy asked, head cocked suspiciously.

"You betcha."

"You ain't joshing me?"

"I gots me a reputation for telling tales, but on this matter, I be as honest and reliable as one of them stained glass window saints," the cotton-topped barber replied, halting and turning sideways to eyeball his companion. "I be the one who lived it, so I must be the expert." He took a couple steps, groaning and click-clicking with each one, then paused again and tapped his brow as he said, "I may be creaky and timeworn, but all my upstairs faculties are still intact."

"I didn't mean nothing, Mr. Whitey."

"I knows that, sonnyboy," he volleyed back, punctuated by a grunt. They were on an early morning jaunt along a ridge above the Rio Chama, supposedly scouting the trail ahead, but the former slave had used that notion as a ruse to be alone with the tadpole. "My life be my life and I knows there be differences, but once upon a time, I was a wee-sprout like you."

"And you were a fisherman?"

"I did me some fishing," Whitey answered perkily. "That swampy creek on the plantation was heaven or some such place for catfish. There were big ones and little ones that tempted and teased us. We always got our fill whenever we had us some time, but there was one dandy-sized granddaddy catfish that was cagey. Within an inch or so, it was as big as you are right now."

"You told me that before."

"And that be where you interrupted me with your disbelief," Whitey said, eyes rolling. "I canst be explaining this here legend properly if'in you ain't gonna let me get to the point. It be a plainspoken yarn I be relating, so you best clean that wax out yer ears and listen up good."

Stace gave him a tight-lipped grin. "Sure thing, Mr. Whitey."

"Me and a bunch of other pickaninnies . . ."

"Pickaninnies?"

"A pickaninny is a nigger child." Whitey shrugged good-naturedly. "I ran with a crew that was full of fun and mischief, and we was always one-upping each other, so it be natural for us to go after that ole catfish and make it a contest of sorts. We was all fired up and full of juice to be the one to catch it. We figured it'd be a banquet of a fish fry once we got it in a skillet."

He made a grumbly noise with almost every gimpy step, but kept taking long strides to stretch his sore legs. "It was summertime, as hot and muggy as soup. There be so much darn humidity you breathed in air and spat out mist, but we was motivated to snag that sucker. All my buddies had their close encounters and there was lots of hits and misses, but we adapted bait and changed tactics, and none of us ever doubted that sooner or later we'd have success.

"On a particular evening marked by coolness, I done did the deed. I had me a sturdy cane pole, and a soggy mixture of cornbread and molasses on a rusty hook. It gobbled that sweet goo in one gulp and I yanked back hard enough to break my back. I pulled and pulled until I got it beached in shallow water, then I was splashing and fighting it like there was no tomorrow.

"That blankety-blank snapped its jaws and swatted its tail at me, but it'd swallowed the hook. I heaved and hoed mightily, yammering hollers for help. Three chums come a-running and it took the four of us to get that whopper onto dry ground. We be carrying on and hooting, then one of them gots a knife and slit its underside open. That mudcat had a treasure in its belly."

"A treasure?" Stace queried, voice squeaking in excitement.

"A gold coin that shined up fine."

"Wow! That would've been neat."

"A Spanish doubloon or some such thing," Whitey said, rubbing his thighs and moaning softly. "We didn't get to hide it or spend it or nothing. Master Fitzgerald heard tell of our haul and confiscated it, then punished us for trying to *steal* his property, is what he told us."

"That weren't right."

"Nope, but that be the way of it," Whitey answered nonchalantly. He stammer-stepped and let out a sorry sounding whine. "It be time we turn-about and get back for breakfast."

"If walking hurts so much, why do it?"

Fitzgerald chortled a burst of grouchy laughter. He continued limping as he nodded and click-clicked whimsically. "You has to keep your walking muscles lubricated, Stace."

"Even when it causes pain?"

"That just be the way of age," Whitey said, eyebrows sinking into a frown. "Walking muscles be different from riding muscles just like stomach muscles be different from heart muscles." He gave another nod. "Working your walking muscles be important, but much more so, you gots to always keep a guard up over your heart muscles, else trouble will bite you."

All of a sudden Stace stopped. His expression hardened into a scowl. His mouth opened and closed twice before a floodgate of emotions were freed and spilled forth. "That's what has happened to me. My heart muscles are hurting bad and I don't know what to do, Mr. Whitey. I'm angry and scared. I miss my mother and it hurts so awful much I want to stomp and shout."

"Let me tell you something about hurting, boss," Whitey said, empathy creeping into his voice. "Hurting has no end. We get some faith and healing and distance enough to kick the past to the past, but nevertheless, we carry every scar until jubilee day when the Lord calls us home to glory. I weren't any older than you, and I saw my mammy and pap get sold and shipped off. I still sees the heart-wrenching in my sleep once and again, so I knows about hurting."

"I'm sorry."

Fitzgerald shook his head adamantly. "No need to be sorry. Better for you to learn from others. Your Aunt Avis knows plenty about hurting, but have you ever heard a single complaint from her?" he asked, raising a finger at him. "That lady had an ornery enough start in life to be beaten down and never get up, but instead, she boldly chose to go forward in hope."

"Aunt Avis is always so optimistic and encouraging."

"She saved this poor nigger's life."

Stace meekly slumped his shoulders. "What should I do?"

"I canst say," Whitey replied curtly. "Early on I made a decision that I'd not be no one's dog. I'd live a life to make my mammy and pap proud. I ain't been anywhere close to perfect, but I's tried and tried to be true, and mostly methinks, they be smiling at me from heaven's shore."

"Will you help me do the same for my mother, Mr. Whitey?"

"With every breath I gots in my body," he said, grabbing hold of him. He enfolded the lad in a bone-crushing hug. Sobs and the spiritual sweat of tears flowed from both of them. After an extended spell they stepped back and smiled, then headed to the campsite. Whitey Fitzgerald had an arm firmly over Stace Hawkins' shoulder and was leaning on him for support.

On Bulldog Mountain, Sally Twosongs was having difficulty breathing. Her lungs were tight and painful. Cramps were centered behind her breastbone and clutching through her torso. The droning noise of the headache had become increasingly strident against her eardrums, but she persistently blocked and ignored it so as to hear from the Creator.

She shivered and shook as though her insides were frothing chunks of ice. Her physical suffering corresponded with a spiritual breakthrough. Excitement had her delirious. The fervor of her prayers and the thinness of the high altitude air combined with dehydration and weakness to put her into a rapturous stupor. Her heart was full and her mind had an enlivened vibrancy that gave her a distinct understanding of happenings elsewhere.

She knew that Charley Jondreau was alone and in danger. That knowledge had a compelling and transparent clarity—she saw him on horseback in a wasteland of gulches and rifts. A cry caught in her throat and she desperately lunged to touch him. Her arms stretched and fingers grasped, eyes gaped open as she kept reaching and reaching to lay hands on him.

Jesse Axler, alert and uncertain, sat off to the side watching and worrying on her. He had his rifle held ready, but wasn't convinced he would even need the Spencer. The situation and her condition took him by surprise because it was so far outside the realm of his experience. He lacked preparedness and had about concluded that he had no inkling of how to assist her.

He'd arrived on-site just before nightfall, but was unable to do anything he perceived as having any real value. He stayed awake to tend the fire and be on guard, but there'd been no dialog with Sally Twosongs. He had made a few attempts, but received shockingly vacant stares, which persuaded him that there was only a slight possibility that she was aware of him being in front of her. Hank, ever faithful and friendly, was antsy and pacing fretfully.

The sun was on the rise. It warmed him, but couldn't extinguish a coldness that had gotten into his bones and made his skin clammy and crawly. Fear clamped onto his innards like a bloodsucker; he resisted the unnerving sensation, but it had persistence and staying power that wore on him. The tricolor dog whined and nudged him. It poked its nose in his chest, then jerked its head to the right. He elbowed it away, but the collie became more and more insistent.

He finally clued in. He took a look in the direction Hank kept pointing, and saw a noble and thick-chested red-tailed hawk perched on a branch of a stumpy evergreen. He studied it, and was amazed by the silent and expressive interplay between the dog and the hawk; it soon became apparent that Hank had developed a communication bond with the bird of prey.

The raptor bobbed its head at him as if in a welcoming greeting. It surprised him and he didn't know what else to do so he returned the gesture. He shifted the Spencer into the cradle of his left arm, then inhaled deeply and felt relaxation ease through his muscles. Jesse Axler had no understanding in reference to the hawk, but was refreshed and heartened by its presence.

The bewitched bobcat was much closer now. It cunningly inched upward, remaining out of sight under the cover of scrubby brush. The evil abiding in it was a ravenous and aggravated bloodlust that would not be sated until the woman with a single braid of black hair was dead. Its anger, inflamed and itchy, had found a previously unknown level of belligerence.

There was nothing left of its character for now it was wholly under the influence of demonic forces. The fiendish impetus clawed ceaselessly at its skull and made calculations in accessing the boy and the dog that were protecting the woman. After dispatching the pair to death, the woman, unable to defend herself, would be an extremely vulnerable victim.

The demented impulse had overwhelming power—it coursed through the wildcat's veins and aroused a maniacal hunger for human flesh. Its tongue slithered and lapped over its lips as violence and savagery gleamed in the dull deadness of its eyes. The feline predator arched its back, then waited to execute the nefarious assignment to kill, kill, kill the woman.

When Delores Solrizo stepped onto the veranda of the Suncurl Café, she was content and simply taking a break to enjoy a cup of coffee in the morning sunshine. As she took a seat in a bentwood rocker she had no hunch that she was about to be drawn into a mystery. She sipped from the over-sized stoneware mug, pleased by the soothing taste. The steaming nectar had a bracing sweetness because she had boosted it with a spoonful of honey.

San Francisco Street was deserted except for a trio ambling in her direction, a couple buggies, and a slow-moving wagon pulled by a team of oxen. She momentarily watched the walkers, then beheld the sky for a lengthy time; it was festooned by several substantial banners of dark gray clouds that were being gathered and folded together into one. Her nose crinkled as she sniffed the air, and she supposed that showers were indeed in the forecast.

"Delores Solrizo?"

She turned her head and saw the three pedestrians standing at the boardwalk—a youthful man accompanied by a lady and gentleman in her age range. "Yes. How can I help you?"

"Jack Whistler, at your service, ma'am."

Delores sat back in surprise and memory gave her a pinch. She studied him. He was a tall and sinewy man, broad-shouldered and slim at the waist. He had a crop of dark brown hair that shaded close to black. He had an aquiline nose and a prominent chin. A lively grin blushed her cheeks and made laughter sparkle in her emerald eyes. "Jack Whistler the acrobat? We shared a stagecoach, did we not? Where have you been and what brings you back to Santa Fe?"

"Here, there and everywhere."

"You were twelve going on thirty, as I recall."

"Now I'm eighteen going on forty, ma'am."

"Still collecting data and facts, I'd surmise."

Whistler nodded and his gray eyes brightened. "Yes, ma'am. One can never have enough information." He then forthrightly made introductions without any fanfare or explanation.

Delores smiled warmly. "Lucinda, Willy. Happy to make your acquaintance."

"Likewise," Willy said, doffing his hat.

"You both must be charmed."

"Whatever do you mean, Delores?" Lucinda asked pointedly.

"Traveling with Jack," Delores replied, a frown forming in response to the snarky tone of the question. "I'm still not sure what Mr. Whistler's story is, but he's surely entertaining."

"Too entertaining for my liking," Lucinda said, surly and disrespectful. "And I've had enough prattling gibberish to last me until death comes knocking and I get put in a box."

"That's rather crude."

"Crude or not, I really don't give a tinker's damn," Lucinda cracked, sneering cheekily. She hiked her skirt up in her fists and stepped onto the veranda. "I made this trip for one reason and one reason only, Delores. Do you or do you not know Deacon Coburn?"

"I do," she answered, eyes narrowing. "I know the man well."

"Did you know him in the Biblical sense?"

"No. Never. Why would you ask such a thing?"

"It's the best way to know a man."

Phips muttered gruffly and cleared his throat. "On that note we better be out of here and leave these ladies alone, Jack. Let's go inside and see if we can scare up some fun."

"There's a pool table," Delores said flatly. "You're welcome to have at it."

Phips nodded, then opened the door and ushered Whistler inside.

"Now maybe we can get down to business," Lucinda said, occupying the bentwood rocker beside her. "Those men insisted we come here straight from the train station. I'm hot, sticky, tired and miserable. You'd be wise not to monkey with me or make it difficult."

"*You'd* be wise to modify your attitude."

"Would I?"

"Common courtesy isn't at all expensive."

"It costs time, so cut the crap, Delores."

"What do you expect from me?"

"Information, plain and simple," Lucinda answered, fluttering the bodice of her dress to fan her bosom. "I need to find Deacon Coburn. Do you know where or how I could do so?"

"You just missed him. He was here last week."

"I'll be damned!"

"Why are you looking for him?"

"Does my reason matter to you?" Lucinda queried, tensing her legs to make the chair move. "Is it mandatory that you have an answer before you will cooperate with me?"

"I've known the man for over twenty years," Delores replied soberly. "He's family, the only big brother I ever had, so you'll have to forgive my inclination to be protective of him. I never heard of you before today. I don't know who you are or where you came from."

"What difference does any of that make?"

"Perhaps none, perhaps plenty."

Lucinda cussed under her breath and fisted her hands on the arms of the rocker. "If you haven't blazed your brand on his ass, I'm not sure why my business with the man is any of your concern." She stood in haughty irritability and stepped onto the thoroughfare. "I'm going to get a hotel suite, soak in a tub, take a nap, then put on fresh clothes from the inside out. I'll be back here later to get the nitty-gritty as to the whereabouts and goings-on of Deacon Coburn."

"If you return in a few hours I'll have a meal prepared for you."

"That'd be nice. We'll get our bearings, Delores. I swear."

The red-headed woman, who a lifetime ago, was infamous as the whore Sweet Flora, leaned forward to watch her visitor sashay away; she wondered what was hidden in her past. The coffee was lukewarm, so she set it down. Her mind was sorting through minutia when her lips slyly crimped. Delores Solrizo now had a suspicion as to the identity of Lucinda Enochelli.

At *WT Ranch,* Naomi Axler was spitting mad. She moved around the kitchen in a rush that had no rationale or goal. She had just finished reading a letter from her niece in Abilene, the contents of which incensed her sensibilities. The missive had obviously been written and put to post before Anna had received her aunt's most recent correspondence to her.

In her anger, Naomi flirted with the idea of getting on a train to Abilene for the express purpose of punching a so-called evangelist in the nose. As satisfying as the errant imagery was to her carnality, she released it and set it free. Compassion swelled in her heart. She sat at the table, breathed a prayer, picked up the pages and read them again.

March 30, 1888
Abilene, Kansas

Dear Aunt Naomi: I am so sorry. I do not want to burden you, but I must share this with someone. I have learned that there is no one here who I can trust and no place for me to turn. Lately I am always full of guilt and shame, and have a need to seek forgiveness for things I have or have not done. Even now I feel as though I must beg your forgiveness. Please grant me patience as I attempt to put into words the darkness that has draped itself over me.

I am smothering in a pit. Despair and misery are my only companions. I keep a brave face on, but it's all mockery because the blackness presses in all around me. I work hard caring for and serving my family, pretending that all is well, but I am plagued by an overpowering sense of condemnation, which I yearn to get past and put behind me.

I am utterly alone. There is no one who will listen or who could possibly understand what is inside me. I am scared and terrified by the cheerless despondency that is my life. Thoughts, over which I have no control, emerge from the bleakness and urge me to harm myself or others, and there are frightening moments when those ghastly notions linger.

Abraham doesn't even try to help me. He thinks I am being silly and overly dramatic. He berates me and belittles my feelings, and is becoming increasingly forceful in the expectations he places upon me regarding my wifely duties in the bedroom. I notice our boys glancing at me oddly because they've picked up on all the hurtful words and actions of their father.

Mr. Mueller vehemently insisted that I call on the elders of the community to anoint me with oil and pray healing over me. It so happened that an itinerant evangelist was holding meetings at the time. Brother Raffens is from Pennsylvania, a roly-poly and florid-faced man who preaches with dogmatic zest and bravado. He had great success. The altar was lined with seekers every night for a week, so the engagement was prolonged for an indefinite period.

After much harrying from Mr. Mueller, I went forward. It was not at all an agreeable or assuring experience. There were overwrought hollers and demonstrations, and calls for me to be delivered and know the peace of God. A cluster of brethren surrounded me, and then, prompted by Brother Raffens, my husband once more confessed our sins of fornication.

It was humiliating. Brother Raffens asked a multitude of questions, and he wasn't at all discreet about it—he claimed he desired to have a clear comprehension of the circumstances. He took pleasure in hearing Abraham say aloud that while we kept company and courted we were not strict enough in setting boundaries and we had sexual intercourse, and that our succumbing to fleshly desires had resulted in my pregnancy and our subsequent marriage.

Everything that had been supposedly dealt with and forgiven years ago when we were disciplined and had to stand before the assembly and affirm our wrongdoing was perversely rehashed. Brother Raffens declared we had to take an axe to the root of our offense by bringing the details into the light of God's longsuffering mercy. All this took place while I was kneeling in the midst of many men, some of whom I had never seen before and certainly did not know.

I was mortified. Prayers were spoken on my behalf that had to do with lust and my sinful nature. The pleading and praying went on for what seemed to be an hour or more. Each one who took a turn found it necessary to enumerate my failings and iniquities, and noisily petition God to blot out my horrible transgressions and affront to his holiness.

Finally, Brother Raffens closed the session in a passionate oratory. I was weeping and shaking uncontrollably. He knelt in front of me, took my hands in his, stared at me full in the face and told me in explicit language that my miscarriages were God's judgment on me for violating his command to be pure and without spot or blemish on my wedding night. His tone and timbre was loud and adamant, rising up to seemingly rattle the rafters of the barn.

He said that God could redeem me and take away the cloud of shame, but his hand was stayed by my enduring obstinacy. I was withholding some unknown bundle from God. Everything was entirely my fault, and there was no mistaking his meaning. The rebellious streak in me had to be subdued and tamed or else mercy and restoration would be denied me. The pacifying of my disposition would occur only as I submitted to my husband in strict obedience.

Aunt Naomi, I am so terribly alone. The pain in my soul is immense and has no end. I cannot be freed or absolved of the bitter words of judgment Brother Raffens decreed. Must the fruit of my body be paid for the sins of weakness that preceded premature intimacy? I never stop grieving and shedding tears for the four *babies that died in my womb. To think that my lapse of virtue is the cause of those spontaneous losses is too harsh an affliction to endure.*

My prayers are useless, so please, PLEASE pray for me.

Sincerely,

Anna

The ire simmering in Naomi Axler boiled anew, as did the aspiration to bash Brother Raffens in the nose. She had to resist the impulse to crumple and rip the letter to shreds. Her mouth was compressed into a thin red line. She went and got her Bible, along with a pen and a stack of flowery stationery, then returned to the table and began composing her response.

The sun was midway to the top of a sky being swept by feathery clouds. Ten miles to the northwest of Wagon Wheel Gap, Caleb Weitzel had his hat pulled low and eyes squinty. He was riding hard and demanding much from the steeldust. The narrow and rocky mountain trail wound its way in and out of shadows, and had a steep drop-off to the left; despite the adverse conditions, Shadrach trotted lithely and showed no signs of weariness or fatigue.

Weitzel hitched up in the stirrups. He spotted spoor he needed to examine more closely. He tightened the reins ever so slightly. The stallion slowed to a walk, then halted. He alighted from the saddle, took three hasty steps and crouched beside a pile of excrement. He hovered a hand over the mound of horse manure, and figured it was less than twenty-four hours old.

He nodded agreeably. This sign coupled with the well-defined hoofprints from a mile or so back made him confident that it was highly probable that the droppings had been deposited by Jesse Axler's soot-gray mare. He stood and searched the area. A few more short strides and he got on his heels again to pick at and run a palm over a relatively flat surface of stone.

A smile touched his lips. There was a divot chunked out of the slate-colored granite; it was made by a horseshoe. He scooped the splinter up and held it loosely as his instincts worked to click all the clues together. He placed the piece in the hole from whence it had been chipped, then rolled forward on the balls of his feet. He was positive he was dead-on the trail.

Not only that—he swiftly came to the conclusion that he knew where he would find Sally Twosongs. That awareness gave him some comfort, however, the apprehension that she would be harmed and he would lose her harassed his mind. Her safety and well-being was of foremost importance to him, and though she had sternly instructed him over and over again to never worry on her, just now, he couldn't prevent or even hinder the sneaky feelings of fretfulness.

Weitzel hopped up and jogged to his mount. The steeldust high-stepped as he swung onto its back. He flicked his hands against its neck. It bolted forward and was at a loping gallop in ten yards, and kept that speed for a furlong as if the footpath was straight and even. When the trail broadened into a spacious clearing from which Bulldog Mountain monopolized the skyline, he prodded the horse to come to a gradual stop. He studied the mountaintop miles away.

There were puffs of smoke. His heartrate increased. The sunrays appeared to become distorted and queerly tinted at the peak. "Up there, Shadrach." He pointed assertively. "We have to get to that summit fast." He bent low and purred a command in its ear. The steed neighed, then stampeded onward into full speed with the vigor and hardiness of a young colt.

"I intend to see buzzards feasting on your corpse, Mr. Crowe."

"That will not happen," the Ute said, gurgling snide laughter. He folded his legs together and readjusted the position of his buttocks on the ground. He got a match from the beaded pouch and struck it against a stone to fire up his pipe. The aroma was cloying and pervasive. He inhaled deeply and held the smoke in his lungs for over a minute, then discharged it in short bursts. "You will scream. You will beg. You will die. I will steal the strength of your soul."

"Crappola."

Crowe shrugged and distractedly fondled the fringes of his leggings. "Your mother had much power and I stole it when I sliced her. She screamed. She begged. She died." He took a series of draws on his pipe and ribbons of smoke wreathed around his head. "Your father too. There was unshakable muscle in his soul, but I killed him. He died squealing like a baby."

"You, sir, are a lying bastard."

Crowe dismissed her words with an arrogant sneer. "The Dawson seed will be gone from the earth." He switched the curved blade knife from one hand to the other. "I will feed on your agony. I will cut off your clothes and make you naked. I will spread your legs wide and stake down your ankles. I will slash your tits until they are no more. I will rape you with my blade. Your womb will spill out in the dirt. I will taste its blood and it will renew life in me."

"You are a slime-sucking maggot who has a surprise or two coming. I will live, you will die," Max said, lividly defiant. Her shoulders hurt; searing slivers of pain cramped down to her bleeding wrists. A jutting knob on the trunk of the juniper tree speared into the small of her back. None of the afflictions prevented her from continuing to twist her forearms to loosen the rawhide thongs. "It will be my delight to spray a goober of snot on your corpse, Mr. Crowe."

He scratched at the flabby folds of wrinkly skin at his midsection. "When I am pleased by all the pain and torment I inflict, and you are dead, I will take time to stand over you and fill your mouth with my piss." He puffed serenely, a sneer bending his lips. "Perhaps I will wait for your man Jondreau to come and tie him down so he can watch all my gladness with you."

"He's not my man."

"Whatever he is, he will come."

"And he will kill you."

"I will kill him, *eh*," he said, emphasizing the mimicry. He stood and waved at a single large crow in the distance. A malicious grin spread across his face as it circled him. "An omen. Yes, I will wait for Jondreau, then we can all be together before my fun and games begin."

The crow cawed and dropped lower. He tapped the smoldering chars from the bowl and placed the pipe and frilled pouch on a tall boulder—leaning against the tabletop rock was a bow blessed by evil, and a clay jar half-full of a concoction of rattlesnake venom mixed with the dried flowers and roots of several toxic plants. Three arrows were situated in the container, the sharp flint tips soaking in the lethal poison. He would only require one, but had alternates ready.

He hissed a shrill whistle. The blackbird dipped its wings and landed near the woman. Its eyes darted as it let out shrieks of glee. He gestured to it and sat on his haunches. It walked to its master, who held out both hands as if he was welcoming an honored guest. His lips parted widely. He offered his right arm and the bird leapt onto it, squawking and fluttering.

"You are the first. I am well pleased by your devotion," Smoky Crowe murmured softly and tenderly. He kissed the crow's beak and petted its back in gentle strokes. "When the sacrifice is made others will hear your heart cry and come in droves to regale me in worship."

"You're insane," Max said, wincing from the burning stress in her shoulder sockets. As much as possible, she sustained the surreptitious task of loosening the leather bindings that had her lashed to the gnarled tree. Her knees were pulled up and her back arched.

Crowe rose to his feet and playfully sauntered to her, yellowy teeth bared in a viciously delightful grin. "My friend wishes to say hello." He did a short and shifty two-step dance, then tossed the bird onto her lap. It shrilled throatily and became a ferocious weapon. It thumped its wings and madly pecked at her, drawing specks of blood from the welts on her cheeks.

Dawson strained backwards and turned away, laboring to thwart the attack. She thrust a shoulder forward and scrunched her head down in an attempt to shield her eyes, but that only riled it all the more. It screeched and clawed at her upper body. She retched up a nasty load of phlegm and saliva, rammed forward as far as she could, and spurted the slop straight into its eyes. "How do you like that, you freakish ghoul?" she asked, laughing crazily.

The crow retreated, yowling and tumbling. It thrashed and flip-flopped spasmodically in the sandy soil. Crowe swore and launched a swift kick that struck her in the stomach. She gasped and spat at him too, but in recoiling from the blow, missed her target. He calmed the bird with soothing words and protectively clutched it to his breast. He thumbed the goop away.

"You will scream. You will beg. You will die. I will steal the strength of your soul," he told her again, fury in his tone as he craned his head to that odd angle so as to fix the milky whiteness of his left eye on her. His affection for the black-winged bird was obvious. He embraced it as one would cradle a newborn, cooing in an unknown language.

Then, with an appalling suddenness, he lovingly fractured its neck. Its body was still convulsing as he took his knife and proficiently slit its throat. Dawson cringed. He hunkered at her feet and pressed the lifeless crow's neck to his mouth to hungrily suckle its blood. Vomit swirled in her belly. She gagged it down, never taking her attention off her captor.

He drank the blood sacrifice until the veins gave no more. He discarded the body. His lips and chin were dripping red droplets. Manic caws were heard on some far horizon. Max Dawson listened and a jagged tremor lanced through her. The clamorous cries of crows were getting louder and louder as more and more joined the flock and it came closer and closer.

The dapple gray was frisky and apprehensive. Charley Jondreau felt the currents of its tension rippling against his thighs. He also noted that the red dun on the lead-line was draggy and exhibiting other traits of skittishness. The horses knew what he knew—the site where he expected to find Max Dawson was fast approaching; likely less than a mile away.

He heard crows—lots of them. The bloodshot eye of the sun was at high noon in blue skies bedecked by papery thin clouds. His shaven head glistened; decades had passed since he'd been hatless so his scalp was scorched. The sunbeams flittering on the cliffs of the gorges and gullies were casting purplish hues that blended to pink on some ridges.

His nostrils were twitchy, his eyes wary. The unmistakable reek of evil prickled the air, but underneath that menacing miasma there was brilliant goodness imposing itself as an imprint at the forefront of his consciousness. Compelling and powerfully intense, he had no difficulty identifying the source; he sensed Sally Twosongs. His heart swelled in courageous tenacity.

He had no doubt or skepticism—her prayers surrounded him. The Navajo princess with whom, for reasons beyond comprehension, he shared a supernatural connection had joined him to assault the heavenlies. Neither the lonesome miles that separated them nor the long years since they were together mattered; much had been washed away in the ocean of time, but the invisible bonds of mysticism that inextricably linked them remained vibrantly alive.

There was no breeze; a stillness deadened and dulled the air, yet he hearkened to her voice on the nonexistent wind—*I will help you*. Memories rushed through him and the veil of yesteryear was torn apart. For the briefest of instants he *saw* what had graced him while he was housed at the Welland County Jail; the straggly girl and the beautiful maiden fortified him.

His eyes twinkled. The fire in his belly burned brighter and hotter. He spread his arms wide and tilted his face skyward in supplication. The man from the Great Lakes region, a proud descendent of Iroquois warriors and Hudson Bay Company trappers, beseeched the sole commander of heaven and earth in a patois mix that paid homage to his bloodlines.

When he was emptied of all self-serving sentiments, he bore through to that sweet spot of surrendered serenity. His backbone hardened. He *knew* the future; the outcome was the fate and fortune for which he had been born, and he was at peace with it. The glimmer in his eyes expanded. A solo teardrop slid down his cheek and his lips puckered in contentment.

He dismounted and had a cursory look around. He needed to find a place to picket the horses, which in badlands on the high desert was commonly a challenge. His eyes searched the surroundings, then he led the animals toward a wide arroyo in the lee of a row of scrub cedars. The dry creek bottom had satisfactory thickets of grass and tufts of other vegetation.

He stripped the gear off and stowed it beneath one of the trees, then put the stallions on long ropes. He stood in front of the dapple gray, took hold of its ears and pressed his forehead between its eyes. "Be faithful, eh. One day we will again ride the wind together."

The horse stomped its hind hoofs. He rubbed its neck before hurriedly departing. He stopped after five hundred yards and built a rock monument marker to point to where the horses were tethered. He checked his pistol's loads, flipped the cylinder shut and returned the gun to its holster high on his right hip. Then, Charley Jondreau brazenly strode onward to confront evil.

For Sally Twosongs, the mountain had become a holy place that consumed all fears and reservations. There was an astounding aura of greenish-orange streamers of light encircling its pinnacle. She was weakened and wearied, but the dazzling atmospheric phenomenon spoke assurance to her soul. Every nerve ending in her body possessed a heightened sensitivity.

Prayers overflowed from her heart the way geysers gushed from underground caverns. The notes of her flute were strong and insistent, rising in a harmonious melody that kept her gradually swaying. Her eyelids recurrently fluttered open for her to be encouraged by the shimmering array of colors crowning the heights of Bulldog Mountain.

The red-tailed guardian shrieked vociferously. She silenced the song. Fatigue slumped her shoulders. She stared at the perch of the stumpy evergreen. "What is it, Mr. Hawk?"

It trilled its steam whistle cry, then leapt off the branch and plunged past close enough for her to feel the draft of its wake. A shivery gasp of amazement broke free from her throat and her heart pounded. She held the instrument to her bosom and watched the bird flap smoothly and mightily as it flew through the multihued tiara encompassing the mountaintop.

The sight dumbfounded her. She shaded her narrowed eyes and leaned back. The hawk ascended the sky as though it were following the pathway of a spiral staircase. She murmured audible wonderment. Each propulsion of its wings carried it higher and higher and higher. And higher. Her neck bent as far as it could, and still the bird of prey went higher and higher.

A stinger of tension tweaked her as the red-tailed hawk became nothing more than a dot. She exhaled an anxious sigh when it disappeared completely. Her heart, already beating rapidly, took on the elements of a racing jackrabbit, thump-thump-thumping faster and faster. She cupped her palm snugger against her brow, straining and stressing to catch a glimpse of the hawk.

She hitched in a gulp when her efforts were rewarded. The dot reappeared, plummeting in what seemed to be a free-fall. She was swiftly able to perceive the hawk's distinctive wingspan. A disturbance struck her ears and it took several seconds for her to identify the sound; the raptor was screeching as it descended in the same pattern as it had soared upward.

Sally Twosongs stayed focused on its flight. The ribbons of gleaming radiance were growing brighter than the sunlight; counterpoint to the illumination was the nearby presence of evil which invigorated her vigilance. The red-tailed hawk landed in front of her, bobbed its head once, then turned around to wait and watch for the heinous trouble that was coming.

Jesse Axler was scared all over again. And this time it was no dream. The behavior of the red-tailed hawk combined with the peculiar display of lights in broad daylight messed with his sensibilities. His palms were damp. He had no idea what to think or do. He was not the only one in such a state—Hank was going loco, spinning around and whining.

He hushed the collie unsmilingly. He gave it a hard-eyed glare that on normal occasions would result in submissive obedience, but not now. The dog continued its exuberance for a spell, then finally plumped onto its buttocks, but its jumpiness could not be contained; every ten seconds, as regular as clockwork, it growled and made low bleating noises.

The bobcat was forty yards away, prowling in the undergrowth around the edge of a scrubby copse of trees. Axler had seen its movement in the moments before the multicolored spectacle materialized out of nothingness, and he knew that the predator had not vacated its position. He had his rifle at the ready as he persisted in patience and determination.

It was a waiting game—a match of wills between him and the wildcat. The wetness of his hands disturbed him, but was not a distraction. His attentiveness was pinned to the responsibility heavy on his shoulders. He had assumed a shooter's stance, flat on his belly with the Spencer aligned on the tangled shrubbery occupied by the feral feline.

Twinges of cramps were clutching at the small of his back. He wanted to get some relief from the annoying pressure, but had no opportunity to do so because the imminent danger kept him motionless. He expected the prowler to attempt to escape or launch an attack; either way, when it scampered from beneath the hedging, he intended to put a bullet in its head.

Hank stood and barked. The red-tailed soldier on guard responded with a short and shrill directive, which caused the dog to snap its jaws. It took a couple steps, then reluctantly dropped onto its haunches. Despite the activity all around her Sally Twosongs didn't balk or falter. She was playing prayers; each eloquent tone had vigor and fullness that reverberated heavenward, seemingly passing through the animated colors to enhance their glowing power.

Axler was entirely discombobulated by all that was happening, but succeeded in staying on task. The kinks had climbed the ladder of his spine and spread outward to become a number of clumpy knots that wanted to yank his shoulder blades together. He gritted his teeth and persevered to resist the urge to flex his muscles in an attempt to release the discomfort.

A rustle of a branch in the underbrush sent a charge through him that grabbed his vitals. He was immediately sweaty and cotton-mouthed. His right index finger eased onto the trigger. He waited and waited. And waited some more—time meant nothing. Then, in unexpected speediness, three things occurred that multiplied fear in Jesse Axler: The tricolor dog woofed, the red-tailed hawk sang an alarm, and the bobcat poked a paw out from under its hiding place.

On a stretch of grassy bottomland along the Rio Chama, Deacon Coburn had withdrawn and was lagging behind the others. His head was throbbing—his teeth were clenched against the pain. He had blind spots in his range of vision, and was dependent on his mount; Gilgal did not disappoint. The silver-dappled buckskin walked along steadily.

The morning had dawned with mist rising from the river, but that burned away before the band of travelers broke camp. By noonday, clouds were bumping against each other like the innumerable thoughts jouncing around his mind. He was reflecting on the past, but getting nowhere fast because the hodgepodge was garbled by the tedious soreness.

He was so far out of sorts that his faith needed to be tangibly bolstered. Every so often he reached forward to finger and feel the stones sewn into the horizontal straps of the bridle as though each one of the twelve had power—perhaps that was true because whenever he touched them, the principles of hope and redemption uplifted him. The small rocks commemorated and honored God's deliverance at a crossroads of life and death.

He had collected the special stones in the shadow of Angel Peak for it was there that Smoky Crowe carved his torso and staked him out to be cooked by the sun. The grim reaper marked him, but he wrenched free of the torture and staggered out of the badlands. His recovery was iffy, but with grace and expert nursing, he recuperated and soon realized that he hadn't changed, but neither was he the same. In the winnowing fire, he had been reborn.

That crucible was worthy of remembrance, hence the memento reminders in the bridle. Now, as the gelding maintained a slow pace, Coburn tugged the brim of his hat lower to shade his eyes. His jaw nearly locked in tension—a burgeoning crate of memories beckoned him to unpack it. He winced even harder. There was solemn resistance in him, but his natural curiosity won out and he began revisiting a pair of recent dreams that had him perplexed.

First, he was seventeen and tenderhearted, alone on a forested hilltop seeking clarity and inner calmness. He wrestled with what his role should be in righting the wrongs of slavery, while on the doorstep of a decision to jump feet-first into the fray. The Old Testament spoke much about judgment and justice, and the graphic imagery of a particular passage in Amos enflamed his motivations: *Take thou away from me the noise of thy songs; for I will not hear the melody of thy viols. But let judgment run down as waters, and righteousness as a mighty stream.*

The Susquehanna River shimmered in the distance. In isolation, he was reading abolitionist articles, and weighing out decisions and consequences when Josiah came along to tell him that their father expected him home for a hog butchering day. The brothers conversed and one thread of discussion led to another and somehow Lucy Elburt got into the mix.

He had not thought of her in years—in fact had most certainly forgotten her, yet there she was, stitched into the fabric of a dream. Upon awakening and in the days afterwards, he vaguely remembered her looks; darkish complexion and raven-haired. The biggest impression remaining was her personality; she did everything with gusto and expressed opinions on all matters. Her mother, adept at promoting her, kept her near him at River Brethren gatherings.

For his part, Deacon Coburn was perfectly polite and a gentleman who went above and beyond in the area of courtesy and decorum, though in a firm and convincing way, made it known that he had no interest in Lucy Elburt, romantic or otherwise. His head was spinning trying to figure why, after thirty-some years, she had surfaced in his consciousness.

That muddled clutter of thinking led him to the visitation that featured the Prophet Eliezer. It bamboozled him for it had emerged from limbo. The madness of the self-proclaimed spokesman for God stuck in Coburn's craw—the self-righteousness linked to a latent insanity and pressed through a sponge of zealous denunciation was all too much to take seriously.

Yet, there was realism about the wild-eyed nightmare that Coburn grudgingly grasped. He had heard similar bombastic garbage from other crackpots, but never elevated to the sinisterly rhetorical zeniths achieved by the Prophet Eliezer. His perversion of God's character was egregious. Even in the fogginess of Coburn's head, the hell-centric tirade sickened him.

His reference to Fredericksburg and Chancellorsville upended Coburn into an emotional cave-in because as a sharpshooter attached to the Army of the Potomac, he had waded through the carnage of those epic bloodbaths. Fredericksburg was mostly a one-sided battle. The Union combatants, led by Major General Ambrose Burnside, launched a series of disastrous frontal attacks against entrenched Confederate defenders that were futile in the extreme.

At Chancellorsville, five months later, the Union Army had General Joseph Hooker in command, but the results were similarly tragic and ineffectual. Under the audacious leadership of General Robert E. Lee the Confederate Army of Northern Virginia, half the size of the attacking forces, out maneuvered, out-foxed and out-fought their blue-coated foes.

The violence and putridly gross inhumanity was horrendous—the casualties and losses in each of the campaigns were mind-numbing. The wailing screams of those dying in a godforsaken wilderness came like a mighty roar from the belly of a leviathan to torment Coburn anew. There was no triumph or pageantry of justice or glory in any of it. And contrary to the Prophet Eliezer's assessment, none of the bloodletting elicited cries of *holy, holy, holy is the Lord Almighty*.

Both dreams, coupled with the remorseless headache and black holes in his vision had Coburn fumbling to interpret his quandary. Frustration ballooned in him. The meaning or reason for it all must have been somewhere out amongst the stars because regardless of his monumental efforts to do so, he could gain no ground in the area of understanding.

The tourniquet of friction imbedded between his temples squeezed harder. Bile soured his stomach and moisture filled his eyes. He gingerly leaned over the saddle horn and began rubbing the stones in the bridle, but then, when he heard Whitey Fitzgerald shout his name followed by a hardy click-click, he jerked back as though he was a child caught in a bit of mischief.

He looked and through blurry lenses saw the barber on his molly mule a hundred or more yards ahead. Deacon Coburn was moderately surprised at how far he had dropped behind his companions. He took hold of the reins and urged Gilgal into an easy trot. The migraine and bothersome stopover in the reality of dreamland calloused and marred his demeanor.

The aroma of freshly brewed coffee filled the kitchen. Naomi Axler poured a mug and placed the pot back on the stove. She had put her anger to work by channeling it in a constructive endeavor. There was calmness and satisfaction in the outcome. She sat at the table and sipped the flavorful beverage as she picked up her handiwork—the reply to her niece's letter was infused with straight talk. A pensive sound slipped over her lips as she began reading through it.

> *April 29, 1888*
> *WT Ranch, Colorado*
>
> *Dear Anna: My heart is broken for you. I desire to stand with you and share your burden. If I could I would reach across the miles to hug you close to my bosom so that you might know that you are not alone. You have no reason to seek my forgiveness or indulgence. I am so sorry that you have been domineered in such an outlandish display of what the church ought never to be; a place of berating and condemning instead of a refuge of redemptive healing.*
>
> *How dare Abraham! How dare Brother Raffens! How dare the River Brethren leadership! That nonsense should have never happened. Your shame and guilt belongs to misguided and self-absorbed men who sought to justify themselves and excuse or make allowances for the lust in their loins by censuring and castigating you.*
>
> *Your grandmother Rebecca had no tolerance for spiritual abuse, which is exactly what you experienced. My mother would have had choice words to put Brother Raffens on his heels. She'd have told him that there was absolutely no foundation in Scripture to give him covering or permission to orchestrate a verbal assault on a lamb seeking the shelter and forbearance of God's peace that passeth all understanding. Shame and guilt-mongering are anathema to the clemency and grace of God that is from everlasting to everlasting.*
>
> *Forgiveness for specific sins is freely given by God whenever we ask for it—once received and accepted, God lifts us up and we move forward with him. There is no jumping over bars set by others or making ourselves right before God by our own efforts; no getting centered through the prism of modern-day scribes and teachers of the law like Brother Raffens and all those supposedly pious brethren who gratified their flesh by belittling you; magnifying your wrongs so as to minimize the darkness of their own sins and transgressions.*
>
> *God is our helper and provider. He yearns to pour blessings upon you. God IS NOT a mean-spirited magistrate who takes delight in your distress and lamentations. Your miscarriages ARE NOT God's chastisement. Do not, however, take my word on these matters. Hear the word of the Lord. It is my insistent prayer that healing and hope will blossom in your heart.*

The Bible I read, dear Anna, makes no mistakes about the issue: "Wash you, make you clean; put away the evil of your doings from before mine eyes; cease to do evil; Learn to do well; seek judgment, relieve the oppressed, judge the fatherless, plead for the widow. Come now, and let us reason together, saith the Lord: though your sins be as scarlet, they shall be as white as snow; though they be red like crimson, they shall be as wool."

That is found in the first chapter of Isaiah. It is a proclamation of God's assurance that if we acknowledge our need for mercy, he will forgive and erase our most deplorable stains of sin. Scarlet and crimson refers to a deep-red tenacious dye from ancient days that was impossible to remove from cloth. Our Enemy will tell us that our sin permanently soils our lives, but that is a lie from the pit of hell. God cleanses us as white and pure as newly fallen snow.

The Bible I read says this: "I am like a broken vessel. For I have heard the slander of many: fear was on every side: while they took counsel together against me, they devised to take away my life. But I trusted in thee, O Lord: I said, Thou art my God. My times are in thy hand: deliver me from the hand of mine enemies, and from them that persecute me. Make thy face to shine upon thy servant: save me for thy mercies' sake. Let me not be ashamed, O Lord; for I have called upon thee: let the wicked be ashamed, and let them be silent in the grave. Let the lying lips be put to silence; which speak grievous things proudly and contemptuously against the righteous. Be of good courage, and he shall strengthen your heart, all ye that hope in the Lord."

These petitioning words are found in Psalm 31. In times of stress we must depend on God to support us. We trust in God's desire and willingness to forgive us, and we take steps of faith to receive and accept forgiveness. God is our protector and defender. Our times are in his hands, which means that we believe that all of life's circumstances are under God's authority and control. He is sovereign and we wait in expectation of his deliverance.

The Bible I read says this: "Have mercy upon me, O God, according to thy lovingkindness: according unto the multitude of thy tender mercies blot out my transgressions. Wash me thoroughly from mine iniquity, and cleanse me from my sin. For I acknowledge my transgressions: and my sin is ever before me. Against thee, thee only, have I sinned, and done this evil in thy sight: that thou mightest be justified when thou speakest, and be clear when thou judgest. Purge me with hyssop, and I shall be clean: wash me, and I shall be whiter than snow. Make me to hear joy and gladness; that the bones which thou hast broken may rejoice. Hide thy face from my sins, and blot out all mine iniquities. Create in me a clean heart, O God; and renew a right spirit within me. Cast me not away from thy presence; and take not thy holy spirit from me. Restore unto me the joy of thy salvation; and uphold me with thy free spirit."

Those are passages culled from Psalm 51, which was King David's pleas for mercy and cleansing after Nathan confronted him about his illicit entanglement with Bathsheba. Remember, not only did David commit adultery, he also conspired and arranged for her husband Uriah to be killed in what appeared to be a battlefield casualty. David had woefully sinned, yet as his sorrow and regret is stripped to the bone, he has confidence in God's benevolence.

God always stands prepared to pour out forgiveness to us. He wants us to be in a healthy relationship with him, therefore he has made provision for our sinful failings. There is no sin that is too terrible or vile that God would withhold forgiveness. We confess and repent of our immorality, and God forgives and tosses our iniquities into the sea of his forgetfulness.

The Bible I read tells a story about how Jesus dealt with a woman caught in the act of adultery. It's in the eighth chapter of John. I just carefully studied it and my heart burned. When they brought the woman to him, the scribes and Pharisees were laying a trap for Jesus so as to accuse him of violating the law of Moses. Those sanctimonious teachers of Israel demanded that she be judged and stoned to death as punishment for her immorality.

Where was the man? It takes two to commit the act of adultery, yet there is no mention of the man in the text, which always unsettles me. Let us dismiss that inequity because Jesus is the focal point through which we see the nature and character of God. He ignored them, stooped low and began to write on the ground. They continued pressuring him to pass judgement, so Jesus stood and said, "He that is without sin among you, let him first cast a stone at her."

Then Jesus returned to the task of writing in the dirt. The script comes alive with grace and mercy: "And they which heard it, being convicted by their own conscience, went out one by one, beginning at the eldest, even unto the last: and Jesus was left alone, and the woman standing in the midst. When Jesus had lifted up himself, and saw none but the woman, he said unto her, Woman, where are those thine accusers? hath no man condemned thee? She said, No man, Lord. And Jesus said unto her, Neither do I condemn thee: go, and sin no more."

Furthermore, the Bible I read is imbued with the supremacy of forgiveness: "This then is the message which we have heard of *him, and declare unto you, that God is light, and in him is no darkness at all. If we say that we have fellowship with him, and walk in darkness, we lie, and do not the truth: But if we walk in the light, as he is in the light, we have fellowship one with another, and the blood of Jesus Christ his Son cleanseth us from all sin. If we say that we have no sin, we deceive ourselves, and the truth is not in us. If we confess our sins, he is faithful and just to forgive us our sins, and to cleanse us from all unrighteousness."*

John, the disciple whom Jesus loved, an eyewitness to the encounter with the wayward woman, wrote those soaring phrases in the opening chapter of his first epistle. It takes humility to recognize and admit our wrongdoing, but we must never fear declaring our sins aloud to God because he already knows them—nothing we can reveal is news to him. Confession frees us from the bondage of sin so that we might have fellowship restored with our Heavenly Father.

My dearest Anna, you have been washed in the blood of Jesus which is a supernatural disinfectant that forever secures you in God's sheltering embrace. When you succumbed to the weakness of the flesh, you confessed and received the full forgiveness of God. What's done is done. God NEVER withdraws or makes amendments to forgiveness. And moreover, take this truth to heart and be cheered: Brother Raffens and those of his ilk, are full of horse dung.

May the presence and graciousness of God grant you every goodness from the riches of glory. In these terribly lonely days of discontent, may our great and loving God, the giver of life and hope, open the storehouses of heaven to bathe you in the balm of serenity as you learn to be content. Know that you are loved and cherished. You are in my prayers always.

Be reconciled to and empowered by the TRUTH of forgiveness.

Much love and prayers,

Aunt Naomi

Her coffee cup was empty. She folded the sheets, being careful to make the creases smooth and sharp. Her Bible was still open to I John. She placed the letter across those pages and pressed her hands together atop them. She closed her eyes, then in tearful silence, Naomi Axler spent more than twenty minutes assailing the gates of heaven on behalf of her niece.

It was midafternoon and in the spacious kitchen of the Suncurl Café, Lucinda Enochelli was polishing off her second bowl of spicy chili con carne and her third thick slice of cornbread. She smacked her lips after nearly every spoonful. The dish was so zesty that her face was flushed and a sheen of perspiration glistened on her brow. She sat on a stool at the island bar across from Delores Solrizo, who had her hands clasped around a tall glass of lemonade.

"That hit the spot," Lucinda said, shoving the utensils aside. "Those beans will surely give my pipes a thorough cleaning, but tomorrow morning on the commode the aftereffects of the peppers are likely going to pucker my arsehole into a torch." She daintily dabbed her forehead with a napkin, then wiped her mouth. "You're a helluva cook, Delores."

"Thank you." She gave a terse nod, then took a tiny drink.

The mood between them was curt and superficial in the extreme. Each was feeling the other out, acting like a pair of fighters feinting and shadow boxing to gain an upper hand against an equally matched opponent. The mistrust and undertow of hostility in the sparring was evident in the glaring stiffness of their posture and the skepticism reflected in their eyes.

Lucinda topped off her lemonade from the ice-filled pitcher. She planted her elbows on the counter and leaned forward. "I'd expect a woman who knows her way around pots and pans, especially one with your curvy shape, would have a line-up of men sniffing around her."

"I've had more than my share of men."

"You sound regretful."

"Some of that lingers in me."

"Did you ever marry, Delores?"

"Yes, as a teenager. The marriage didn't last."

"Did hubby step out on you one too many times?"

"No."

"You were the one stepping out?"

"It's a convoluted story, Lucinda."

"I'm listening."

"But I'm not talking, am I?"

"You got something to hide?"

"Not at all."

"Everybody is hiding something, Delores."

"Everybody?"

"You bet your sweet ass."

"So what canard have you got hidden?"

"Nothing that is any of your concern."

Delores smiled slyly. "Did you ever marry?"

"Nope."

"Why not? You're a handsome woman."

"Men are good for one thing only," Lucinda replied tartly. She lifted her tumbler and had a long pull of lemonade. "And you don't have to marry 'em to get sweaty with them."

"That's true enough."

"You know about getting sweaty, do you?"

"More than I care to remember."

"There's those regrets I heard earlier."

"That's a fact, Lucinda."

"What's *your* story, lady?"

"I tell you mine, you tell me yours?"

"Not quite."

"Why not, Lucinda? All brass and no courage?"

"Enough of this jibber-jabber," Lucinda said, eyes narrowed and glowering. The tension intensified as her glare became inflexible. "What can you tell me about Deacon Coburn?"

"That'll take us down a whole new avenue of jibber-jabbering," Delores answered in an even and obliging tone. "One that will require you to provide some information." She never balked or gave any indication that she would. "For starters, how are you connected to Deacon?"

"I knew him before the war."

"How so? As a lover? A friend?"

"What are you, a copper?"

"Just someone safeguarding her big brother."

"That's balderdash."

"Why do you need to find him?"

"It's a convoluted story, Delores."

"That's the way it's going to be?"

Lucinda smirked. "I don't get your meaning."

"Why do you need to find him?" Delores asked again, uncompromising.

"He's a friend, if you must know."

"And you just want to say hello for old times' sake?"

"I have something for him."

"What exactly?"

"Something that belongs to him."

Delores softened her expression. She tilted her head, eyebrows rising. "Deacon has a sister at a horse ranch near Wagon Wheel Gap in Colorado. He visits her every few years."

"His sister?"

"Yes. Naomi Axler."

"I was told he also had a daughter."

"Abbey Langton. I'm not sure where she and her son could be found," Delores said, low and velvety. "*WT Ranch* is your optimal possibility." She drained her glass and set it down. A minuscule grin put pressure on the edges of her mouth as a mischievous sparkle flickered in her eyes. "I know your secret, ma'am. Lucinda Enochelli is not the name you carried as a babe."

"Mayhap not."

"There's no mayhap about it."

"I guess you'd know, smartass that you are, Delores."

"You're from a River Brethren community in Pennsylvania."

"Am I?"

"Your true name is Lucy Elburt."

"Is it?"

"Indeed, yes."

"That's all interesting news to me, Delores."

"Are you saying I'm wrong?"

"Neither here nor there."

"What are *you* hiding, Lucinda?"

"None of your damn business," Lucinda replied huffily. "My reasons for finding Deacon Coburn are honorable, so to hell with you." She slammed off the stool, grabbed her handbag and stomped onto the back stoop. She hitched her skirt up over her thighs and sat on the steps, then rolled a cigarette, fired it up and smoked obsessively. When she crushed the third ciggy, there and then, Lucinda Enochelli decided to regroup by taking a vacation trip to San Francisco.

The colors were fantastic and bizarre; ghostly, even. Rolling columns of reds and oranges were in unison with greens and yellows; tendrils wisped and curled like a whirlwind of fire from the heavens enfolding itself upon Bulldog Mountain. The eerie presence of the nimble lights merrily dancing had Caleb Weitzel flabbergasted; a man of faith who accepted the ambiguity and conserved a healthy agnosticism for the inexplicable, he had his heart submerged in hope.

He was riding hard toward the capricious singularity. It fueled his imagination, which raced through a gamut of explanations that ran from the optimistic to the catastrophic, though the later likelihood was immediately evicted by a scroll of promises contained in ancient words gifted to the world through the lives of trustworthy Hebrew mediums.

A spectacular idea popped into his head and he chuckled in agreement. The scintillating hues at the mountaintop were a sign that God was there and in control—a theophany comparable to the pillar of fire at night and obelisk of cloud by day that guided the Israelites after elite manifestations of the miraculous delivered them from the bitter bondage of slavery in Egypt.

Fearlessness sharpened his resolve. The horse, already running dangerously fast over arduous terrain, heaped more muscle into its exertions. He felt inspired as he mulled over truths about God: His powerful arms were protective and lifted high in glorious strength; righteousness, justice, unfailing love and unparalleled integrity were the foundation of his throne. Weitzel was exhilarated; the thoughts filled him with a quivery knowledge of the Almighty One.

He bore down in the saddle as the incline increased in steepness. The reins were relaxed in his palms because over the course of years and more miles than could ever be counted, his mount had time after time proven its know-how. The two had a collaborative relationship that was energizing, seamlessly appreciative of each other's instincts and intentions.

The footing became a gravelly mix of loose soil, but Shadrach never ceased or even slowed in straining and stretching its gait as it gobbled up real estate in huge graceful strides. Its muscular body was steamy and lathered in the whitish foam of perspiration as its chest heaved and its heartbeat pumped like oiled pistons of industrial machinery.

A blaze of trepidation flared in Weitzel. He scowled in surprise, his attention alternating between the trail and the destination bathed in streaming ribbons of phenomenal light. He spotted the pitfall a blink of an eye too late. A deep rut obscured at a hairpin turn. At the last possible instant the stallion reacted to the peril, but despite herculean efforts could not sidestep it.

Its left front hoof struck the furrow, which spawned a tumultuous chain of events that transpired in the ferocity of a split-second. The horse collapsed from under him, and Weitzel was airborne. He hit the ground and bounced onto his feet even as Shadrach regained an upright position, lame and limping. It whinnied and stamped its hind legs angrily.

Weitzel promptly knelt to examine its foreleg. He stroked and flexed it, and muttered a complaint as he elected to complete the journey by putting boot-heels to work. He stood and had a decisive look, calculating there was another mile or so to where he could now undoubtedly see tapers of smoke rising from a campfire. He stood in front of the horse and gave it a signal by brusquely holding up a hand. "Stay, Shadrach. I'll be back with Sally Twosongs."

The steeldust shook its head and neighed vigorously. He replicated the brisk hand gesture and imperative in a deeper voice. He withdrew his rifle from its scabbard, then turned and started away. Shadrach would have none of it, blowing a mist of hot breath before blatantly disobeying the order. The horse followed and belligerently nuzzled his shoulder. He grabbed onto the bridle and got in its face to communicate in no uncertain terms that it was to stay put.

Shadrach bared its teeth and nipped at him. He shied away, gape-eyed in disbelief. The premier stud of *WT Ranch* bucked and kicked wildly in protest, rearing up on its hindquarters to thrash the air with its front hoofs. He put his hands on his hips and his expression crunched in curiosity; its whole body was aggressively refusing to obey. He jabbed a finger under its nose, but the animal continued to insistently refuse to respect the directive.

Weitzel took a knee once more and studied the injury—as far as he could tell no bones were broken. The damage amounted to bruises and a probable sprain. "If you're going to be bullheaded about it I retract the command. Let's finish the rescue mission together."

Shadrach snorted and nodded thrice. Weitzel massaged the stung area for several minutes and while doing so prayed, asking God to provide an outpouring of healing and an anointing of strength. Then, Caleb Weitzel holstered the firearm and pivoted into the saddle. He whispered forcibly to the steeldust. Shadrach stepped lively, demonstrably favoring the wounded limb, but within a hundred yards, it was sprinting onward and upward at a gutsy canter.

Charley Jondreau was huddled down in a shady hollow of a gently sloping rise. Scrubby sagebrush was all around him. He was within shouting distance of his objective. Ahead and to the left was an opening to a canyon from which a legion of crows cawed discordantly. He cared nothing for the blathering commotion because the red-tailed hawk coasted above him.

His fingers were interlocked while his thumbs kept twiddling like tumbling dice. Relaxation and awe of the future seeped through him, as though he was alone meditating in the sanctuary of some stone-walled cathedral. He was at ease and at peace; no qualms whatsoever regarding the imminent showdown with a purveyor of evil sanctioned by the false god whose native language had vowels and consonants layered in lies.

A whiff of tobacco smoke tickled his nostrils, but was instantaneously displaced by the pungent smell of the skunk. His eyelids shuttered and the veins in his neck bulged. His vertebrae fused rock-hard and his breathing stilled. He saw Sally Twosongs sitting at a campfire playing her flute. He heard the melody of her prayers. Her face shone like the face of an angel.

He stretched forth a hand to touch her. All at once she brought the song to conclusion, grasped the instrument to her bosom and stared straight at him. Their gaze locked as surely and solidly as a cast-iron bolt sliding into its latch. He acquired the potent force emanating from her dark eyes. Her mouth broadened into a strikingly placid smile and she said, "I will help you."

Then she was gone. Charley Jondreau was freed from the extrasensory revelation. He gasped a lungful of air. His hands had not changed position; his thumbs were speedily making a perpetual circular pattern. He moistened his blistery lips and stood. The red-tailed hawk cried high above him, filling him with explosive vitality and a razor-edged willpower.

He removed his knife from its sheaf, effortlessly flipping it from one hand to the other, valuing its flawless balance. He opted to hold it ready to throw in his right, knowing that he could switch hands and quick-draw the revolver all in the same fluid motion. He took a gander at the eastern horizon where thunderheads were amassing. A shrewd grin chased over his lips and he chuckled lowly. Then Charley Jondreau stalked forward to meet the enemy.

Sixty or more crows were clustered together in juniper trees and on the ground, forming a crooked arc around the woman as though she was bound on stage in an amphitheater. The noise of their jubilant quacks and caws was an ever-present din that rose to the sky like the confused and salivating joy of a motley choir drunk on the sacramental wine of expectation.

Smoky Crowe was in his glory. He strolled amongst the rabble of worshipping disciples as a victorious emperor who had conquered and ravaged vast territories. He had the stiff bearing of royalty receiving praise and laurels from adoring citizens. As a scepter he carried a rattlesnake that writhed and twisted around his forearms, spitting hisses and flicking its tongue.

Every few steps he paused for lengthy intervals to interact with the birds. He would do so with bunches of them on weather-beaten trees and also, at more than one stop, he singled out an individual crow and carried on a vocal exchange as one might do upon rendezvousing with a long-lost relative at an unanticipated locale. The inflection of his voice was reverent; each feathered devotee he nattered to ducked its head to listen in a subservient manner.

He put the snake around his neck and over his shoulders as if it was a living scarf to keep him warm from the nonexistent cold. The rattler slithered and twitched its tail, its jaws opening and closing drowsily. Crowe sauntered to his strawberry-blonde prisoner and squatted lewdly in front of her. He cupped a hand over his crotch and gluey drool dripped from his mouth.

"Are you having fun, scumbag?"

"I am," the Ute answered, grinning.

Dawson smiled, unrepentantly provocative. "As am I."

"You lie."

"Do I?" she queried, shifting against the trunk of the tree. Her wrists were stinging to the point of numbness from her continual wrangling to stretch or slacken the leather straps. "I am more than overjoyed watching a lunatic play the thug because he thinks he frightens me."

Crowe grunted. His eyebrows shot up as his lips parted even wider to flaunt the unsightly ugliness of his choppers. He finessed the snake into his hands and suspended it aloft. "What if I introduce you to *this* friend of mine?" He tossed it on the ground; its weight produced a brief billow of dust. It slunk over her boots and coiled alongside a clump of sagebrush. He sneered at her. "You must have shit in your pants or luck on your side for my comrade to ignore you."

"Neither, actually."

"No shit, no luck?"

"You must have shit between your ears. Period."

Crowe growled laughter. "For someone who will soon taste my vengeance, you have much bluff and fancy talk. Your mouth runs like watery bowels." He pulled a curved blade knife from a sheaf affixed to his leggings. "I grow weary waiting for your man Jondreau. I will make sport of you for entertainment until he comes, or I just decide the time for blood is now."

"Do whatever cranks your gears, Mr. Crowe," Max said, caustic and fiery-eyed. "But I guarantee you'll not get what your heart desires. I swear there's no chance that I will scream or beg. As far as it is possible for me you will not get any jollies due to weakness on my part."

"Bold talk from a kitten." He gained his feet and took a couple steps so as to straddle her legs. She unleashed a kick at his groin, but he blocked it and delivered a walloping backhand to her cheek that whiplashed her head. He then sat on her knees and gave a playful bounce.

"You, sir, are psychotic."

Crowe clamped the blade between his teeth and grabbed the lapels of her jacket. He yanked her as far forward as possible. Her face squashed in a contorted grimace. He slammed her back as belching chuckles snarled deep in his throat; the humming rumble was monstrous. He pressed in close to delicately sniff her hair, which was a tousled and matted jungle.

Her black Stetson, with the rattlesnake band fashioned from a kill she'd made near San Antonio when she was fourteen, had been knocked off and lost in her capture. She was detached and unresponsive as his fingers messed and toyed with her tresses. His rancid scent, a vinegary mingling of urine, sweat and tobacco, sank into her nasal passages like grease.

He sat upright and removed the knife from his mouth. His tongue slid over his lips, then he leaned in again and licked at dried clots of blood on her face. The grossly unnatural sound of his merriment continued unabated. A hand was on her breasts, crudely clinching and squeezing each one through the flannel shirt. "I will slice these off and feed them to my crows."

Max Dawson remained uncompromisingly defiant. Her eyes blazed as his molestation became more and more contentious. A button popped off the red-checkered shirt, then another. And another. Her left teat was getting brutally and thoroughly worked over. His loathsome burps of amusement were in her ears; the slobbery wetness of gooey spittle on her neck.

He abruptly ceased and jerked back as though his hand had been bitten by an unseen scorpion. His normal eye widened and a gleam flashed in it. He carefully traced his right hand over the waist length jacket and felt the outline of what she had concealed in its inside pocket. He glowered in delight and made a move to retrieve it, but just then, a strident aria pealed from the uproarious chorus as a crow soloed, striking shrill and frenzied notes.

Crowe stood as the frantic bird swooped at him. His head tilted oddly. His left eye enlarged and protruded. A teardrop of mucus trickled from it. He uttered a string of unintelligible phrases. The agitated bird dipped its wings and landed on his shoulder. He conversed with it, nodding as he did so. It squawked in his ear, then flew back to its branch.

Crowe glared at her. "Jondreau this way comes."

"And he will kill you."

The Ute soothsayer ignored her. He went to the rattlesnake and crouched on a knee to charm it. Kindness was in his tone as he lifted it up. His words became a guttural incantation that hit its crescendo when he blissfully throttled the serpent in his bare hands. His face lit up like a jack-o'-lantern. He twisted until it was asphyxiated, then took his knife and lopped off its head. He voraciously slurped and drank its fluids. The darkness within enveloped him.

He disposed of the dead snake by flinging it at a dwarfish cedar. He scarpered to his feet and began spinning around and around in some ritualistic dance that aroused the crows. It was as if the birds were collectively infected by a crazed brain fever. The flock blundered from perches to flap and fly in erratic patterns and become a screeching black tempest.

Crowe's bass voice rumbled louder and louder as his twirling revolutions increased in speed. Then, as spontaneously as it started, the rotating shimmy ended in a strutting two-step that carried him to the tabletop rock where his pipe and frilled pouch rested. He extended his arms high over his head. The blackbirds became pacified in a rushing hurry. It was only moments before the colony flitted to previous spots and were soundlessly immobile.

He deferentially removed the three arrows from the jar of toxic poison. After checking each arrowhead he selected the shaft that would deliver death. His left eye pulsed. He fitted the arrow into the string of his bow. He took up a defensive position with a narrow escape route behind him, then Smoky Crowe awaited the powers of light that were aligned against him.

The ghostly colors were mystifying—an ever moving curtain-like wall that blended shades of reds and oranges together with greens and yellows on a celestial palette that appeared to be teetering precariously at the summit of Bulldog Mountain. Audible cracks and frenetic undertones were intermittently heard from inside the energetic anomaly.

Jesse Axler had never seen anything like it. His imagination wanted to leap at various whys and wherefores to explain the peculiar oddity, but he repudiated any inkling to give in to the temptation. He was flattened on his belly, struggling to not be distracted by the luminescent exhibition as he sighted down the barrel of the rifle. He had it targeted on a dense growth of underbrush forty yards below; the gradual slope of distance was barren terrain.

The red-tailed hawk, as stalwart and sharp-eyed as a Pinkerton bodyguard, stood in front of Sally Twosongs, who was swaying in rhythm to an inner symphony. Plugged into a spiritual dimension, she was oblivious to occurrences around her. Her eyes were half-closed as her lips briskly mouthed silent prayers from her heart. Trembles visibly coursed through her, and every few minutes she almost doubled over as if slugged by tremendous pain.

Axler was torn. He caught a glimpse of her suffering each time she folded like a bent pin, and felt like he should do something about it. He doubted that he had anything to offer to assist her, but just the same, an urge to make an attempt to do so wrapped around his conscience like a tightened length of barbwire pricking him. The earnest impulse to abandon his firing position to help the distressed woman had his stomach trussed up in granny knots.

He had to trust his gut, which informed him that his principal responsibility was to shoot or shoo the wildcat. Seeing to the physical care of Sally Twosongs would have to wait until the primary menace fled the scene or was dispatched to death. He gnashed his teeth and summoned intestinal fortitude to stay single-mindedly focused on the bobcat's hiding place.

Hank paced between him and the feathered protector, growl-whining continuously; the sounds and actions of its anxiety were disruptive to his concentration, but Axler had given up trying to keep it still and quiet. The collie had herded him and kept him safe as a child; the two had a rich history of embarking on adventures, and he was grateful to have the dog at his side now, but realized that the onus of dealing with the feline predator was on him.

He murmured in a breath. He wiggled his ankles to alleviate cramps, then slightly adjusted the angle of his legs. His heartbeat felt like a hot poker striking his ribcage. He hitched in another whisper of air, and was surprised when the tension in the middle of his back suddenly released as surely as vapor being swept away by a gust of wind.

A smile bit at his lips and his eyes flickered in excitement as his determined vigilance paid off. He spotted a rustle of movement in the hedgerow. And another. Thrills whipsawed through him when he saw the grayish-brown speckled pattern of the cat's torso. A paw inched from beneath the cover, and then, as if it was propelled by a medieval catapult, the bobcat hurtled from the undergrowth at full speed. It zigged one way, zagged the other.

Axler accurately lined it up, gave it a wise lead and pressured the trigger. The Spencer vibrated in his damp hands, then he was on his feet. His careful aim had failed; the bullet sailed away and struck only air. He had the cat in the gun's sights again, but it was speeding faster and faster in its zigzagging attack route, increasing the difficulty of the shot.

Closer and closer it came. Every lesson Axler had ever learned about shooting cascaded through his head in a flurry of disjointed splinters. His trigger finger was itchy. Each moment he had a chance to put *that* finger to its task, the lightning-like predator crisscrossed in the opposite direction he had anticipated. Beads of sweat were forming a line along his eyebrows.

Incredibly the bobcat sped up even more; it was a careening blur. Then, pandemonium erupted. The raptor shrieked with such ear-splitting shrillness that Axler lurched in his footsteps. Hank howled and charged the wildcat. The domesticated dog and feral feline slammed together less than ten yards from the twelve-year-old. The rifle never left his shoulder as fur flew, growls snarled and jaws snapped in a tempestuous storm of a battle.

Hank was old and worn out, plagued by arthritis and other degradations of age, but it fought with the intensified strength and shrewdness of a pooch in its prime that had been bred and born for the desperate and violent abandon of the fight. The advantage went back and forth. Hank would have the bobcat pinned, then in a hissing and clawing fury, the dog would be in jeopardy, yelping and fighting back to prevent the deadly teeth from sinking into its throat.

The coppery scent of blood thickened the air. Axler smelled it. His throat seemed to be clogged and closed off by the unruliness of his thumping heart. The muscles in his shoulders and chest were as taut as tightropes. His bottom lip was being chomped on by his top teeth. He kept trying for a shot, but because of the riotous combat no gap of opportunity opened.

The red-tailed hawk, its wings arched and feathers disheveled, was high-stepping and calling out in screeches that were either cheers or instructions to enable the tricolor guardian to terminate the dangerous enemy. Axler sidled toward the bird of prey to put himself in front of Sally Twosongs. His eyelids were blinking—the colorful lights, flamboyant and alive, flashed brighter and brighter, and became so dazzling in radiance that he had to squint.

The bobcat let loose a scream of agony. It was on its back, wiggling combatively to be free, but its legs pumped and slashed at nothing as vitality left its body and its lifeblood flowed into the gravelly dirt. Hank had it down and was viciously biting its throat; blood spurted like a fountain as the feline's death throes petered out to a panting whimper; then silence.

Hank was not yet finished punishing it. The long dormant instinct for wildness had been awakened and now, needed to be satiated. The dog put its front paws to spiteful work, digging at the cat's midsection as though it expected to remove its heart. That dizzying overkill gave rise to a latent savagery that belied the collie's gentle disposition; it locked its jaws on the scruff of the wildcat's neck and ferociously tossed its lifeless body around as if it was a bag of rags.

"Hank!" Jesse shouted at the top of his lungs. No response. "*Haaaank!*"

The dog stopped. Its head cocked as it dropped its vanquished foe. Its bushy tail wagged in fits and starts. Awe-filled curiosity and indecision animated its eyes. The loyal and beloved pet hesitantly backed away from its kill as though it was a shocking new discovery. It cried a feeble whine, then took several cumbersome sideward steps before flopping lopsidedly.

Axler ran to his lifelong friend and knelt. His breath and voice were trapped in his gullet. Tears seared and distorted his vision, but not enough to deny the gruesome mutilation. Through tousled clumps of hair, he saw deep and jagged gashes on its chest and underbelly. The pumping seepage of blood was prodigious. He stroked the thick collar of luxuriant hair around its neck, and watched its spirit depart from its pleading and expressive eyes. He shuddered.

He wept stifled sobs and sat holding the dog for he knew not how long. A chirping peep from the red-tailed hawk brought him back to his senses. He slid the corpse off his lap and stood with his Spencer in hand. And though the bobcat was dead, with his chin trembling and cheeks stained by tears, Jesse Axler squeezed the trigger once more and put a bullet in its skull.

In the echo of the gunshot, he heard the pounding of approaching hoofbeats.

The thunderheads in the east were growing larger and darker. Charley Jondreau noted the black-veined clouds as he crept closer and closer, making no effort to conceal his position. His strides were cautious and discreet, but the heroic boldness written on the tablet of his heart carried him forward. There were no obstacles before him, no trail of regrets behind him.

He stiffened and stopped at the entrance of the canyon from which a squadron of crows were raising a clattery ruckus. He inclined to the left and entered. At the far end, fifty or so yards away, Smoky Crowe stood, armed and standing tall, naked from the waist up. Jondreau's steps were springy, his muscles in accord with the mission; he was a willing and ready vessel.

He took in all the details of the battleground. There were no surprises. He considered the scattered groups of crows in the juniper trees; he realized the cawing birds could be a diversion if Crowe ordered them to attack, but astutely dismissed that possibility because of an enlightened assurance as to the aftermath of the confrontation. He saw his partner; Dawson was bound, bruised and bloodied, but unbent and undefeated. Her face was reddened and blotchy.

Ice water flowed through him. "Any complaints, Max?"

"I'm alright, Charley," she said, sass and contempt competing for dominance in her voice. "All boisterous threats and promises of mayhem from a bullying waste of skin."

"His death will come soon."

"Kill him now, Charley."

"It will be a good outcome, eh. I have *seen* it."

"Gut him like a pig."

Charley Jondreau was face to face with Smoky Crowe. Ten yards separated them as they cautiously assessed possible frailties in each other. An enormous surge of volcanic power sizzled between them; the positive of good smashed and sparked against the negative of evil. The dead odor of singed ozone was an invisible fog that scorched the air. The one-eyed Ute witch had an arrow slotted in his bowstring which was drawn back and ready to be released.

"You are the dragon, eh."

"I am the great prophet."

"You are squadoosh," Charley said, bopping up on the balls of his feet. His hips were loose and relaxed, while his right hand held the knife poised to sling it. A smile, so subtle as to be undetectable, grazed his lips. "Nothing more than a counterfeit abracadabra artist."

"I am the messenger of death."

"The Great Spirit is the author of life and death."

"I am the herald of the dark one."

"I will kill you, eh."

"I am indestructible."

"You are a pillager. Pillagers die."

"I am indestructible," Smoky Crowe reiterated, head craning crookedly. The milky white sickness of his left eye roiled and pulsated incessantly. "I will ascend the mountains and walk upon the clouds. You have no power to stop me." He leered an exultant grin. "Your Navajo princess will not, cannot save you from the hellfires of damnation and victory."

"You will die here today, eh."

Crowe tossed his wispy hair and barked laughter. "Die?" He shuffled his feet in a parade of a dance as a nightmarish yowl tore from his throat. The bloodcurdling blare bounced off the rock walls and incited a bedlam of hoarse croaking from the flock of blackbirds. "Die?" he asked again, shaking his head. "The powers of light shall never destroy the realms of darkness."

"Light displaces darkness, eh. Darkness cannot hide from light."

"Lies."

"Men prefer darkness to light because their deeds are evil, but light triumphs for it is good and pure, eh. Light always triumphs," Charley said evenly. He casually adjusted his stance so his shoulders were squared. The fingers of his right hand jiggled on the handle of the knife. "One day when the sun is no more, sacred light will shine victorious across the ages."

"More lies."

"Truth," Charley replied, smiling coolly. The daylight grew turbulent with thunder and the smell of burnt ozone became profoundly oppressive. He rocked bouncily on his heels. His head jerked and his eyes went cold and vacant; for a fleeting flicker nothing could be seen except the whites. His eyelids quivered, then his eyes were normal—keenly fixed on his adversary. "But the one who was born Cheveyo knows nothing of truth, nothing of light, *do you*?"

Crowe shrank back, startled and disconcerted. "Who *are* you?"

"The man who will kill you, eh," Charley answered, pleased and content. "The outer darkness of weeping and wailing will be your eternal abode, to which you can go now." His right hand blurred so fast as to be unseen. The knife flew straight and true as he pulled his pistol.

Crowe fired the poison-tipped arrow. The twang of the catgut bowstring was heard above the chaotic disorder of overexcited crows. The projectiles, a steel blade and a flint arrowhead, passed each other in mid-flight. Everything became an unglued mishmash of shouts and screams, which were supplemented by horrendous cackling and flapping wings.

The blade struck Smoky Crowe just left of center in his chest—it sank to its hilt. As he juddered backwards and clutched at the knife a blast of gunfire rang out. The hunk of hot lead demolished the living evil of his ghoulish eye and exited in a spray of blood and brains. Jondreau stood strong to watch him die. Crowe entered the underworld's everlasting fires in a thrashing conniption—the phantasm outcry of a banshee filled the emptiness of the badlands.

Peals of thunder crackled, followed by a slivery second of deathly frigid silence. Crowe dropped to his knees, then sprawled spread-eagle with his tongue jittering in the dirt. Somewhere far off a lone coyote mournfully howled a yap-yap-yapping lament. Charley Jondreau exhaled a convulsive gasp and stutter-stepped awkwardly. He holstered the six-shooter.

At the instant that Charley Jondreau's knife got buried in Smoky Crowe's heart, Deacon Coburn took a tumble off Gilgal. It happened like this: Despite the ongoing difficulties of blind spots and black holes in his vision, which he adapted to and managed to keep hidden from the others, he was riding lead on a craggy trail rising up from the bank of the Rio Chama.

A blinding light lanced behind his eyes and he reeled backwards. He was falling and falling, arms flailing and legs kicking as he crash landed in a crumpled heap. Pain, of the kind that transmitted fiery contractions from the top of his head down his spine and across his torso, had a relentlessness that provoked a cruelly violent seizure.

He squirmed and palpitated with quaking tremors which had him spewing foam from his mouth as his head smashed repeatedly against the rocky ground—finally, blessedly the severe fit of spasms passed and he became as rigid and still as a felled oak tree. He was slumped on his back, limbs folded crookedly, eyes slammed shut and mouth dangled open.

Inside his head, a kaleidoscope of shape-shifting colors swirled so speedily that, though he was unconscious, he felt like he was spinning out of control. He floundered and struggled to find a way out, but the puzzling assortment of whirling shades and hues had him in its grip. Time reversed itself and in the workings of the spiraling rainbow the past was revived.

Disremembered images were so real that in his extreme tussle for equilibrium and stability he straightway wanted to reach out and touch them; mirages of his childhood at play with his siblings, conversations with his mother, his youthful idealism and the conflict with his father, Blackjack Gallagher and his daughter Alice, the gory battlefields of the war, Angela Langton and a letter painstakingly written to her, the only woman he had ever loved.

The iridescent episode unloosed him and he was in the Angel Peak badlands, emaciated and ragged, a tall and rangy scarecrow of a man clinging to saddlebags and armed only with a pistol while being surrounded and trapped by a renegade band of Utes led by a one-eyed warrior with a booming voice. He had proven to be a worthy quarry and made them adapt tactics, but now, there were no more ruses to be exploited and no escape.

He was beaten and subjected to knife-blade trickery and debauchery. His chest and back was mangled by the leader; each slicing cut, even in this out of season chain of memories, caused his jaw to lock and his body to clench. The blood squirted and his tormentor giggled in delight. He tilted his head to a rightward angle so as to fix his malignant eye on his victim.

"Aaaarg!" the Ute yelped, pitching and stumbling as a bullet entered his brain through the entrance of the deviant eye socket. A shroud of darkness buried Coburn and he was smothering. He boxed to be free of the pitch-black gloom. Misery rammed behind his breastbone, as though his ribs were being screwed tighter and tighter. He scuffled and scrapped to breathe.

A rushing wind of a gasp billowed into his lungs. From the middle of the bleak murkiness imprisoning him the malformed grayish-white eye of the vengeful Ute pulsed—it was alive and throbbing and lunging at him, but then, in an eruption of brightness, it blinked shut forevermore. Coburn wobbled and began swimming up out of the desolation toward familiar voices.

"He be breathing?"

"It's ragged and thin, but yeah."

"What can we do?"

"We be doing it."
"Is he going to die?"
"Dear God, no!"
"Don't jump to bad conclusions."
"He be a tough old coot."
"I'm scared. Really scared."
"No reason for fear, boss. He be coming around."

Coburn felt his head and shoulders get lifted. His eyes squished open. The headache had been vanquished; the pain and blind spots had also passed on. He was calm and clear-eyed. The constriction in his chest had relaxed, and though discomfort lingered, his intake of oxygen was as it should be. He moistened his lips, then weakly said, "Evil has been overcome by good."

"What you say?"

"I thought I was a goner, Whitey." Deacon muttered, dry and croaky.

Avis Lahay was on her knees cradling his head in her lap—Whitey Fitzgerald was stooped over him on one side, while Daniel Twosongs squatted on his heels on the other. Stace Hawkins stood off to the side, tears trickling down his cheeks. Each one had a raw expression of apprehension, but it was the upset of the boy that plucked Coburn's emotions. The lines around his eyes rumpled as he forced a smile and gave the youngster a convincing thumbs up.

"What you say?" Whitey asked once more, click-clicking.

"Evil has been overcome by good."

"Chaarleeey!"

Max Dawson shouted a tick of time before Smoky Crowe's arrow found its mark. She almost dislocated her shoulders as she strained against the bindings. Agony flamed in her joints and the clarion shriek of her voice ripped membranes in her larynx. She kept straining against the tree trunk, helplessly hoping that the onslaught was a sunstroke induced hallucination.

She hollered his name again and again, but he was in a glassy-eyed zone of grit and acted as though he didn't hear her. The poison arrowhead was implanted deep in his belly, the shaft a grotesque extension of his body that wavered with each spastic step he took. A murder of crows were flapping and squawking as he hobbled over to their master's body. The largest bird had tipped into an emotional outbreak in which it fussed immeasurably louder than the others.

Jondreau glowered at the hysterical culprit, then retrieved his knife from Smoky Crowe's heart. In sheer calmness he grabbed a fistful of his straggly white hair, and hoisted his head and shoulders off the ground to slit the dead man's throat from ear to ear—he did so with such a brawny thoroughness that he almost decapitated the satanic enchanter.

"Evil can never be dead enough, eh," he said, grimness woven into his voice. He wiped the blade clean on his mortal enemy's leggings, then stood as tall as he possibly could and put the knife in its sheaf on his left hip. The blackbirds were going berserk, carrying on and caterwauling so rabidly that downy tufts of feathers floated like puffy springtime pollen. He singled out the noisiest one, drew his revolver and shot it in one effortless motion.

The black-winged bird fell in a fluttering thud. Every other crow immediately shut its craw, which resulted in an eddy of silence that rippled throughout the badlands. Silence; creepy and unnerving silence. Jondreau returned the pistol to its home, then as the arrow jerked around spookily, he waved his arms at the stupefied birds. "Be gone!" he ordered, gasping.

Wings pummeled like heavy drumbeats as the panicked flock took flight as one to become a fast-moving cloud skedaddling across the sky in a headlong streak toward the western horizon. At that precise instant, the haunting thunderheads which had gathered and were rumbling in the east, began to split apart and disperse with a rapidity that defied natural law.

Jondreau clutched at his belly and almost toppled. He staggered for several weaving steps, then righted his balance. His stance was wide, his shoulders rounding into a slouch. He saw his partner wrestling to break the fastenings that secured her to the juniper. "The horses are there," he said, pointing in the general direction as to where the animals were picketed.

"Forget the horses, Charley. Get here so I can help you."

"I will help you," he answered as he galumphed over to her. His footsteps were plodding and unpredictable. "There's no help for me, but from the Great Spirit. I have *seen* it, eh."

"My God! Why, Charley? Why?"

Jondreau got to her, but in his haste and changeable stability, almost tripped and crashed over her legs. He had to lean hard against her to get onto a knee and withdraw his knife. The blade was razor-sharp, but he was weakened. It took tense seconds to cut the rawhide from her wrists. As soon as she was free he sagged onto his back and stared longingly skyward.

Dawson crouched beside him. She gingerly touched the arrow at its entrance point. The blood was pumping out in a perfectly atrocious excess. She wanted to grab and yank the shaft to remove it, but realized that'd be futile. "My God! Why, Charley? Why?" She placed a hand on his cheek. "This is madness! This cannot be the way it ends. My God, Charley, my God!"

"Peace is mine, Max."

"You shouldn't have come to rescue me."

"I ain't outguessing fortune, eh."

"Damnit, Charley!"

"You'd have done for me."

She pinched her mouth to tamp down a torrent of tears. Her heart felt like it was being garroted by a thin wire; the ever contracting tautness made her wiggle restlessly. She stared into his eyes—the connection between them, forged in sunshine and storms during a decade of riding trails together, had a far-reaching impact on her perspective. She took hold of his hands as waterworks busted the dam of her resolve. "All of this is a wrong mistake, Charley."

"Unless a seed falls to the ground and dies there is no life, eh."

"Meaning what?"

"I give you life, Max. Go live it."

"Without you?"

"The Great Spirit has someone for you."

She sniffled. "Domestic bliss? Please. That's crazy."

"Different, not crazy. I have *seen* it."

"You're going to die, Charley."

"Just stepping through a doorway, Max."

"What can I do for you?"

"A pile of rocks, I suppose."

"Any words . . . prayers?"

"Respect, is all."

"You own every ounce of respect I got until *my* dying day, Charley."

"No tears remembering me, eh."

"I can't make that promise. Look at me blubbering."

"You have been my closest friend."

"Likewise."

He tried to breathe deeply, but merely gurgled a blood-speckled mist. He nodded to her. "Only great love will cause a man to give up his life for his friend. Live free and be courageous. I will catch you on the other side, eh." His eyes disappeared in his head and then, in an utterance not his own, he told her, "*Leave it alone, Badger. Sometimes the price to purchase pieces of justice is too damn high. Find your own trail and live a life that makes a difference.*"

An electrifying jolt knocked her onto her keister—she was shaken and addled down to the soles of her feet. Those were her father's words and *his* unforgettable voice. She had the fidgets and was shillyshallying. She clambered forward to speak to Charley Jondreau, but his eyelids were shut and his jaw slack for he had departed his earthbound shell of flesh and bones.

Max Dawson froze inside as she went into shock.

When Charley Jondreau wheezed his final labored breath, Sally Twosongs recoiled and grappled to latch onto handholds in the air that did not exist. She reached and grabbed over and over in an almost angry furor of passion. Her dark eyes bulged. Whimpers of unnatural sounds emerged from her mouth as an invisible vortex took hold of her. Swaddled inside the tunnel of air, she was carried away in the spirit and was high and lifted up in the heavenlies.

She looked and saw a multitude celebrating a circle dance around a golden throne, upon which sat the triumphant Lamb slain before the foundation of the world. He appeared as the Son of man, clothed in a spotless garment. His face was as bright and beautiful as the noonday sun; his eyes flamed like shards of fire and his flowing hair was purer than the whitest snow.

His voice was a resounding trumpet or the mighty rushing of many waters. *"Fear not; I am Alpha and Omega, the beginning and the ending. Which is, and which was, and which is to come, the Almighty. I am the first and the last: I am he that liveth, and was dead; and behold, I am alive forevermore, Amen; and have the keys of hell and death. To him who overcometh I have given hidden manna and a white stone with a new name written on it that only he knoweth."*

Sally Twosongs was on her knees in awestruck worship. A chanting song saturated the atmosphere, rising and falling with such spontaneity that unrestrained joy flooded her soul. The leaves of palm branches were quavering and undulating amongst the throng of tribes surrounding the throne; thousands and thousands and thousands, of a number no one could count. Her heart was humbled and overwhelmed by the panoramic pageantry of praise and adoration.

Nations that existed in the forgotten realms of antiquity were side by side with nations from a future she could in no way comprehend. Her eyes were aglow in concentration; her ears on alert to hear every note and phrase of the melodious harmony. The metrical drumbeats, from a percussion section that was an all-inclusive representation of cultural traditions, were in unison with the myriad choir and the ensemble of horns, flutes, bagpipes, harps and lyres.

Sally Twosongs had difficulty processing the totality of the spectacle or containing the thunderstruck sensation that burned through her like tingly embers. Her attention was now drawn to a glorious army of angels. The attendants stood round about the throne and sang out in voices akin to the roar of a waterfall. *"Amen: Blessing, and glory, and wisdom, and thanksgiving, and honor, and power, and might, be unto our God for ever and ever. Amen."*

The teeming mass of humanity, diverse and attired in apparel characteristic of every kindred clan and ethnicity, responded with an exuberant heel to toe honor dance. Each ritual step was presented in graceful elegance and persuasive foot-stomping. The whacking drums increased and decreased in speed and loudness as the dancers sprang and skipped in individual displays of ancestral folklore that somehow melded together in a breathtaking mosaic.

She got caught up in the primal rhythms and wanted nothing more than to hop to her feet and join the grandeur of the sanctified powwow, but when she attempted to do so was suddenly skewered by an excitement that transfixed her—Charley Jondreau came into view, his visage decorated with charcoal and stripes of radiant paint, an arm raised in supplication. She immediately called his name, but it stuck in her throat and remained unheard.

He shuffled free from a cluster of high-steppers to take a turn leading. He was clothed in ceremonial Iroquois regalia; a formal feathered skullcap, wampum jewelry around his neck, a ribbon shirt, breechcloth and leggings. His feet were encased in intricately beaded doeskin moccasins and he held a hawk-feather fan over his heart. He twirled in a flourish as his upper body bobbed and weaved, his face encircled in rays of light.

She felt a wave of heated emotions and tried to shout louder and louder, but not a squeak came forth. He crouched low and spun around in a dipping whirl that began slow and measured, but careened to an abrupt end when he saw her. He proudly strode to within a few inches of her, and though engulfed in the euphoric glorification of the Kingdom, for a transient moment that bridged the expansive chasm of time and space, he was alone with the Navajo princess.

Jondreau touched the tip of the hawk-feather fan to his forehead. "Thank you for helping me. Peace is mine, eh. I will see you again when your time on earth is no more." He bowed at the waist and beamed a bottomless smile, then in a swirling burst of double-tapping two-steps he rejoined the circle dance while jubilant cries and hoots whooped from his voice box.

Sally Twosongs wept hot tears, her heart beating so forcefully that the noise of it buffeted her eardrums. The exultant scene around the golden throne was swept away by a maelstrom of wind that picked her up and returned her to the campsite on Bulldog Mountain, though in reality and unknown to her, she had never physically been away from it. She was semiconscious, and thrusting her arms up and outward in a swimming motion as she keeled over.

Shivers tossed her about for several moments. She was burning up with fever and sweating profusely; her skin clammy, her braided hair grungy. Her teeth were chattering. She inhaled a panting lungful, and all at once the tremors passed. Her body and breathing calmed to a near deathlike stillness. She felt a presence and hands on her. Her eyes creaked open.

A faint smile cracked her lips. Her husband was at her side holding her hand and stroking her brow. Jesse Axler sat at her feet. Her gaze slanted to the mountaintop. The spectral aura of aurora borealis was no more. Her head turned slightly. The red-tailed hawk was prissily cleaning itself on its perch in the stubby evergreen. She sighed gratefully for all was as it should be.

Midway through the next day, Max Dawson came to the end of her emotions. Her heart was as desiccated and dry as her body, but not even a smidgeon of quit had the temerity to rise up in her. She persevered through the effects of her ordeal, which included dehydration along with cuts, bruises and a soreness in her joints that felt like flaming torches.

She sat placidly on the ground beside the mound of rocks that was her partner's grave as she watched a half-dozen vultures pick at the disappearing remains of the unholy terror whose wanton depravity was legendary. Even before burying Charley Jondreau, she had dragged the Ute witch's body to a weathered knoll of desert terrain some twenty-odd yards away.

The red-headed scavengers distracted and amused her on a superficial level, but no amount of entertainment could ever provide any relief from the aching in her soul. Her senses had been shattered into jagged scraps and reassembled to become a serrated-edged bereavement that mercilessly sawed and razed her. There was wreckage within a horrid aloneness crying out—wreckage and aloneness that she had wrought by an accumulation of choices.

She could not reconcile success with the loss. The sum of the victory did not add up to a justifiable total on the balance sheet of her life. She had done everything necessary and more to keep a vow to her father to see Smoky Crowe dead. *You can bet your money on me, Daddy.* She had not relented. Through all the desperate chances and against the odds, she was unswerving in her odyssey and remained ever true to her nickname and the character bred in her bones.

Now, at the graveside of a gallant and honorable man who had fought the good fight in every circumstance, the rubble and flotsam floating around the wasteland inside her had no practical meaning or purpose. Seeing Smoky Crowe's corpse picked clean by buzzards could do nothing to vindicate or even come close to alleviating the wreckage and aloneness.

She leaned forward to rest a hand on one of the boulders that entombed the man who she had ridden alongside of for ten memorable years. "It's a helluva end, Charley," she said in a virtually inaudible rasp from deep in her throat. Her belly growled hungrily. She puckered and sucked her cheeks in and out to stimulate a dab of saliva just to have something to swallow, but that was not to be for her tongue and the roof of her mouth were parched and cracked.

Her bloodshot eyes were focused on the burial place. She cursed mildly. The last words Jondreau had spoken haunted her. Lonesome futility coerced her to cry, but that was not possible because her tear ducts were drained. She fisted her hands so forcibly that fresh blood seeped from the swollen wounds on her wrists. "My God, Charley! How could you know?"

She slumped back. Her mind was jumping and flitting from one jangled thought to another. A hitch caught in her throat and her lungs contracted in a tremulous ripple that caused her breathing to come in short and irregular spurts. Her hand tentatively reached into the left inside pocket of her jacket. She gripped the leather wallet and pulled it out.

Shakiness impaired her fingers as she fumbled to grab hold of the only note her father ever wrote her. The singularly compelling message had been passed along to her at the Suncurl Café in Santa Fe when she was on the trail after her mother had been cold-bloodedly butchered by Smoky Crowe. She had never shared it with or shown the small sheet to anyone. The crease of its one fold was worn. She handled the paper with care and read the sentences aloud.

> *Leave it alone, Badger. Sometimes the price to purchase pieces of justice is too damn high. Find your own trail and live a life that makes a difference.*

"Dear God, Daddy," she said in a shuddery gasp. "I never shirked my duty, but damnit, I doubt I'll find much hope for a life in any of this crappola." She returned the short letter to its secure nook, then the billfold to its slot. She glanced at the ugly cusses feeding and came to a conclusion; the embodiment of evil known as Smoky Crowe was undeniably dead enough.

The sun was a straight-up scorcher. She licked her blistery lips. An idea popped into her head—a notion that she instantly resisted and attempted to dismiss, but it hammered at her with an insistence that could not be refused. She tried moistening her lips again as she got to her feet. Her strides were intense and decisive; she went to the exact site where Charley Jondreau had stood strong while an arrowhead in his belly worked to fulfill its lethal objective.

Her eyes narrowed and she studied the sandy soil for memento reminders. She dug a filthy handkerchief out of a front pocket of her raggedy trousers, then knelt to engage in a rite learned by listening to the man from

Conoy Creek. She methodically selected twelve smooth stones, passing by or discarding those that did not stir sensations of excellence in her heart.

When she was satisfied with her collection, she bundled the keepsakes in the kerchief and tied it in a knot. She had no particular plan for what she would do with the tokens, but having them gave her some encouragement. She had one final look at the vultures, then walked away on a course to find the horses, where she would drink from the canteens and mend for a spell. After that, she intended to go to *WT Ranch*, but destiny would intervene to redirect her.

April 30, 1888

Dear Diary: Twilight is falling from the sky. We are settled in a grove of cottonwoods. I am at the water's edge on the trunk of a tree growing sideways off the sloping bank. The pretty colors of the sunset are glittering on the rippling Rio Chama. A truly beautiful and peaceful evening that makes me want to file the memory of it away for a rainy day.

After all the chores were completed Deacon went off for a walk through the woods. He had his Bible in hand, so I expect he was on the search for reflective solitude. Supper is being prepared, supervised by Daniel and his expert spicing. Whitey and Stace spent an hour fishing this afternoon and caught several good-sized trout, which just now are being seasoned.

The horses and Whitey's mule are staked on a grassy stretch of overgrown meadow. We adults are getting spoiled rotten because Stace has taken over most of the tasks in regards to our livestock. He makes me so proud hour by hour—Brenda would be impressed by his choice to shoulder responsibility simply from following the example of his elders.

Deacon and Whitey have been kindhearted in walking alongside him. Daniel, too. Just about every night around the campfire Daniel has a story for Stace that has a moral lesson. The details come from his childhood or have to do with an escapade he had on his travels. Of course, Whitey chimes in here and there to provide commentary or exclamation points. It is delightful listening to them yarn. I contemplate the tales when I'm all-snug in my bedroll.

Spending the days on horseback and nights sleeping under the stars is good for my soul. I am processing and thinking through so much. My heart is full of joys and worries. The joys come from all the terrific relational experiences. To think that these companions are family is often too wonderful for me to comprehend. We care for each other in a consequential manner that inspires me. The bond between us gets strengthened with every passing mile.

Stace is really coming out of his shell. We rode side by side for most of the morning and we chatted about a wide variety of topics. It refreshed me because there was no undercurrent of tension, so I wasn't on pins and needles or overthinking anything. One discussion led to another with little or no prompting from me. He had lots to say and initiated most of our dialog.

He even opened up and shared some of his feelings and what's in his head about his mother's death. He told me that though his heart hurts and he still wonders about many whys, he is striving to come to terms with the mournful sadness, and what it all means because, and I quote, "Mr. Whitey explained some stuff about hurting and I've been stewing on it."

He spoke with a maturity that startled me. He stated that going forward he's going to buckle down and never do anything that would embarrass his mother in heaven. What was amazing is that he said all this dry-eyed and with no tremble in his voice. Meanwhile, I was biting the inside of my bottom lip a-plenty while batting my eyelids to chase away teardrops. I had to pull my skimmer low and avert my eyes to way off in the middle distance.

My worries, despite what I just wrote, mostly have to do with Stace and me. Will I be able to be the surrogate mother I must be to guide and direct him through the ups and downs of life? Can I teach him to always use his head and learn how to reason for himself? I gleaned so much wisdom from Mom, Whitey and Deacon—will he follow my example? I pray so.

Deacon concerns me. He has had a headache almost every day we have been on the trail. For how long before we were together, I do not know. He downplays the issue. Whenever anyone mentions it or asks about his level of discomfort, he shrugs and says all is well. Whitey gets on his case as only Whitey can do, which is humorous, but still, after yesterday's episode when he blacked out and had some kind of seizure, my worry for him skyrocketed.

Afterwards, when he returned to consciousness and recovered from the sudden attack of the shakes, Deacon was his usual closemouthed self. Try as we might we could get nothing out of him. He simply kept asserting that he was alright and all would be fine. We pressed him, but he had no explanation for the Bible verse he referenced: *Evil has been overcome by good.* Today he claims that there is no headache or any carryover from the worrisome incident.

I don't know. I retain an abiding uneasiness for him that has to be released into God's hands because that is the territory over which the Lord has complete dominion. We have no clue as to what may be coming around the next corner in our lives. The future is unknown. And that's the way God intends it. If we were to know all that was going to transpire in our lives, then there wouldn't be any incentive for us to take God at his word and trust him step by step.

I am seeking direction about the kind of life I want to build for me and Stace. Seeing him come alive on the trail and his natural aptitude for horses has me weaving a daydream that I have harbored since the first time I sat in a saddle. To be employed at a thriving horse ranch has been a secret passion of mine and now I seriously consider it as a real possibility.

What would our lives be like if we relocated to WT Ranch? The fact that we will winter there is fortuitous. If in visiting and doing jobs with the crew, we determine there is work and a place for the two of us, then I will be inclined to make the move, but I cannot let selfishness be the one to make the call. This has to be a matter where I hear the counsel of others, and most importantly, be on the same page written for me before one of them came to pass.

I am praying about it; hard praying. I WILL ONLY raise the subject in my journal. The fleece I am laying out for the Lord is this: If the idea is broached by Caleb or Sally Twosongs, and is enthusiastically affirmed by Pete and Naomi, then that will be a positive indicator to take us to the next level of confirmation. Mom, Whitey and Deacon have to be in agreement. And I suppose Stace, too—I guess I'm kind of assuming he'll be genuinely eager for the move. That's all I got, which is good because I hear and smell fish sizzling.

Avis Lahay closed the maroon leather daybook with its pattern of interlinked circles engraved on its edges. She put the fountain pen in its spine. She stretched. The sun was a half circle drizzling pinkish shades across the western horizon. She lost herself within its marvelous splendor and gave thanks. Stillness filled her senses for she understood that the Supreme Artist who was painting such a magnificent skyscape was also the holder of all her tomorrows.

~ ~ ~

~The End~

www.ingramcontent.com/pod-product-compliance
Lightning Source LLC
Chambersburg PA
CBHW070314230426
43663CB00011B/2122